THE

CONSTITUTIONAL HISTORY

OF THE

PRESBYTERIAN CHURCH

IN THE UNITED STATES OF AMERICA.

BY

CHARLES HODGE, D.D.

PROFESSOR IN THE THEOLOGICAL SEMINARY, PRINCETON, NEW JERSEY.

PART I.

1705 TO 1741.

PHILADELPHIA:
PRESBYTERIAN BOARD OF PUBLICATION,
No. 265 CHESTNUT STREET.

PREFACE.

SOMETIME during the past summer, the Rev. Dr. Hoge, of Ohio, wrote to one of his friends in Philadelphia, stating that a work was greatly needed, which should give a distinct account of the character of the present controversies in our Church. He conceived that in order to the proper exhibition of the subject, the documentary history of the formation of the first Presbytery, of the adopting act, of the great schism, of the union of the two Synods, and of the formation of our present constitution, should be clearly presented to the public. The gentleman to whom this letter was addressed submitted it to a meeting of clergymen and laymen, who all concurred in the opinion that such a work ought to be prepared, and united in requesting the undersigned to undertake the task. A request from such a source the writer did not feel at liberty to decline. He soon found that the work was far more extensive than was at first supposed. If the documentary history of the leading events connected with the origin and progress of our Church was to be given at all, it was clearly right that it should be done in the best manner the materials at command would allow. These materials, though in some respects very defective, were ascertained to be too numerous and too important to be compressed within the limits of a pamphlet. The plan was, therefore, enlarged, and the writer was led to undertake a general review of the history of the Presbyterian Church in the United States. The design of the work is to exhibit the true character of our Church; to show on what principles it was founded and governed; in other words, to exhibit historically its constitution, both as to doctrine and order. He has, therefore, ventured to call the work "A Constitutional History of the Presbyterian Church." His readers will not expect more than this title promises. To trace the rise and progress of our Church in different parts of the country; to detail the controversies, struggles, revivals and declensions which have attended its course, is a work far too extensive for the time or resources of the present writer. It is indeed greatly to be desired that some competent person would undertake the task. If this cannot be done, it would be comparatively easy for different persons to collect and arrange the rapidly perishing materials of the history of our Church in those portions of the country with which they are most familiar. Such a history for Virginia and the Southern States; another for Kentucky and the West; and another for the Middle States, could not fail to be instructive and interesting. No one who has not attended to the subject can be aware of the necessity of this work being done soon, if it is to be done at all. Every year carries with it into forgetfulness the knowledge of important facts. Much has already been lost, which the men of the last generation might have preserved. It is our duty to save as many of the memorials of the past as we can, for the sake of those who come after us.

Recent events have led to various speculations on the origin and constitution of our Church. It has been said, that we owe our ecclesiastical existence to Congregationalists; that the condition of ministerial communion among us was assent to the essential doctrines of the Gospel; and that the Presbyterian form of government which our fathers adopted was of a very mitigated character. As these statements relate to the fundamental principles of our ecclesiastical compact, they deserve to be investigated. To ascertain how far we are indebted for existence as a Church to Congregationalists, the writer was led to inquire what foundation was laid for a Presbyterian Church in the character of the early settlers of our country. This inquiry was extended so far as to form an introductory chapter by itself, which may be considered as too long if viewed in relation to the contents of the present volume. It is hoped, however, that this objection will not be considered of much weight, if the probable extent of the whole work be taken into view. The next subject of investigation was the actual character of our Church before the year 1729, as far as it can be learned from its history and records. This required an examination into the origin of our early congregations and ministers, and into the standard of doctrine and form of government which they adopted. As to the first of these points, great difficulty has been experienced in gaining satisfactory information. The reader has the results of as thorough a search as the circumstances of the writer permitted him to make. The exhibition of the form of government was comparatively an easy task; since the records of the original Presbytery and Synod furnished the materials on which the decision of that question must be made.

The third chapter contains the review of our history from 1729 to 1741. As the act by which the Westminster Confession of Faith was adopted by the Synod as their standard of doctrine, was passed in 1729, this seemed to be the proper place to exhibit in full the testimony furnished by the records, not only as to the true interpretation of that act, but as to the condition of ministerial communion in the Presbyterian Church.

It is intended, should God permit, to continue, in a second volume, this history from 1741 to 1789. This will require an exhibition of the causes of the great schism, an investigation of the doctrinal and constitutional questions involved in that controversy, and of the principles on which the Church was settled at the time of the union of the two Synods. Whether the work shall be continued in a third volume, embracing a review of our history from the formation of the General Assembly to the present time, must depend on circumstances over which the writer has no control.

The author is bound to acknowledge his obligations to Dr. Green and to Dr. John McDowell, for allowing him access to records and documents in their possession. The former of these gentlemen as chairman of the committee appointed some years ago to write the history of the Church, had received from various sources, a great number of short sketches of the history of particular congregations and Presbyteries. Of these documents much use has been made in the investigation of the origin of our early churches. They are referred to, in the subsequent pages, as authority under the general title MS. History.

CHARLES HODGE.

Princeton, March, 1839.

CONTENTS.

CHAPTER I.

INTRODUCTION.

CHAPTER II.

PRESBYTERIAN CHURCH FROM 1705 TO 1729.

CHAPTER III.

PRESBYTERIAN CHURCH FROM 1729 TO 1741.

THE

PRESBYTERIAN CHURCH, &c.

CHAPTER I.

INTRODUCTION.

Recent division of the Presbyterian Church.—Distinctive opinions of the two parties.—American Presbyterianism essentially the same with that of Scotland, and of the French Protestants.—Sources of knowledge of the early character of our Church.—Obscurity of its early history.—Presbyterian settlers of this country.—I. The Puritans.—The English Puritans were generally Presbyterians—Many of those who came to this country were Presbyterians.—Their settlements out of New England.—II. The Dutch—their settlements.—III. The Germans.—IV. The French Protestants.—V. Scotch and Irish.—The persecutions of the Scotch under Charles I. and II.—The settlements of the Scotch and Irish in this country.—Conclusion.

THE controversies which have so long agitated the Presbyterian Church, have, at length, resulted in its separation. It would not be easy to state, in a manner satisfactory to both parties, the points of difference between them. It may, however, be said, without offence, that the one party is in favour of a stricter adherence to the standards of the church, as to doctrine and order, than the other. On the one hand, it has been contended that the Westminster Confession of Faith was adopted as the Confession of the Presbyterian Church only in a very qualified manner, and that the proper condition of ministerial communion is nothing more than agreement in those points, which are "essential and necessary in doctrine, worship, or government."* As it regards church order, it is said that American Presbyterianism is something very different from the Scottish system; that our higher judicatories have only judicial and advisory powers; that is, the right to hear and decide appeals, complaints, and references, and to give advice; that the General Assembly, especially, is nothing

* Dr. Hill, after quoting the adopting act of 1729, in which the language quoted in the text occurs, exclaims, "Noble, generous-hearted Presbyterian fathers!" And in commenting upon Dr. Green's strictures upon that act, he asks, "Does my venerable friend admit of no distinction between essential and non-essential doctrines of the Gospel? And does he believe that every word and every sentence in our Confession of Faith contains essential doctrine? This is not the old divinity we were taught in olden times. If I mistake not, our present Confession of Faith does the same in amount. (See Book of Discipline, ch. v. sec. 13, 14, 15.) 'Heresy and schism *may* be of such a nature as to infer deposition; but errors ought to be carefully considered, *whether they strike at the vitals of religion*, and are industriously spread; or *whether they arise from the weakness of the human understanding*, and *are not likely to do much injury.*'" From this it appears that Dr. Hill considers the "adopting act," and our present constitution as requiring nothing more than agreement in the essential doctrines of the Gospel.

THE CINCINNATI JOURNAL contains a series of articles on the early history of our Church, the ninth number of which embraces a long extract from a letter by Dr. Halsey, published in 1836. In that letter Dr. Halsey endeavours to show that the conditional adoption of the Confession of Faith is "the distinctive peculiarity of our Church—an avowed standard principle." What degree of latitude of construction, ought, in his judgment, to be allowed, may be learned from the following passage. "They (*i. e.* our fathers) believed that visible union and communion among Christians was a divinely-appointed duty, and they laboured to fulfil it on such terms as did not merge Christian character. What was essential to this they maintained, what was not essential they treated accordingly; leaving us an example that we should follow their steps." That this relates to ministerial communion is evident from the whole drift of the letter, and from what immediately follows the passage just cited. "It may be asked how this distinctive peculiarity of our Church should ever be lost to the sight of her members? The history of our Church supplies the answer. In the hostilities of 1741, the 'old-side' in Philadelphia became possessed of the original records, which became sequestered. The original 'adopting act' lived but in tradition, and the reproaches of adversaries. Meanwhile, those who questioned its propriety, taught their own views of 'the adopting act,' representing it absolute not conditional."

but an appellate court and advisory council; that our several courts are, as to their existence and action, entirely independent of each other.* It is asserted that "Congregationalism was the basis of Presbyterianism in this country;" and that "had Congregationalists never entered the field beyond the bounds of New England, Presbyterianism would scarcely have existed in this country, except in name." It is not to be supposed, however, that all the brethren who are now considered as "New School" adopt, to their full extent, either of the extreme opinions above stated.

On the other side, it is contended that our church, ever since it had a constitution at all, has been strictly Calvinistic in doctrine, and purely Presbyterian in government; that is, that such were the requirements of the judicatories of the Church. The condition of ministerial communion was not merely agreement in the essential doctrines of the Gospel, but the adoption of that system of doctrine which is contained in the Westminster Confession and Catechisms. A great distinction has always been made between ministerial and Christian communion. We are bound to regard and treat as Christians, all whom, in the judgment of charity, we believe to be the children of God. Accordingly, assent to the Westminster Confession of Faith is not required of the private members of the church; nor are private Christians subjected to discipline for any error not regarded as subversive of Christianity. But of those who aspire to be teachers or rulers in the church much more has been required. It is not enough that such should be Christians. They must be sound in the faith. To secure this end, the church has required their assent to her doctrinal standards as containing the system of doctrines taught in the word of God. And by system of doctrine, according to the lowest standard of interpretation, has been understood the Calvinistic system as distinguished from all others. There are indeed many, whose views of subscription are such, that they could not adopt the Confession of Faith, unless they were able to receive every distinct proposi-

* See "Presbyterianism, by a member of the New York Bar." The American Biblical Repository, July, 1838. See also Dr. Hill's paper No. 2, on the Great Schism.

tion which it contains. This may be right; but it is believed that no attempt has ever been made to enforce the discipline of the church against any individual who was not believed to reject some of the distinctive features of the Calvinistic system as contained in our Confession.

With regard to church order, it is contended that our church adopted from the beginning, and has ever continued to exercise that form of government which had been previously adopted in Scotland, Ireland, Holland, and among the Protestants of France. This system was every where, in all its distinctive and essential features, the same.* It required the government of individual

* See "The Form of Presbyterian Church Government, agreed upon by the Assembly of Divines at Westminster; examined and approved, Anno 1645, by the General Assembly of the Church of Scotland," &c. In this directory it is declared, that the ordinary and perpetual officers of the church are pastors, teachers, and other church governors and deacons.

"In a single congregation there ought to be one at least, both to labour in word and doctrine, and to rule. It is also requisite that there should be others to join in government.

"It is lawful, and agreeable to the word of God, that the church be governed by several sorts of Assemblies; which are congregational, classical, and synodical.

"It is lawful, and agreeable to the word of God, that the several Assemblies before-mentioned have power to convene, and call before them any person within their several bounds, whom the ecclesiastical business which is before them doth concern.

"They have power to hear and determine such causes and differences as do orderly come before them.

"It is lawful, and agreeable to the word of God, that all the said Assemblies have some power to dispense church censures.

"Synodical Assemblies may lawfully be of several sorts, as provincial, national, and œcumenical.

"It is lawful, and agreeable to the word of God, there should be a subordination of congregational, classical, provincial, and national assemblies for the government of the church."

These few extracts from the Westminster Directory, will serve to show the nature of the Scottish and English system of Presbyterianism. The French system was just the same. In the discipline of the Reformed Churches of France, it is said,

"In every church there shall be a consistory composed of persons who shall have the government of it: viz. pastors and elders."

congregations to be vested in the pastor and elders, and not in the brotherhood. It required the association of several particular churches under one Presbytery, composed of ministers and elders. It provided for provincial and national Synods, composed of delegates from the lower courts, and recognized as belonging to Synods, the authority of review and control, and the right to set down rules for the government of the church.

When it is said that we adopted the Scottish system, the expression is used in its ordinary and proper acceptation. When two countries or two churches are said to have the same system of government, it is not implied that they have the same laws in all their details. We, for example, have some rules about the reception of foreign ministers, the forms of process, statistical reports, &c., which are peculiar to ourselves. The Church of Scotland has a multitude of rules relating to tithes, patronage, &c., which arise out of its peculiar circumstances. So, also, the French Churches have rules about schools and colleges which may not be found in the Scottish books. Still the Church of Scotland considers itself as adopting the same system of discipline as the Protestants of France, and no authority is more frequently quoted by Scotch writers than the *Ratio Disciplinæ* of the French churches. The question is not about any particular laws or rules, but about principles of government. Are our courts "as to their existence and action entirely independent of each other?" Are the acts of our Synods, when not judicial, merely advisory? or have our judicatories the right to set down rules for the government of the church?

For the union of churches, it provides that there shall be *colloquies* or *classes*, formed by the authority of the provincial synod, and composed of the ministers and an elder from each church.

The authority of the classis is subject to that of the provincial synod, and that of the consistory to the classis.

The provincial synod is a convention of the ministers of a province, together with one elder, or at most two, chosen by each consistory.

The national synod, it is provided, may consist of deputies, ministers and elders, in equal proportions, chosen by the provincial synods.

The national synod shall have power to decide definitively on all ecclesiastical matters.

The power claimed for Synods, using the word in its general sense, is nothing more than what, in express terms, is said to belong to them in the Confession of Faith. It is by no means an unlimited power. It relates merely to matters of government; for all legislative powers in "matters of religion," or in things affecting the conscience, our church has, with one voice, uniformly disclaimed. It is, moreover, restricted by our present constitution within very narrow limits, much narrower than those within which our old Synods were accustomed to move. It is in the sense thus explained, it is maintained, that our church did, from the beginning, adopt the Scottish system of government, and has maintained it ever since. It is difficult to know what is meant, when it is said, "the Presbyterian systems of the French Huguenots and of South Britain, were much more mild than those of Holland and Scotland, where they had the civil authority to protect them and enforce their enactments." * Such remarks are frequently made. It is said that we adopted a system more allied to the mild form of Presbyterianism prevalent among some of the Reformed Churches, than to that of Scotland.

It is a great mistake to suppose that French Presbyterianism was more mild than that of Scotland, as would abundantly appear from a review of Quick's "Synodicon, or the Acts, Decisions, Decrees and Canons of those famous national councils of the Reformed Churches in France." There were twenty-nine of these Synods held at irregular intervals, in the course of a hundred years, as per-

* Dr. Hill's Historical Sketches, No. 7. The systems were however the same. The Scotch adopted and ratified the form of government matured in South Britain, and which was there for a time established. Neal, in his History of the Puritans, says, "it may not be improper to set before the reader in one view, the discipline which was settled in the Kirk of Scotland and subsists at this time." He then gives a view of the system which would suit the Presbyterianism of Holland, of France, or of this country, just as well as that of Scotland; omitting, of course, mere matters of detail, as the number of Parishes, Presbyteries, and Synods, the ratio of representation, the right of the Universities to send members to the Assembly, &c. As to all essential matters, the system is as much French and American as it is Scottish. See vol. iii. p. 381.

mission could be obtained from the government. The first was held in 1559, the last in 1659. The revocation of the Edict of Nantes, of course, put a stop to all such assemblies, and consummated that long train of persecutions, by which the Reformed Churches in France were nearly extirpated. It is said that, in ten years, two hundred thousand French Protestants suffered martyrdom, and about seven hundred thousand were driven from the kingdom. Few portions of the Christian church have higher claims on the sympathy and respect of Protestants than the Reformed Churches of France. They were, however, rigidly Calvinistic, and strictly Presbyterian, and those who do not respect these characteristics, cannot respect them. Some idea of the kind of Presbyterianism which prevailed in France, may be gathered from the following facts. The provincial Synods were obliged to furnish their deputies to the national Synod, with a commission in these terms: "We promise before God to submit ourselves unto all that shall be concluded and determined in your holy Assembly, to obey and execute it to the utmost of our power; being persuaded that God will preside among you, and lead you by his Holy Spirit into all truth and equity by the rule of his word, for the good and edification of his Church, to the glory of his great name; which we humbly beg of his Divine Majesty in our daily prayers." Quick, vol. i. p. 478. On the next page is the following record: "The Confession of Faith of these Reformed Churches in the kingdom of France, was read word by word, from beginning to the end, and approved in all its articles by all the deputies, as well for themselves as for the provinces that sent them, and all of them sware for themselves and provinces, that they would teach and preach it, because they believed that it did perfectly agree with the word of God; and they would use their best endeavour, that as it had been hitherto, so it should be evermore received and taught in their churches and provinces." This Confession contains forty articles, and occupies nine folio pages; and when it is remembered that it was drawn up by Calvin, it may be conceived what doctrines it contains. It became the custom to have the Confession read and readopted at every national Synod. The record is nearly in the same form every time; it was read "word by word, and re-examined in every particular point and article;" and the deputies "swore" or "protested" for themselves and principals, "to live and die in this faith."

That the French churches agreed with those of Holland in doctrine and discipline, is evident from the fact, that when the deputies from the Dutch Churches appeared in the national Synod, held in 1583, and tendered the "Confession of Faith and body of church discipline, owned and embraced by the said Churches of the Low Countries, this Assembly," it is recorded "having humbly and heartily blessed God for that sweet union and agreement, both in doctrine and discipline, between the churches of this kingdom and of that republic, did judge meet to subscribe them both; and it did also request those, our brethren, their deputies, reciprocally to subscribe our Confession of Faith and body of church discipline; which, in obedience to the commission given them by their principals, they did accordingly; thereby testifying mutual harmony and concord in doctrine and discipline of all the churches in both nations." Vol. i. p. 143.

When the canons of the Synod of Dort were published, they were presented to the national Synod of France, held 1620. From the record relating to this subject, the following is an extract: "This Assembly, after invocation of the name of God, decreed that the articles of the said national council held at Dort, should be read in full Synod, which being read accordingly, and every article pondered most attentively, they were all received and approved by a common unanimous consent, as agreeing with the word of God and the Confession of Faith of these our churches—for which reason all the pastors and elders deputed unto this Assembly, have sworn and protested, jointly and severally, that they consent unto this doctrine, and that they will defend it with the utmost of their power even to their latest breath. And this Assembly ordaineth that this very canon be printed and added to the canons of the said council, and that it shall be read in our provincial Synods and universities, that it may be approved, sworn, and subscribed to, by the pastors and elders of our churches, and by the doctors and professors in our universities, and also by all those that are to be ordained and admitted into the ministry, or into the professor's chair in any of our universities. And if any one of these persons should reject, either in whole or in part, the doctrine contained in, and decided by the canons of the said council, or refuse to take the oath of consent and approbation; this Assembly decreeth, that he shall not be admitted into any office or employment, either in our churches or universities." Quick's Synodicon, vol. ii. pp. 37, 38.

In the Synod, 1644–45, it was reported "by certain deputies of the maritime provinces, that there do arrive unto them from other countries, some persons going by the name of *Independents*, and so called, for that they teach every particular church should of right be governed by its own laws, without any dependency or subordination unto any person whatsoever in ecclesiastical matters, and without being obliged to own or acknowledge the authority of colloquies or Synods, in matters of discipline or order; and that they settle their dwellings in this kingdom; a thing of great and dangerous consequence if not in time carefully prevented. Now this Assembly fearing lest the contagion of this poison should diffuse itself insensibly, and bring in a world of disorders and confusions upon us, all the provinces are therefore enjoined, but more especially those which border on the sea, to be exceedingly careful that this evil do not get footing in the churches of this kingdom," &c. &c. p. 467.

There are many acts of these Synods which would make modern ears tingle, and which prove that American Presbyterianism in its strictest form, was a sucking dove compared to that of the immediate descendants of the Reformers. To maintain truth and order in the church in those days of conflict, it required a sterner purpose and firmer conviction than are commonly to be met with at the present time, when many are wont to change their church and creed almost as readily as they change their clothes. This account of the French church has been given, because, as will appear in the sequel, there was at an early period, a strong infusion of French Presbyterianism into the churches of this country, and it is well to know something of its character.

The Scottish system is now spoken of with disapprobation, and its early advocates are called "sectarian bigots." This is certainly

2

not the way in which our fathers were accustomed to speak on this subject. In a minute adopted in 1751, the Synod of New York say, "We do hereby declare and testify our constitution, order, and discipline to be in harmony with the established Church of Scotland. The Westminster Confession, Catechisms, and Directory for public worship and church government, adopted by them, are in like manner received and adopted by us. We declare ourselves united with that church in the same faith, order, and discipline. Its approbation, countenance, and favour, we have abundant testimonies of."* In their address to the General Assembly of the Church of Scotland, written in 1753, in furtherance of the efforts of Messrs. Gilbert Tennent and Samuel Davies, in behalf of the college of New Jersey, they say, "In the colonies of New York, New Jersey, Pennsylvania, Virginia, and Carolina, a great many congregations have been formed upon the Presbyterian plan, which have put themselves under the synodical care of your petitioners, who conform to the constitution of the Church of Scotland, and have adopted her standards of doctrine, worship, and discipline." Again: "Your petitioners, therefore, most earnestly pray that this very reverend Assembly would afford the said college all the countenance and assistance in their power. The young daughter of the Church of Scotland, helpless and exposed, in this foreign land, cries to her tender and powerful parent for relief."† Whose language is this? Not that of the "Old-side" Synod. If it was, it might be regarded as a matter of course. It is the language of the "New-side" Synod; of that body which, according to the popular representation, were opposed to the Scottish system. It is the language of the Tennents, Blair, Pemberton, Davies, Burr, Finley,‡ and others. Yet it is language which those, who think they adopt their principles, will not now bear.

Both parties in our church have appealed to its early history in

* Minutes of the Synod of New York, page 11 of the Appendix.

† Minutes of the Synod of New York, Appendix, pp. 13, 16.

‡ It appears from the minutes, that all the gentlemen mentioned were present when one or the other of the aboved-cited declarations was made, and most of them on both occasions.

support of their peculiar opinions. It is the object of this work to review that history, in order to show that our church has always demanded adherence to the system of doctrines contained in the Westminster Confession of Faith and Catechisms, as the condition of ministerial communion; and that it has ever claimed and exercised all the distinguishing powers of Presbyterian government. The arguments in support of this position will be drawn from the origin, from the official declarations and constitution, and from the history of the church. As there have, at different periods, been many persons connected with the Church of England, who disliked Episcopacy; so there have, doubtless, been many connected with the Presbyterian Church who disliked its principles, and were far from complying with its demands. The question, however, is not about the opinions of individuals, but the avowed principles of the Church.

It is admitted that the early history of the Presbyterian Church in the United States is involved in great obscurity. The reason of this fact is obvious. Presbyterians did not at first emigrate in large bodies, or occupy by themselves extensive districts of country. In New England the early settlers were Congregationalists. The history of that portion of our country is, therefore, in a great measure, the history of that denomination. The same remark, to a certain extent, is applicable to the Dutch in New York, the Quakers in Pennsylvania, the Catholics in Maryland. The case was very different with regard to the Presbyterians. They came, as a general rule, as individuals, or in small companies, and settled in the midst of people of other denominations. It was, therefore, in most instances, only gradually that they became sufficiently numerous in any one place to form congregations, or to associate in a Presbyterial capacity. It is true their increase was very rapid; partly by the aggregation of persons of similar principles, though of different origin, and partly by constant immigration. This peculiarity in the history of American Presbyterians arose, in a great measure, from the fact, that the persecution which drove so many of the early settlers to this country, fell, in the first instance, heaviest on the Independents and Quakers; and when it came upon the Presbyterians, (at least those of Scotland,) it did not drive them so generally from their own country, but led to a protracted struggle for liberty at home, a struggle which was eventually crowned with success.

Owing to the circumstances just referred to, we are obliged, in tracing the early history of the Presbyterian Church in this country, to review the colonial history of the several States, and gather from their records the scattered and imperfect intimations they afford of the origin of our own denomination. There is one preliminary remark, which must be constantly borne in mind. The Puritans were not all Congregationalists. The contrary impression has indeed become very general, from the fact that the Puritans settled New England, and that Congregationalism became there the prevalent form of church discipline. Hence it seems to be confidently inferred, that all emigrants from Old, or New England, bearing that designation, must have carried Congregationalism with them wherever they went. Hence too, it is taken for granted, that if a minister came into our church from New England, he could not be a Presbyterian. This is a great mistake. The Congregationalists or Independents were a mere handful, compared with the whole number of the Puritans. This term was applied to all who were desirous of a greater degree of purity, in ceremonies, discipline, or doctrine, than they found in the established Church of England. The first Puritans, under Elizabeth, scrupled about the church vestments. They had no difficulty as to the doctrines of the church; they were willing to submit to Episcopacy, but they could not reconcile themselves to the "idolatrous gear," as they called it, which had so long been the distinguishing badge of the Popish priesthood. This was the first cause of schism in the English Church. It is true many Puritans reluctantly submitted to the imposition of the clerical habits, and retained their standing in the Church. This was the case with Grindal himself, afterwards Archbishop of Canterbury. A majority of the members actually present in the convocation, held 1562, as they were desirous of a further reformation, were stigmatized as Puritans.* All the most eminent churchmen were on their side, as Jewel, Grindal, Sandys, Nowell. Archbishop Parker, and Cox, Bishop of Ely,

* Neal, Hist. of the Puritans, vol. i. p. 211.

stood almost alone on the other side; sustained, however, by the authority of Elizabeth, whose will was law.* The hold which the Puritans had upon the people is manifest from the frequent majorities which they commanded in parliament, even during this despotic reign.† The main controversy was as yet about ceremonies. Had the use of the habits and a few ceremonies been left discretionary, both ministers and people had been easy; but it was the compelling these things by law (as they told the Archbishop) that made them separate.‡ It was thus that the first and most scrupulous class of Puritans were ejected from the church.

When Whitgift was made Archbishop, in 1583, he tightened the reins of discipline, and of course increased the number of dissenters. He published three articles, which all who enjoyed any office or benefice in the church were obliged to subscribe. The second of these articles declared that the Book of Common Prayer "contained nothing contrary to the word of God." This, large numbers could not assert, and hence were suspended or deprived. Many, however, still remained in the church, who either escaped the imposition of the articles, through the favour of their bishops, or subscribed with such explanations, as satisfied their consciences. Hitherto, doctrinal matters had not entered into the controversy. The faith of the Reformers was still the faith of the church. Whitgift, the great persecutor of the Puritans, was a most strenuous Calvinist; as were Grindal before him, and Abbot after him. James I., who had sent deputies to the Synod of Dort, and had urged on the persecution of the Remonstrants, suddenly became, under the influence of a few favourite ecclesiastics, a convert to Arminianism. This, however, did not change the faith of the church or of the nation. Even "Oxford," at this time, says Le Bas, the biographer and eulogist of Laud, "bore a greater resemblance, in many respects, to a colony of Geneva, than to a Seminary of Anglo-Catholic Divinity." § As Arminianism, from this

* Hallam's Constitutional History of England, vol. i. p. 237.

† Ibid. vol. i. ch. 4.

‡ Neal, vol. i. p. 252.

§ Le Bas' Life of Archbishop Laud, p. 5.

time, became the doctrine of the high church and court party, Calvinism was identified with Puritanism. One of the earliest parliaments under Charles I., "took up the increase of Arminianism as a public grievance. It was coupled in their remonstrances with Popery, as a new danger to religion, hardly less terrible than the former." * Under the administration of Archbishop Laud, the Puritan party rapidly increased. It was the fate of that prelate to appear at a time when his spirit and principles were in direct opposition to those of the people whom he attempted to govern. He was for receding to the very confines of Romanism; they were getting alienated even from Episcopacy. He laid peculiar stress on matters of ceremony; they were becoming more and more enamoured of simple forms of worship. He was most despotic in his ideas of government; they were determined to be free. Every parliament met but to demand a redress of grievances, (of which those arising from the bishops formed a prominent part,) and was dissolved only to have their burdens rendered more intolerable. This conflict ended as might have been expected. The principles of Laud brought himself and his unhappy master to the block. During all this time, opposers of the government were called Puritans; a term not expressive of any one set of opinions, so much as of one common object. Episcopalians, who refused to read the book of Sunday sports; Presbyterians, who objected to the power of the bishops; Independents, who rejected all government in the church, beyond that of a congregation over itself, were all Puritans. Subsequent events proved that the second of these classes was much the most numerous of the three. Even as early as the time of Elizabeth, a large portion of the clergy of the

* Hallam, vol. i. p. 551. The house passed the following resolution: "We the commons in parliament assembled, do claim, protest, and avow, for truth, the sense of the articles of religion which were established by parliament in the thirteenth year of our late Queen Elizabeth, which by the public act of the church of England, and by the general and current exposition of the writers of our church, has been delivered unto us. And we reject the sense of the Jesuits and Arminians, and all others that differ from us." See Neal vol. ii. p. 213.

established church were Presbyterians in principle. They were unwilling to separate from the church as long as unity could be preserved, and were willing to submit to Episcopacy, rather than be guilty of schism. They endeavoured, to a certain extent, to associate in Presbyteries, without separating from the establishment. As early as 1572, a Presbytery was formed on these principles at Wandsworth; and other associations of the same kind were instituted in different parts of the kingdom.* Travers drew up in Latin a form of government, entitled "The Discipline of the Church as described in the Word of God," which was printed at Geneva in 1574. It was subsequently translated into English, and revised by Cartwright.† This discipline, which is published at length by Neal in the Appendix of his history, is completely Presbyterian. It was subscribed by above five hundred beneficed clergymen, as agreeable to the word of God and to be promoted by all lawful means.‡ Thus early and thus numerous was the Presbyterian party in the Church of England.

When the arbitrary measures of Charles I. drove the nation into rebellion, the partisans of the court were of course Episcopalian; the opposite party was, or became, in the main, Presbyterian. It is not easy indeed to ascertain the proportion which the parties in the Long Parliament, opposed to the government when it first assembled, bore to each other. Of the Presbyterians, there appear to have been two divisions; the one strenuous for their whole system, the other willing to admit Archbishop Usher's plan,§ either

* Neal, vol. i. 314. Hallam dates the more extended effort to establish a Presbyterian government within the church in 1590. See vol. i. p. 158.

† This work was soon suppressed; the Archbishop having advised that all the copies should be burnt. It was republished in 1644, with the title, "A Directory of Government anciently contended for, and as far as the time would suffer, practised by the first non-conformists in the days of Queen Elizabeth, found in the study of the most accomplished divine, Mr. Thomas Cartwright, after his decease, and reserved to be published for such a time as this. Published by authority." Neal, vol. i. p. 439.

‡ Neal, vol. i. p. 471.

§ This plan provided for the government of the church by Presbyteries and

from preference, or as a compromise. A bill was brought forward by Sir Edward Dering for the utter extirpation of Episcopacy, which passed its second reading by a vote of 139 to 108.* Yet this gentleman afterwards advocated the plan of Usher. There is no doubt that many Presbyterians would have acquiesced in this scheme which was essentially Presbyterian, could it have harmonized the conflicting parties in the kingdom. When all hope, however, of a compromise was at an end, they became more strenuous in advocating their own system. When the compact came to be formed with Scotland, all the members of the commons who remained at Westminster, to the number of two hundred and twenty-eight, and between twenty and thirty peers, subscribed the solemn league and covenant.† This no doubt, was done by many from motives of policy; but it is to be hoped that the strong declarations in favour of Presbyterianism which that covenant contains, were not insincere on the part of the great majority. When the parliament called together the Westminster Assembly of Divines, in 1643, of the one hundred and twenty clerical, and thirty lay members, of which it consisted, not more than six or seven were Independents, a few were Erastians, and the remainder, with the exception of some Episcopalians, who soon retired, were Presbyterians.‡ Of these Presbyterians there were the same two divisions, which were just mentioned as existing in parliament. That this Assembly was a fair representation of the state of parties among

Synods, under the presidency of a suffragan or bishop. A vote in favour of this plan passed the house in the summer of 1641.

* Hallam, vol. ii. p. 158, who says he suspects the greater part of those who voted for this bill only wished to intimidate the bishops. He adds, however, in a note, "Clarendon tells us, that being chairman of the committee to whom the bill was referred, he gave it so much interruption, that no progress could be made before the adjournment. The house, however, came to a resolution that the taking away the offices of archbishops, bishops, chancellors, and commissaries out of the church and kingdom should be one clause of the bill." This does not look like mere intimidation.

† Hallam, vol. ii. p. 225.

‡ Neal, vol. iii. ch. 4. Chambers' Life of Bishop Reynolds, and Lightfoot's Debates in the Westminster Assembly.

the opposers of the government, subsequent events sufficiently proved. The Presbyterians became completely predominant, and their form of government was established by law, a measure to which the Independents did not object, though they insisted on freedom for themselves. That the English Presbyterians were sufficiently decided, is evident from the fact that the Assembly asserted the *jus divinum* of Presbyterianism. To this the parliament very properly demurred, and required the declaration to be put in the form in which it now stands in the Directory, viz. "that it is lawful and agreeable to the word of God, that the church be governed by congregational, classical, and synodical Assemblies." With this the English Presbyterians were as little satisfied as the Scotch. Against this declaration the London ministers, as well as the mayor and common council, earnestly remonstrated.* The Independents

* Neal, vol. iii. pp. 290, 291. One great point of difference between the Assembly and the parliament related to the power of the civil magistrates in relation to the church. The Presbyterians had passed a resolution declaring that Jesus Christ had established a form of government for the church "distinct from the civil magistrate." With this the parliament were by no means satisfied. They claimed an authority in the church as extensive as that which had been exercised formerly by the king and parliament combined. The Assembly was called merely to give advice; they were expressly denied any jurisdiction, power, or authority ecclesiastical, whatsoever. Accordingly, Episcopacy was abolished, the directory for worship enjoined, Presbyterianism established, all by act of parliament. The church had nothing to do with it. This was in strict accordance with the English method, which has been almost completely Erastian since the time of Henry VIII. The church cannot act with authority; the form of government, the articles, the liturgy, all derive their binding force from the civil rulers. The church is the creature of the State. To assert the independence of the church has always been regarded as the height of clerical arrogance. See Hallam's remarks on Cartwright's opinions, vol. i. p. 252. The power of self-government the Church of England has never enjoyed. Every sentence of a spiritual judge is liable to be reversed by a civil tribunal. Its bishops are appointed, and their number increased or diminished at pleasure, by the government. Since the power has passed out of their own hands the high-church party begin to complain bitterly of this thraldom. See British Critic, No. 43, and various numbers of the Oxford Tracts. It was on this principle of subordination to the civil authority that Presbyterianism was established by the Long Parliament; as provision was

were a small minority in parliament, among the clergy, and in the nation. Their strength was in the army. They no doubt increased greatly under Cromwell; but at his death, when the ejected members resumed their seats in parliament, the whole kingdom was in the hands of the Presbyterians. At the restoration of Charles II., "The Presbyterians," says Neal, who was very far from being their friend, "were in possession of the whole power of England; the council of state, the chief officers of the army and navy, and the governors of the chief forts and garrisons, were theirs: their clergy were in possession of both universities and of the best livings of the kingdom." Another proof how numerous and important the Presbyterians were considered, is, that it was deemed advisable in order to conciliate them, to allow Charles II. five months after his return, to issue a declaration in which so many reductions of Episcopal power, and so many reforms were promised, as to make the hierarchy very little more than it would have been, had Archbishop Usher's plan been adopted. This declaration was designed, says Hallam, merely "to scatter dust in men's eyes." The motion in parliament to give it the force of law was lost by a vote of 183 to 157.* Instead of compromise, the harshest measures were soon adopted. The act of uniformity was passed which required re-ordination of those who had been presbyterially ordained; "assent and consent to all and every thing contained, and prescribed, in and by the Book of Common Prayer," and the profession of the doctrine of passive obedience. This the Presbyterians could not submit to, and were consequently ejected from the ministry of the church, to the number of about two thousand. These, of course, were only the most conscientious, or the most decided. Multitudes who had taken the covenant, conformed, and retained their stations. This was the case with Dr. Reynolds, a man of great learning and excellence, who was made Bishop of Norwich. Among those who were ejected, were Baxter, Calamy,

made for an appeal from the censures of the church to a civil tribunal. Neal, vol. iii. pp. 297, 303. It is hard to see how this can be avoided in any country where ecclesiastical censures are followed by the forfeiture of civil rights.

* Hallam, vol. ii. p. 435.

Manton, Bates, Meade, and many others scarcely less distinguished for their learning, piety, and zeal.*

Reference is made to these familiar historical events to correct the impression that the Puritans were generally Congregationalists. Every body knows, indeed, that such was not the fact, yet from our peculiar associations with the term, it is commonly taken for granted, that all who, as Puritans, emigrated to this country to avoid the persecutions which they suffered at home, were Congregationalists. The truth, however, is, that as the great majority of Puritans in England were Presbyterian, so no inconsiderable proportion of those who came to America, preferred the Presbyterian form of church government.† The question will naturally be asked, If this be so,

* The representation given above of the prevalence of Presbyterianism among the Puritans of the reign of Charles I. is not so strong as that which may be found in the works of authors, who cannot be suspected of partiality. Mr. Bancroft, in his History of the United States, speaking of the state of England, at the close of the first civil war, says: "The majority (of parliament) was with the Presbyterians, who were elated with the sure hope of a triumph. They represented a powerful portion of the aristocracy of England; they had, besides the majority in the Commons, the exclusive possession of the House of Lords; they held command of the army, they had numerous and active adherents among the clergy; the English people favoured them. Scotland, which had been so efficient in all that had thus far been done, was entirely devoted to their interests, and they hoped for a compromise with their sovereign. . . . . And what compromise should be offered by the Independents? How could they hope for superior influence, when it could be gained only by rising above the Commons, the peers, the commanders of the army, all Scotland, and *the mass of the English people?*" pp. 9, 10. This superior influence they did gain by the genius of Cromwell, by forcibly ejecting the majority of parliament, and by the devotion of the army. "A free parliament would have been their doom," says Mr. Bancroft. "Had peace never been broken, the Independents would have remained a powerless minority; the civil war gave them a rallying point in the army." p. 12.

† Neal admits, vol. ii. p. 468, that "in the reigns of Queen Elizabeth and King James I., the Puritans were for the most part Presbyterians." He adds, however, that "from the time that Arminianism prevailed in the church, and the whole body of Calvinists came to be distinguished by the name of doctrinal Puritans, both parties seemed to unite in a moderate Episcopacy." There is no doubt much ground for the latter remark. When the erroneous doc trines, the popish ceremonies, the exceeding tyranny of the high-church party

how came Congregationalism to be generally established in New England? The answer is, that the first settlers were Congregationalists. They belonged to that division of the Puritans, which, departing farthest from the established church, first felt the necessity of setting up for themselves. In coming to this country, they came with the determination to carry out their principles, and thus the mould into which the additional settlers were cast, as they successively arrived, was fixed at the beginning. Again, the master-minds among the early Puritans in this country, by whom their civil and ecclesiastical polity was determined, were principally Congregationalists. And, thirdly, as the Puritan Presbyterians were willing, for the sake of the great ends of peace and union, to unite with the Episcopalians in a modified form of Episcopacy; so for the same important objects, they were willing to unite with the Independents in New England, in a modified form of Congregationalism. Such was the intimate union between Church and State, established in the New England provinces, that it was hardly possible that dif-

under Charles I., had driven almost the whole of the better part of the church, as well as of the nation, into the ranks of the Puritans, there were among them many who were sincerely attached to Episcopacy, and who desired nothing more than the correction of the abuses of that system. With these, the Presbyterian Puritans were generally disposed to make common cause, and to settle the Church, on the plan of what was called "primitive Episcopacy;" according to which the bishop was little more than the presiding officer of a Presbytery, an episcopus præses, and not episcopus princeps having the sole power of ordination and discipline. This is perfectly consistent with their decided preference for their own plan of government; and it accounts for the statement so often made by historians, that the parliament had at first no design to overturn the hierarchy, and that the majority of the Westminster Assembly, at first, were favourable to moderate Episcopacy. This may be very true, when they had to answer the question, What church discipline is best suited to the present state of England, so nearly equally divided between Episcopalians and Presbyterians? But when called to answer the question, Which system is the best and most agreeable to Scripture? their answer was very different. The early and decisive votes in the House of Commons against the continuance of Episcopacy, the zeal with which parliament, the Assembly, and the majority of the people, declared in favor of Presbyterianism, when all hope of an accommodation with the Episcopal party was at an end, shows clearly what their opinions and preferences were.

ferent ecclesiastical organizations could exist without producing confusion and difficulty. This union between Presbyterians and Congregationalists was, doubtless, the more readily effected, inasmuch as with the exception of the first colony from Holland, the emigrants had not enjoyed any separate ecclesiastical organization at home. They were almost all members of the established church. The ministers were, with rare exceptions, beneficed clergymen of the Church of England, who had been suspended for want of conformity, generally, in relation to matters of ceremony. Whatever, therefore, might have been their individual preferences, they had not become wedded by habit to any particular sytem.

It might be confidently inferred from the opinions of the English Puritans, as stated above, and from the circumstances which led to their emigration, during the reigns of James I. and Charles I., that many of them would bring with them a preference for Presbyterianism. It is estimated that about twenty-one thousand two hundred emigrants arrived in New England before 1640.* Cotton Mather tells us that previous to that same year four thousand Presbyterians had arrived.† In another place, when speaking of the union effected between the Congregationalists and Presbyterians in London, about the year 1690, he says, the same union and on the same terms, had subsisted between these two denominations in New England, for "many decades of years;" that is, almost from the very first settlement of the country.‡ This mixed character of the people seems also to be recognized in the address of Increase Mather to King William. He begged him to consider that, "in New England they differ from other plantations; they are called Congregational and Presbyterian; so that such a governor will not suit with the people of New England, as may be very proper for other

* Bancroft's History of the United States, vol. i. p. 415. The number of inhabitants in New England is said to have decreased rather than increased between 1640 and 1660. Holmes, vol. i. p. 361.

† Magnalia, vol. i. p. 73. From the connexion in which this fact is mentioned, it is doubtful whether these Presbyterians were from England or Scotland. In either case, their influence must have been considerable.

‡ Magnalia, vol. ii. p. 233.

English plantations."* Of the two thousand Presbyterian ministers cast out of the Church of England, by the act of uniformity in 1662, a considerable number, it is said, found a refuge in New England.† The colony of Connecticut, in writing at an early period to the lords of trade and plantations, tells them, "the people here are Congregationalists, large Congregationalists, and moderate Presbyterians, the two former being the most numerous." This form of expression evidently implies, that the latter class bore a large proportion to the former. The principal friends and patrons of this colony in England were Presbyterians; particularly Lord Say, an original patentee of the colony, to whom they often express their obligations, and to whose influence, and to that of the Earl of Manchester, another leader of the Presbyterian party, they were in a great measure indebted for the restoration of their charter.‡ Trumbull, speaking of the Assembly which drew up the Saybrook Platform, says, "Though the council were unanimous in passing the platform of discipline, yet they were not all of one opinion. Some were for high consociational government, and in their sentiments nearly Presbyterians; others were much more moderate and rather verging on Independency."§ The result of their labours proves that the former class had greatly the ascendency.

The influence of Presbyterian principles in New England is, however, much more satisfactorily proved by the nature of the ecclesiastical systems which were there adopted, than by any statements of isolated facts. These systems were evidently the result of compromise between two parties, and they show that the Presbyterian was much stronger than the Independent element. The two leading points of difference between Presbyterianism and Congregationalism, particularly as the latter exists at present, relate to the mode of government within the congregation, whether it should be by elders or the brotherhood, and to the authority of Synods. As to both these points the early discipline of the New England churches approached much nearer to Presbyterianism than it does at present. Elders, indeed,

* Magnalia, vol. i. p. 180.

† Holmes's American Annals, vol. i. p. 384.

‡ Trumbull's History of Connecticut, vol. i. p. 248. § Ibid. vol. i. p. 487.

were a regular part of the organization of the churches of the Independents, even when totally disconnected with Presbyterians. A tendency, however, soon manifested itself on the part of the brethren to dispense with their services, and take the keys into their own hands.* Mr. Wilson, one of the first ministers of Boston, lamented, on his death-bed, as among the sins of the people, opposition to elders, and "the making light of, and not subjecting to the authority of Synods, without which the churches cannot long subsist."† The venerable Eliot entertained the same opinions. "There were specially two things, which he was loth to see, and yet feared he saw, falling in the churches of New England; one was a thorough establishment of ruling elders in our churches;" and the other "a frequent repetition of needful Synods."‡ In the Cambridge Platform, which was drawn up in 1648, it is said, "The ruling elder's office is distinct from the office of pastor and teacher." He is "to join with the pastor and teacher in those acts of spiritual rule, which are distinct from the ministry of the word and sacraments committed to them," &c. In a subsequent Synod, it was agreed, 1. "The power of church government belongs only to the elders of the Church." 2. "There are certain cases, wherein the elders in their management of their church government, are to take the concurrence of the fraternity;" namely, in elections, and admissions, and censures. 3. "The elders of the church are to have a negative on the votes of the brethren," &c.

As to Synods, the Cambridge Platform denies to them in sec. iv. ch. 16, the right to perform any act of "church authority or jurisdiction;" but adds in sec. v., "The Synod's directions and determinations, so far as consonant to the word of God, are to be received with reverence and submission, not only for their agreement therewith (which is the principal ground thereof, and without which they bind not at all,) but also secondarily, for the power whereby they are made, as being an ordinance of God appointed thereunto in

* "I came from England," said one of the early inhabitants of Boston, "because I did not like the lord-bishops; but I cannot join you because I would not be under the lord-brethren." Magnalia, vol. i. p. 221.

† Ibid. p. 285.

‡ Ibid. p. 501.

in his word." This is very near the Presbyterian doctrine, which teaches that the decisions of Synods are binding on those voluntarily connected with them, when made in reference to things within their jurisdiction, and not contrary to the word of God, or any constitutional stipulations. The subsequent Assembly which met at Cambridge, carried the power of Synods fully up to the Presbyterian doctrine, if not beyond it. The second proposition on this subject, determined in that body, is in these words: "Synods duly composed of messengers chosen by them, whom they are to represent, and proceeding with a due regard to the will of God in his word, are to be reverenced as *determining* the mind of the Spirit concerning things necessary to be received and practised, in order to the edification of the churches therein represented." The third proposition is, "Synods being of apostolic example, recommended as a necessary ordinance, it is but reasonable that their judgment be acknowledged as *decisive*, [in or of] the affairs for which they are ordained; and to deny them the power of such judgment is to render a necessary ordinance of none affect."* Here it is evident that the Presbyterial element in those churches predominated.† May it not without offence be asked, whether it would not have been better, in conformity with this doctrine, to allow the church to govern itself, instead of referring so much power to the civil magistrate, as was done by the great and pious men who founded Massachusetts? Their memory deserves to be held in perpetual veneration, and their errors should be treated as the errors of a parent. Filial piety, however, permits us to learn wisdom from the mistakes of our

* Magnalia, vol. ii. p. 213, and also 200 and 201.

† "Under the first charter (of Massachusetts), Synods for suppressing errors in principles or immoralities in practice, or for establishing or reforming church government and order, had been frequent; but under the new charter no Synod had been convened." An attempt was made to have one called in 1725, but "opposition was made to the measure by the Episcopal ministers, who applied to England for its prevention. In the absence of the King, the lords-justices sent over instruction to surcease all proceedings; and the lieutenant-governor received a reprimand for 'giving his consent to a vote of reference and neglecting to transmit an account of so remarkable a transaction.' The proposal was therefore relinquished; and no subsequent attempt has been made for a Synod." Holmes's Annals, vol. ii. p. 115.

fathers. Those excellent men ought not to be quoted, as is so often done in our days, as the advocates of the independence of each separate congregation. They had suffered so much from the tyranny of ecclesiastical rulers at home, that they went to the extreme of denying to church courts, armed with nothing but moral and spiritual censures, their legitimate authority. But feeling the necessity for some authority superior to that of a single congregation over itself, they devolved it upon the magistrate. The Cambridge Platform, which denies the binding force of the decisions of a Synod, declares that not only idolatry and blasphemy, but heresy and open contempt of the word preached, "are to be restrained and punished by the civil authority." And further, "If any church, one or more, shall grow schismatical, rending itself from the communion of other churches, or shall walk incorrigibly and obstinately in any corrupt way of their own, contrary to the rule of the word; in such case the magistrate is to put forth his coercive power, as the matter shall require." The very same rules, enforced by mere ecclesiastical censures, which the Presbyterian Synod were so much reproached for making, and which led to the schism of 1741, were made in Connecticut by the legislature and enforced by civil penalties.* The controversy, therefore, between the fathers of the New England churches, and those of the American Presbyterians, would be not as to the necessity of a general authority in the Church, but as to where it should be lodged.

The churches of Connecticut appear to have had, from the beginning, more of a Presbyterian influence among them than those of Massachusetts. Hooker, the patriarch of Connecticut, said with great earnestness shortly before his death, "we must settle the consociation of churches, or else we are undone."† He also, it appears, laid peculiar stress on the importance of ruling elders.‡ The Saybrook Platform, accordingly, comes much nearer to the Presbyterian model than that of Cambridge. The former declares, 1. "That the elder or elders of a particular church, with the consent of the brethren of the same, have power, and ought to exercise church discipline according to the rule of God's word, in relation

* Trumbull, vol. ii. p. 163. † Ibid, vol. i. p. 479. ‡ Magnalia, vol. i. p. 316.

to all scandals that fall out within the same," &c. 2. "That the churches which are neighbouring to each other, shall consociate for mutual affording to each other such assistance as may be requisite, on all occasions ecclesiastical," &c. 3. "That all cases of scandal, that shall fall out within any one of the aforesaid consociations, shall be brought to a council of elders, and also messengers of the churches within the said circuit, i. e. the churches of one consociation, if they see cause to send messengers when there shall be need of a council for the determination of them." Art. 5 declares, "That when any case is orderly brought before any council of the churches, it shall be heard and determined, which (unless orderly removed from thence) shall be a final issue; and all parties therein concerned shall sit down and be determined thereby." "If any pastor or church doth obstinately refuse a due attendance and conformity to the determination of the council," after due patience, "they are to be reported guilty of a scandalous contempt, and dealt with as the rule of God's word in such case doth provide, and the sentence of non-communion shall be declared against such pastor and church." In giving, therefore, the exercise of discipline to the pastors and elders, and in making the determinations of councils definitive and binding, on pain of non-communion, the Saybrook Platform, unanimously approved by the Assembly which prepared it in 1708, and adopted by the legislature as the discipline of the churches established by law, comes very little short of Presbyterianism. It is very evident, as this Platform was a compromise between two parties, being less than the one, and more than the other wished to see adopted, that one party must have been thorough Presbyterians. That they were, moreover, the stronger of the two, is evident from the Platform approaching so much nearer to their system, than to that of the Independents.

It is, therefore, a most unfounded assumption that the Puritans were all Congregationalists, or that the emigrants from England or the New England colonies, who joined our church, as a matter of course, were disaffected to our form of government.*

* At a later period, Presbyterian sentiments, it is believed, were very prevalent among the clergy of New England. President Edwards, and his son

Though New England was the home of the Puritans, they did not confine themselves to that region of country. With the adventurous spirit which has always been one of their leading characteristics, they extended at an early period, their settlements in various directions. Long Island, from its proximity to Connecticut, was soon occupied by emigrants from the older colonies, and by settlers direct from England. The Dutch having occupied the western end of the island, these English settlements were principally towards the central and eastern portions. Before the commencement of the last century several churches had been organized, whose ministers, in many instances, were from England.*

the President of Union College, Dr. Strong, of Hartford, Dr. Dwight, are all understood to have adopted those sentiments. And, indeed, it has often been said by New England men, that the great majority of the clergy in that region of country would gladly see Presbyterianism adopted among them; but that the people, as might be expected, were opposed to it. There has, however, no doubt been a great change in the opinions of the ministers on this subject within the last ten years.

* The church at South Hampton was originally formed at Lynn, Massachusetts, and consisted of Rev. Abraham Pierson, from Yorkshire in England, and some other persons. They removed to Long Island and settled the town of South Hampton, in 1640. Hazard's MS., who quotes Winthrop, p. 204. This Mr. Pierson, who was a Presbyterian, removed with his people to Connecticut, and thence to Newark, N. J. See MS. History of Newark, by Dr. McWhorter. The first permanent minister of South Hampton was, according to MS. History of the church, Rev. Joseph Fordham, from England. This congregation placed itself under the care of the Presbytery of Philadelphia in 1716. See Minutes.

The first settlement of East Hampton was in 1649. Most of the inhabitants came from England; some were from Salem, and some from New Haven. About 1660, Rev. Thomas James became their pastor. MS. History.

The first minister of Southold was Rev. John Young, from England, who was settled about 1652. Their next minister, Rev. Joshua Hobert, was also from England. MS. History.

Huntingdon was settled by a number of people from England, and by emigrants from New England. The first minister was Rev. Eliphalet Jones, a Congregationalist from New England. "The Church of Huntingdon appears to have been conducted on the Congregational plan until April 8th, 1747, when the Rev. Messrs. Ebenezer Gould, Nathaniel Mather, Ebenezer Prime, Sylvanus White, and Samuel Buell, agreeably to previous appointment, met

Smith, in his History of New York, written in 1756, gives the following account of the inhabitants of Long Island, at that period. In King's county, opposite New York, "the inhabitants are all Dutch." In Queen's county "the inhabitants are divided into Dutch and English, Presbyterians, Episcopalians, and Quakers." Suffolk county, "except one small Episcopal congregation, consists entirely of English Presbyterians." *

The Puritans do not appear to have made much impression upon New York before the early part of the last century, but in East Jersey their settlements were numerous and important. In 1664, a company from the western part of Long Island purchased a tract of land and laid out the town of Elizabethtown. There were, however, but four houses in the place, when Philip Carteret, in 1665, arrived as governor of the province, from England, bringing with him about thirty settlers.† The first colony, therefore, must

to consult the interests of the Redeemer's kingdom, and the prosperity of the churches under their care; and after much deliberation, they adopted the Presbyterian form of government, in a manner which does them much honour as Christian ministers of the Gospel, as may be seen at length in the introduction to their Presbytery book." MS. History. In the MS. account of the Church of Bridgehampton, it is said: "The Presbytery of Long Island, formerly known by the name of the Presbytery of Suffolk, was constituted or formed April 3d, 1747." There is a confusion in these accounts which it is not easy to clear up. Frequent mention is made of a Presbytery of Long Island, in the minutes of the Synod of Philadelphia, pp. 17, 18, and onward; and also, at a later date, of a Presbytery of Suffolk. There is, however, frequent inconsistency in names of the Presbyteries in the early records. They appear sometimes to be named from the places where they happened to meet.

Jamaica was settled about 1656, chiefly by emigrants from New England. The first minister was Mr. Walker; the next Mr. Prudden. In 1692, Rev. Mr. Hubbard was called, who, in Smith's History of New York, is always called a Presbyterian; and the congregation, through their long conflict with the Episcopalians, about their property, which the latter most unjustly endeavoured to wrest from them, is styled a Presbyterian church. See Smith's History. In 1712, Rev. Mr. McNish, a member of the Presbytery of Philadelphia, became their pastor.

* Smith's New York, p. 114. He probably used the word Presbyterian in a wide sense.

† Gordon's History of New Jersey, p. 28.

have been small. Much about the same time, Woodbridge, Middletown and Shrewsbury were settled, in a good degree by emigrants from Long Island and Connecticut. Newark was settled in 1667 or 1668, by about thirty families principally from Brandford in Connecticut. As the New England Puritans were some of them Congregationalists and some Presbyterians, it is not easy to ascertain to which class the emigrants to East Jersey belonged. It is probable that some preferred the one form of church discipline, and some the other. Those who settled at Newark were Presbyterians. The Rev. Abraham Pierson was, it is believed, episcopally ordained in England, whence he emigrated to this country with a number of followers. After several previous attempts at settlement, they fixed themselves at Brandford, in Connecticut. Being dissatisfied, however, with the union between the colonies of New Haven and Connecticut, they removed to Newark. After continuing the pastor of the church there for about twenty years, Mr. Pierson was succeeded by his son, who was subsequently appointed the first president of Yale College. "These two ministers, tradition relates, were moderate Presbyterians, but the son more especially. He had imbibed moderate Presbyterianism from his father, and when at Cambridge College, he had received strong prejudices against Plymothean independency; and after his father's death he was for introducing more rigid Presbyterianism into Newark." * It appears, from the narrative just quoted, that this attempt of the younger Pierson was sustained by some Scotch members of the congregation, and opposed by others recently from Connecticut, who were in favour of the Saybrook Platform. It is probable that this difficulty led to Mr. Pierson's removal. In 1715, the church of Newark appears in connexion with the Presbytery of Philadelphia.†

* MS. History of Newark by Dr. McWhorter. The doctor says that an aged elder, then eighty-six, stated that there had been a church session in Newark from the earliest time he could remember, and that he always understood there was one from the beginning.

† The township of Woodbridge was settled from 1660 to 1665. "The inhabitants were emigrants from Scotland, but principally from New England.

The Puritans were not very successful in their attempts to form settlements upon the Delaware. In 1640, the colony of New Haven made a large purchase on both sides of that river and sent out about fifty families to make a settlement.* As this country, however, was covered by a previous claim of the Dutch, the trading establishments of the New Haven colony were broken up by the Hollanders, and the people scattered. In 1669, application was made by New Haven to the commissioners of the united colonies to make plantations on the Delaware, but the proposal was declined; and it was left to the New Haven merchants to dispose of the land which they had purchased, or to plant it as they should see cause.† Some permanent settlements, however, at a subsequent period, were made upon the Jersey side of the Delaware. Fairfield, for example, was settled about 1690, by a number of persons from the town of the same name in Connecticut. This fact is ascertained from the law creating the township of Fairfield, passed in 1697. Cape May was also a Puritan settlement, of which their records contain indubitable evidence.

In the southern colonies, there are here and there traces of Puritan settlements, but not sufficient either in number or extent, to exert much influence on the character of the rising population. Maryland was at first a Catholic colony, but being settled upon the principles of general toleration, the number of Protestants soon greatly exceeded that of the Romanists. Lord Baltimore

Their first pastor was Rev. Mr. Wade, of whom so much is said in the early minutes of the Presbytery of Philadelphia. In 1714, they invited Mr. John Pierson from Connecticut, who remained with them forty years. It was in his time, and by his influence, that this congregation obtained a royal charter of incorporation under the name and title of the First Presbyterian Church in Woodbridge; and did then take legal possession of the tract of land given by the proprietors of the province for a parsonage at the first settlement of the town. During Mr. Pierson's time there was no session in this church. He managed the affairs of the congregation without elders." MS. History of Woodbridge.

* Trumbull's History of Connecticut, vol. i. 119. Gordon thinks the number of settlers much overrated. History of New Jersey, p. 18.

† Holmes's Annals, vol. i. 348.

"invited the Puritans of Massachusetts to emigrate to Maryland, offering them land, and privileges, and 'free liberty to religion;' but Gibbons, to whom he had forwarded a commission, was 'so wholly in the New England discipline,' that he would not advance the wishes of the Irish peer; and the people, who subsequently refused Jamaica and Ireland, were not now tempted to desert the Bay of Massachusetts for the Chesapeake." * The Protestant population which so soon gained the ascendency in Maryland, were no doubt of various religious sentiments. It would seem, however, that the Episcopalians predominated, either in number or influence, since when the bishop of London sent over his commissary in 1692, the provincial assembly divided the colony into thirty parishes, sixteen of which were supplied with ministers and provided with livings.†

Virginia was so completely an Episcopal province, and the laws against all non-conformists were so severe, that we can expect but few traces of the Puritans in her early history. Unity of worship was there preserved, with few exceptions, for a century after the settlement of Jamestown.‡ There were, however, some Puritan families in the colony from the beginning, and others arrived at a later period, and there were also a few settlers from Massachusetts. As early, however, as 1633, severe laws were made for the suppression of Dissenters, who had begun to appear in the colony.§ In 1643, it was ordered, "that no minister should preach or

* Bancroft's History of the United States, vol. i. p. 253.

† Holmes, vol. ii. p. 12. Bancroft in his account of Maryland, uses the word Puritan for Protestant, as he applies it to all who opposed the Catholics, and unjustly disfranchised them. During the time of the Long Parliament and of Cromwell, these people seem indeed to have been Puritans in the English sense of the word. They passed an act confirming liberty of conscience provided it did not extend to "Popery, Prelacy, or licentiousness" of opinions. As the Independents pride themselves on being the earliest friends of liberty of conscience, it is probable they will not aspire to the honour of being the authors of that act. The mention of Prelacy and licentiousness of opinion seems to indicate rather that class of Puritans, who, in England, were opposed equally to bishops and sectaries.

‡ Bancroft, vol. ii. p. 190.

§ Holmes, vol. i. p. 269.

teach publicly or privately, except in conformity to the constitutions of the Church of England, and non-conformists were banished from the colony." * A Congregational church had been gathered by the labours of ministers from New England, and increased in 1648 to the number of one hundred and eighteen persons; but the governor, who had already banished its elder, now enjoined on Mr. Harrison its pastor to depart from the country.† During the time of Cromwell, a spirit of greater moderation prevailed; but on the restoration of Charles II., the assembly revived all the laws against separatists. Strict conformity was demanded, and every one was required to contribute to the support of the established church. The whole liturgy was to be read, and no non-conformists might teach either in public or private, on pain of banishment. In 1663 these laws were made still more severe. Attendance on the meetings of non-conformists was punished by severe fines, and the rich were obliged to pay the forfeitures of their poorer brethren. Ship-masters were punished if they brought dissenters into the colony.‡ The separatists against whom these laws seem to have been mainly directed, were Quakers and Baptists. It was not until after the commencement of the eighteenth century, that other denominations than the Episcopal obtained permanent footing in Virginia, protected by the English toleration act. The Presbyterian church in the Atlantic portion of the State was, in a great measure, built up by those who had been previously Episcopalians; and in the portion beyond the mountains, by the Scotch-Irish emigrants from Pennsylvania.

Under the name of Carolina, Charles II. granted to the Earl of Clarendon and his associates, the district of country between Virginia and Florida, and from the Atlantic to the Pacific. When the first emigrants sent out by the proprietors arrived, they found a small colony of New England men already established on the south side of the Cape Fear river. This colony, however, did not prosper, and although it received some accessions from New England, the people were soon nearly absorbed in the colonies estab-

* Bancroft, vol. i. p. 207. † Holmes, vol. i. p. 346.

‡ Bancroft, vol. ii. p. 200.

lished by emigrants from Barbadoes and the Bermudas.* The earliest settlers of this part of Carolina were principally refugees from Virginia; men who endeavoured to escape from the oppressive laws of that province against all non-conformists. They were probably mostly Quakers; at least the earliest religious teachers and meetings were in connexion with their society. As Puritans, when sufficiently numerous, were seldom long without the regular ministrations of the Gospel, the fact that there was no stated minister in North Carolina before 1704, and no church until 1705,† proves that their influence was very small.

South Carolina was settled about 1670, under the direction of the proprietors. The first colony came from England with the governor, "William Sayle, who was probably a Presbyterian;" the people, however, it is presumed were principally Episcopalians. The country was rapidly filled up with settlers from various quarters, but no mention is made of the Puritans as among the early colonists, except that a church organized in Dorchester, Massachusetts, removed in 1696 and settled on the Ashley river.‡ Rev. John Cotton, from Plymouth, son of the celebrated John Cotton of Boston, removed to Charleston in 1698, and gathered a church there.§ At an earlier period, 1683, Blake, brother of the famous admiral, brought over from Somersetshire a company of dissenters who settled in Charleston.‖ To what denomination they belonged is not mentioned. The predominant influence in South Carolina, either from the number of its adherents, or from their influence, was with the church of England, which in 1703 was established by law. I have thus endeavoured to trace the influence of the Puritans, beyond the limits of New England, in the early settlement of our country. It appears they were predominant on Long Island, numerous in East Jersey, few and scattered on the Delaware, and dotted at certain distant intervals along the southern coast.

The Dutch come next under consideration, for although they have been so numerous as to form by themselves, a distinct ecclesiastical organization, yet being Calvinists and Presbyterians, they

* Bancroft, vol. ii. pp. 137, 151.

† Ibid. vol. ii. p. 164.

‡ Holmes, vol. ii. p. 34.

§ Ibid. 42.

‖ Bancroft, ii. 172.

have in many parts of the country entered largely into the materials of which our church is composed. It was by the Dutch that the Hudson, the Connecticut, and probably the Delaware rivers were discovered. In 1613, they erected a few huts upon Manhattan Island; and in 1623, a more permanent establishment was there effected. They built a fort on the Delaware, and another on the Connecticut, laying claim to all the intervening country. In 1629 and 1630, they purchased the land on both sides of the Delaware, and commenced a settlement near Lewistown. In 1638, the Swedes arrived and purchased the land from the mouth of the Delaware to Trenton, and established themselves on Christiana creek. Several successive bodies of emigrants having arrived from Sweden, they extended their settlements as far as where Philadelphia now stands.

The few English families, emigrants from New England, who had been allured thither by the climate or the facilities for traffic with the Indians, were either driven away or submitted to the Swedes.* The Dutch viewed these colonists as intruders, and in order to maintain their claim to the soil established themselves, in 1651, at New Castle. The Swedes, in 1654, attacked and reduced that settlement, but were themselves in the following year conquered by the Dutch, who became complete masters of the Delaware.† In the mean time the Dutch settlements were rapidly extended along the Hudson, as high as Albany and the western end of Long Island. In New Jersey they had settlements in Bergen, around Newark, on the banks of the Raritan, near Shrewsbury, and were mixed with other settlers in various parts of the eastern section of the State. When the Dutch possessions were conquered by the English, in 1664, the number of inhabitants was probably not far from ten thousand. The Dutch were also among the early settlers of Maryland.‡ And in 1671, almost immediately after the settlement of Charleston, South Carolina, two ships arrived

* Bancroft, ii. 288.

† The Swedes amounted to about seven hundred, when conquered by the Dutch. Bancroft, vol. ii. p. 298.

‡ Bancroft, vol. i. p. 236.

there with Dutch emigrants from New York, who were subsequently followed by others of their countrymen from Holland.*

The German emigrants, though never forming a distinct government, as was the case, not only with the Dutch, but even with the Swedes, were far more numerous than either, and have exerted a powerful influence on the character of our country. Gov. Hunter of New York brought over with him, in 1730, three thousand German emigrants, who had fled to England to escape the persecution which they suffered in their own country.† They also formed a settlement to the west of Albany, on the German Flats. Their emigration to Pennsylvania commenced as early as 1682 or 1683, when Germantown was settled by them. In subsequent years they came in such numbers, that it was estimated in 1772, that one third of the population of the province, which was then between 200,000 and 300,000, consisted of them and their descendants.‡ In the year 1749, twelve thousand German emigrants arrived, and for several years nearly the same number arrived annually.§ From Pennsylvania they extended themselves into Virginia and Maryland. Their settlements in Carolina were also extensive. In 1709, upwards of six hundred Germans arrived and settled Newbern,‖ and were probably Swiss Germans, from the name which they gave their new home. Between 1730 and 1750, says Dr. Ramsay, South Carolina received large accessions from Switzerland, Holland, and Germany; Orangeburg, Congaree, and Wateree, receiving a large portion of the German emigrants. Numbers of Palatines arrived every year.¶ In 1764, five or six hundred were sent over from London, and had a separate township of land assigned to them.** And a few years later three hundred families, who had previously settled in Maine, removed and joined their countrymen who had

* Bancroft, vol. ii. p. 171.

† Smith's History of New York, p. 139.

‡ Proud's History of Pennsylvania, vol. ii. p. 273. § Ibid. p. 273, 4.

‖ Williamson's History of North Carolina, vol. i. p. 184.

¶ Ramsay's History of South Carolina, vol. i. p. 11.

** Holmes, vol. ii. p. 268.

fixed themselves in the south-western part of Carolina.* Other settlements were made at an earlier period in Georgia.† ‡

The Welsh, from their numbers, deserve particular notice. The principal settlement of them at an early period, was upon the left bank of the Schuylkill, in Pennsylvania. They there occupied three townships, and in a few years their numbers so increased that they obtained three additional townships.§

The persecutions to which the French Protestants were exposed during the reign of Louis XIV., consummated by the revocation of the edict of Nantes in 1685, drove hundreds of thousands of those unhappy people from their native country. They found a home in the various cities of Holland, Germany, and England, and large numbers of them came to this country. They were so numerous in Boston as to have a church by themselves in 1686.|| In New York, when yet under the dominion of the Dutch, they formed so large a portion of the population, that the laws were sometimes promulgated in their language as well as in that of the Hollanders.¶ In Richmond county, they and the Dutch made up almost the entire population; and they were settled also in considerable numbers in the counties of Westchester and Ulster.** Scattered emigrants fixed themselves, in greater or less numbers, in the provinces of Pennsylvania and Maryland, but their principal location was in the Southern States. In 1690, King William sent "a large body" of them to Virginia, where lands were assigned them on the James river; others removed to Carolina and settled on the

* Holmes, vol. ii. p. 306. † Ibid. p. 142.

‡ With regard to the Germans in Pennsylvania, Mr. Andrews, in a letter dated October 14, 1730, says, "There is, besides, in this province a vast number of Palatines, and they come in still every year. Those that have come of late are mostly Presbyterian, or as they call themselves, Reformed; the Palatinate being about three-fifths of that sort of people. There are many Lutherans and some Reformed mixed among them. In other parts of the country, they are chiefly Reformed, so that I suppose the Presbyterian party are as numerous as the Quakers, or near it."

§ Proud's History of Pennsylvania, vol. i. p. 221.

|| Holmes, vol. i. p. 446. ¶ Bancroft, vol. ii. p. 302.

** Smith's History of New York, pp. 213, 215, 218.

Santee.* In 1699, and the following years, six hundred more are mentioned as settling in Virginia.† Soon after the settlement of Carolina, Charles II. sent two ships with about two hundred French Protestants, to introduce the culture of the productions of the south of Europe.‡ From 1685 onward, the number of French emigrants to Carolina was very considerable; "fugitives from Languedoc on the Mediterranean, from Rochelle, and Saintonge, and Bordeaux, the provinces on the Bay of Biscay, from St. Quentin, Poictiers, and the beautiful valley of Tour, from St. Lo and Dieppe, men who had the virtues of the English Puritans without their bigotry, came to the country, to which the tolerant benevolence (?) of Shaftesbury had invited the believers of every creed."§ This emigration continued far into the succeeding century. In 1752 it is stated upwards of sixteen hundred foreign Protestants arrived in South Carolina.‖ In 1764 two hundred and twelve arrived from France.¶ The descendants of these numerous French Protestants have become merged almost entirely in the Episcopal and Presbyterian churches.

"The history of American colonization is the history of the crimes of Europe." The Scotch Presbyterians had not escaped their portion of the persecutions, which all opposers of Prelacy, in Great Britain, experienced during the reigns of James II. and Charles I. It was not, however, until the restoration of Charles II. that the measure of their wrongs and sorrows was rendered full. James had been educated a Calvinist and Presbyterian, and when leaving Scotland to ascend the vacant throne of Elizabeth, he assured his countrymen of his love for their church, and of his determination to support it. He had, however, hardly crossed the Tweed before he began to manifest his aversion to a form of church discipline which he regarded as essentially republican. The submissive demeanour of the English bishops, and their high doctrine as to the power of kings, confirmed a conversion which had already taken place. The Scottish presbyters were accustomed to urge him

* Holmes, vol. i. p. 479. † Ibid. vol. ii. p. 47.

‡ Bancroft, vol. ii. p. 172, and Dr. Ramsay's History of South Carolina.

§ Ibid. p. 181. ‖ Holmes, vol. ii. p. 190.

¶ Ramsay's History of South Carolina, vol. i. p. 19.

to repent of his sins; the English bishops, on their knees, assured him he spoke by the immediate assistance of God. It is not wonderful, therefore, that James adopted the cause of the latter, and made it his own. He knew enough, however, of the people whom he had left, or had sufficient respect for their opinions, to induce him to proceed with some degree of caution in his attempts to bring the ecclesiastical polity of Scotland into harmony with that of England. His more unhappy son determined to effect at once, and by authority, what his arbitrary but timid father was content to accomplish gradually, and with some appearance of co-operation by the church. He first ordered a book of canons to be published and enforced, on his own authority altering essentially the constitution of the church; and then a liturgy, copied in a great measure from that of England, but altered by Laud, so as to bring it into nearer conformity with the Roman missal. This he ordered should be used by all ministers on pain of suspension. It was resisted in all parts of the kingdom, and by all classes of the people, from political as well as religious motives. It was not merely a form of prayer, but an absolute despotism, which the people opposed. If the king, without the concurrence of the nation or the church, could introduce the English liturgy, why not the Roman mass? These arbitrary measures excited an opposition which "preserved the liberties and overthrew the monarchy of England."

* Hallam, vol. iii. p. 427. This result might doubtless have been accomplished in some other way; for it is hardly to be supposed that Englishmen could have been reduced to a state of bondage by such monarchs as the Stuarts. Still, in the providence of God, it was the struggle of the Scotch for the liberty of their church, which was the means of preserving the liberties of England. Charles had succeeded in governing the latter kingdom for twelve years without a parliament. When the Scotch formed their national covenant, that is, a voluntary agreement to sustain each other in resisting the arbitrary measures of the king, and prepared to oppose force by force, Charles found it absolutely necessary to summon a parliament. The Scotch being in arms in the north, the friends of liberty in the House of Commons were emboldened in their opposition to the court, and entered on that course which soon ended in the overthrow of the monarchy and of the established church.

The Scotch have been greatly, and, to a certain extent, justly blamed, be-

Unjust as was the conduct of this unfortunate monarch, it appears mild and honourable when compared with that of his son. Charles II., at the time of his father's death, was a friendless fugitive. The Scotch offered to receive him as their king, on condition that he should pledge himself by oath to regard and preserve their Presbyterian form of church government. To this he assented. When he arrived in the kingdom he subscribed the covenant; and again at his coronation, under circumstances of much more than usual solemnity, he swore to preserve it inviolate. The Scotch, accordingly, armed in his defence; but, divided among themselves, and led by a general very unfit to cope with Cromwell, they were soon defeated, and Charles was again driven to the continent. When he returned in 1660, he voluntarily renewed his promise to the Scotch, by whom his restoration had been greatly promoted, not to interfere with the liberty of their church. No sooner, however, was he firmly seated on his throne, than all these oaths and promises were forgotten. Presbyterianism was at once abolished, and Episcopacy established; not such as it was under James I., when bishops were little more than standing moderators

cause, instead of being satisfied with securing the liberty of their own church, they insisted on the overthrow of that of England. It should be remembered, however, that intolerance was the epidemic of the age. The Episcopalians enforced the prayer-book, the Presbyterians the covenant, the Independents the engagement. The last being more of a political character than either of the others, was, so far, the least objectionable. It was, however, both in design and in fact, what Neal calls it, "a severe test for the Presbyterians." Besides, the rigid doctrine of the exclusive divine right of Presbyterianism, and an intolerant opposition to Prelacy, did not prevail among the Scotch until they were driven, by persecution, into extreme opinions. When they found Episcopacy, in their own bitter experience, associated with despotism and superstition, and, in their firm belief, with irreligion and Popery, it is not wonderful that they regarded it as a bitter root which could bear nothing good. Their best apology is that which they themselves urged at the time. They considered it essential to the liberty of their church and country that the power of the bishops should be destroyed in England. The persecutions which they had already endured, and their just apprehensions of still greater evils, sprang from the principles and conduct of the English prelates. How well founded this opinion was, the atrocities consequent on the restoration of Charles II. and the re-establishment of Episcopacy, abundantly proved.

of the Presbyteries, but invested by the arbitrary mandate of the King, with the fulness of prelatical power. An act was passed making it penal even to speak publicly or privately against the King's supremacy, or the government of the church by archbishops and bishops. A court of high commission, of which all the prelates were members, was erected and armed with inquisitorial powers. Multitudes of learned and pious ministers were ejected from their parishes, and ignorant and ungodly men, for the most part introduced in their stead.* Yet the people were forced, under severe penalties, to attend the ministrations of these unworthy men. All ejected ministers were prohibited preaching or praying except in their own families; and preaching or praying in the fields was made punishable with death. Any one, though the nearest relative, who should shelter, aid, or in any way minister

* The testimony of bishop Burnet, who was living in Scotland at the time, and had the best opportunities for gaining correct information, is very candid and explicit on this subject. When urged to accept of a benefice, he said, "that he would not engage with a body of men, who seemed to have the spirit and temper of inquisitors in them, and to have no regard for religion in any of their proceedings."—History of his own Times, vol. i. p. 228. In another place he says, "He who had the greatest hand in the change (*i.e.* archbishop Sharp) proceeded with so much dissimulation, and the rest of the order was so mean and so selfish, and the earl of Middleton, with the other secular men who conducted it, were so utterly impious and vicious, that it did cast a reproach on every thing relating to religion, to see it managed by such instruments." Dr. Cook, in his History of the Church of Scotland, says of the Episcopal clergy of this time: "The great majority of those chosen, were men in every respect despicable. As preachers, they fell far below their predecessors. . . . . Copying the manners of those by whom they were appointed, they not only threw aside the decencies of the clerical life, but they disgusted, by the most scandalous dissoluteness and vice, those whom they should have instructed and reformed." Vol. iii. p. 271. He refers as his authority for this representation to the contemporary writers, Burnet, vol. i. pp. 229 and 307. Wodrow, vol. i. pp. 156, 7. Naphtali, pp. 171 and 181. As Leighton, so distinguished for all excellencies, was one of the Scottish prelates of this day, so there were doubtless many of the inferior clergy of exemplary character. As Leighton, however, was at length forced by the atrocities of his associates to lay down his office, so many of the better portion of the clergy were ultimately driven from their posts.

to the wants of those denounced, was held liable to the same penalty as the person assisted. All landholders were required to give bond that their families and dependents should abstain from attending any conventicle. To enforce these wicked laws torture was freely used to extort evidence or confession; families were reduced to ruin by exorbitant fines; the prisons were filled with victims of oppression; multitudes were banished and sold as slaves; women and even children were tortured or murdered for refusing to take an oath they could not understand; soldiers were quartered upon the defenceless inhabitants and allowed free license; men were hunted like wild beasts, and shot or gibbeted along the highways. Modern history hardly affords a parallel to the cruelty and oppression under which Scotland groaned for nearly thirty years. And what was all this for? It was to support Episcopacy. It was done for the bishops, and, in a great measure, by them. They were the instigators and supporters of these cruel laws, and of the still more cruel execution of them.* Is it any wonder, then, that

* "The enormities of this detestable government," says Hallam, "are far too numerous, even in species, to be enumerated in this slight sketch; and of course, most instances of cruelty have not been recorded. The privy council was accustomed to extort confessions by torture; that grim divan of bishops, lawyers, and peers, sucking the groans of each undaunted enthusiast, in hopes that some imperfect avowal might lead to the sacrifice of other victims, or at least warrant the execution of the present." Again, "It was very possible that Episcopacy might be of apostolical institution; but for this institution houses had been burned and fields laid waste, and the gospel been preached in the wilderness, and its ministers had been shot in their prayers, and husbands had been murdered before their wives, and virgins had been defiled, and many had died by the executioner, and by massacre, and in imprisonment, and in exile and slavery, and women had been tied to stakes on the sea-shore till the tide rose to overflow them, and some had been tortured and mutilated; it was a religion of the boots and the thumb-screw, which a good man must be very cool-blooded indeed if he did not hate and reject from the hands which offered it. For, after all, it is much more certain that the Supreme Being abhors cruelty and persecution, than that he has set up bishops to have a superiority over Presbyters." Const. Hist. vol. iii. pp. 435 and 442. The wonderful subserviency and degradation of the Scottish parliament during this period must strike all readers with astonishment. This fact is partially explained, and the disgrace in some measure palliated by the

the Scotch abhorred Episcopacy? It was in their experience identified with despotism, superstition, and irreligion. Their love of Presbyterianism was one with their love of liberty and religion. As the Parliament of Scotland was never a fair representation of the people, the General Assembly of their church became their great organ for resisting oppression and withstanding the encroachments of their sovereigns. The conflict therefore which in England was so long kept up between the crown and the House of Commons, was in Scotland sustained between the crown and the church. This was one reason why the Scotch became so attached to Presbyterianism; this too, was the reason why the Stuarts hated it, and determined at all hazards to introduce prelacy as an ally to despotism.*

peculiarity of its constitution. The controlling power was virtually in the hands of the bishops, who were the creatures, and, of course, the servants of the crown. The lords of the articles were originally a committee chosen by the parliament for the preparation of business. But Charles I., without any authority from parliament, had the matter so arranged, that "the bishops chose eight peers, the peers eight bishops; and these appointed sixteen commissioners of shires and boroughs. Thus the whole power was devolved upon the bishops, the slaves and sycophants of the crown. The parliament itself met only on two days, the first and last of their pretended session, the one time to choose the lords of articles, the other to ratify what they proposed." Hallam, vol. iii. p. 428. This arrangement was renewed after the restoration of Charles II.

* The first Confession of Faith prepared by Knox and his associates, asserted explicitly the right and duty of the people to resist the tyranny of their rulers. This was the result of the Reformation being carried on by the people. In England it was carried on by the government. Hence the marked difference between the principles of the two churches as to the liberty of the subject and the power of kings. The General Assembly of 1649 declared, 1st. That as magistrates and their power are ordained of God, so are they in the exercise thereof, not to walk after their own will, but according to the law of equity and righteousness. . . . A boundless and unlimited power is to be acknowledged in no king or magistrate. 2d. That there is a mutual obligation betwixt the king and his people. As both are tied to God, so each of them is tied the one to the another, for the performance of mutual and reciprocal duties. 3d. That arbitrary government and unlimited power are the fountains of all the corruptions in the Church and State. Compare these

Considering the long-continued persecution of the Scotch Presbyterians, just referred to, the wonder is that they did not universally forsake their country. The hope of regaining liberty at home, however, never entirely deserted them; and in their darkest hours there were occasional glimpses of better things to come, which led them to abandon the designs of emigration which they had formed. A company of thirty noblemen and gentlemen had contracted for a large tract of land in Carolina, as an asylum for their persecuted countrymen, when the hope of the success of the English patriots, engaged in the plot for which Russell and Sydney suffered, led them to relinquish their purpose. Still, though the

sentiments with the declarations and oaths issued and enforced by the Scottish bishops. They were the principal authors of the arbitrary laws above referred to. They all voted for the famous assertory act of 1669, which declared the king's supremacy in all ecclesiastical matters, in virtue of which the ordering and disposal of the external government and polity of the church belonged to him as an inherent right of the crown; and that his orders respecting all ecclesiastical persons and matters are to be obeyed; any law, act, or custom to the contrary notwithstanding. Cook, vol. iii. p. 314. They eagerly supported an act imposing an oath, (at first designed only for office-bearers in the church and state, but which came to be almost universally enforced,) "which no man who had not made up his mind for slavery, could swear." It declared the King to be supreme governor over all persons and in all causes, civil and ecclesiastical; that it was unlawful to consult or determine upon any subject relating to church or state without his express permission, or to form associations for redressing grievances, or take up arms against the King, or to attempt any alteration in the political or ecclesiastical constitution of the kingdom, &c. *Ibid.* 368. This reference to the arbitrary principles and atrocious cruelties of the Scottish bishops, is not made with the ungenerous design of casting odium on Episcopacy. The odium belongs to the men and to their principles, and not to Episcopacy. Those prelates were introduced by the King, in opposition to the wishes of the people. They owed every thing to the prerogative. They could stand only so long as the power of the King should prevail over the will of the nation. It is no wonder, therefore, that they magnified that power. Had the case been reversed, had Episcopacy been abolished and Presbyterianism introduced by despotic authority, we might have seen Presbyterians the advocates of prerogative, and bishops the asserters of liberty. As it was, however, prelacy and despotism in Scotland were inseparable; neither could live without the other: so they died a common death.

emigration was not so great as might under such sufferings have been expected, it was very considerable.

What portion of the four thousand Presbyterians who, according to Mather, came to New England before 1640, were from Scotland or Ireland, his account does not enable the reader to determine. At a later period, a hundred families from Ireland settled Londonderry in New Hampshire. They brought with them the Rev. James McGregore as their pastor, "who remained with them until his death, and his memory is still precious among them. He was a wise, faithful and affectionate guide to them both in civil and religious concerns."* In 1729, a church was organized in Boston, composed of Scotch and Irish, which continued Presbyterian until 1786. The Rev. Mr. Moorhead was their first pastor, "an honest, faithful, and laborious minister."† Other emigrants settled at Pelham and Palmer. There was a church also at Hampton.‡

At what time the Scotch and Irish began to emigrate to New York, it is not easy to ascertain. Smith says, the inhabitants of the city, in 1708, were "Dutch Calvinists, upon the plan of the church of Holland, French refugees on the Geneva model, a few English Episcopalians, and a still smaller number of English and Irish Presbyterians."§ Having increased in numbers, they "called Mr. Anderson, a Scotch minister, to the pastoral charge of their congregation: and Dr. John Nicolls, Patrick McKnight, Gilbert Livingston, and Thomas Smith, purchased a piece of ground and founded a church." (p. 209.) That the members of that congregation were principally Scotch may be inferred from the following facts. Of the four gentlemen who were the original pur-

* Holmes, vol. ii. p. 99.

† MS.

‡ MS. The same account states that the church in Newburyport became Presbyterian under the influence of Mr. Pierson, who left Connecticut about 1743. All these churches were probably included in the Presbytery of Boston, as may be inferred from "A fair narrative of the proceedings of the Presbytery of Boston, against Rev. Robert Abercrombie, late minister of the Gospel, at Pelham, in a letter to Rev. John Moorhead, Rev. Jonathan Parsons, and Rev. David McGregore, committee of said Presbytery." Boston, 1757.

§ History of New York, p. 186.

chasers of the ground for the erection of the church, Dr. Nicolls was a native of Scotland,* he had the principal and almost exclusive control of the pecuniary affairs of the church, and is spoken of by Mr. Pemberton, "as one of its principal founders, and its greatest benefactor." Mr. Patrick McKnight was from the north of Ireland; Mr. Gilbert Livingston was Scotch by birth or immediate descent;† Mr. Thomas Smith's origin is not known. The Rev. Mr. Anderson, their first pastor, settled in 1717, was a Scotch minister ordained by the Presbytery of Irvine. In 1720, a petition was presented to the president of the council for an act of incorporation, and would probably have been granted, but for the active opposition of the vestry of Trinity church, as the council to whom the president referred the application, reported in its favour. This application was made by "Mr. Anderson, Presbyterian minister, and Patrick McKnight, John Nicolls, Joseph Leddel, John Blake, and Thomas Inglis, in behalf of themselves, and the rest of the Presbyterian congregation in the city of New York." The petition states, that the applicants had purchased a piece of ground and erected a convenient house for the worship of God, "after the manner of the Presbyterian church of North Britain." It further details the inconvenient way in which they were obliged to vest the title to their property in certain individuals, to be held by them until the congregation should be incorporated "as one body politic in fact and in name, for carrying on their said pious intentions, and the free use and exercise of their said religion in its true doctrine, discipline and worship, according to the rules and method of the established church of North Britain." They therefore pray the president, "by letters patent under the great seal of this province, to incorporate them by the name of the ministers, elders, and deacons of the Presbyterian church in the city of New York."‡

* Dr. Miller's Life of Dr. Rodgers, p. 134.

† It is believed that the whole Livingston family, in this country, trace their descent from the celebrated Scotch clergyman of that name.

‡ This is one of the churches which is most frequently and confidently claimed as originally Congregational in its composition and character. The above statement shows that this was not the fact. It was originally a strict

The account which was published of their long and fruitless efforts to obtain an act of incorporation, is entitled "Case of the Scotch Presbyterians," &c. There can, therefore, be no doubt as to the origin and early character of this congregation. A portion of the people being dissatisfied with Mr. Anderson's strictness as a Presbyterian, were, by the trustees of Yale College, erected into a separate congregation. This interference gave great umbrage to the Presbytery of Long Island, and much is said in reference to it in our early records. This new congregation did not long continue. Most of its members, it is believed, returned to the old church.

Presbyterian church, having elders and deacons from the beginning, as the above application was made, March 4, 1719–20. It was not until after Mr. Pemberton's settlement that elders were laid aside. In the records of the trustees of that church, commencing with the year 1740, there is an account of the congregation from the beginning, in which mention is made of "the elders, deacons, and session-room;" and in the account of the difficulty with Mr. Pemberton, it is said, "*at present*, by reason of the death of some, and the removal of others, we have not one lay elder or deacon." Of course they had these officers before. Again, the trustees enter a protest against Mr. Pemberton's claim to sit with them and take part in the temporal affairs of the church; in which they say, "the power in this church and congregation may be considered under the usual similitude of three keys, the key of doctrinal instruction, the key of discipline and government, and the key of the cash. The first, they say, belongs to the minister, the second to the minister and elders, "either alone or with the deacons, which we do not determine;" and the third to the trustees. For these facts the writer is indebted to the kindness of James Lenox, Esq. of New York. The difficulties in this church were of very long continuance, and arose from various sources. A part of the people were dissatisfied with Dr. Nicolls' management of the pecuniary affairs, and complained to the Synod on the subject; and a committee was sent, in 1727, to endeavour to arrange this matter. It was then agreed that the property should be vested in certain ministers in Edinburgh, to be held by them for the benefit of the Presbyterian congregation in New York. Another source of trouble was, the difference of opinion about psalmody; and another related to discipline and government. As far as this last point is concerned, instead of a few Scotchmen entering a Congregational church and trying to make it Presbyterian, as has been represented, the reverse happens to be the case; Congregationalists entered a Presbyterian church and then were unwilling to submit to its rules. How far this is analogous with the case of our church at large, remains to be seen.

At a subsequent period, about 1756, when the majority of people determined, with permission of the Synod, to introduce the use of Watts's hymns, a portion of the Scotch members withdrew, and formed the church of which the Rev. John Mason became the pastor.

Holmes mentions the arrival of between four and five hundred emigrants from Scotland at New York, in 1737.* The county of Ulster, in 1757, was inhabited by "Dutch, French, English, Scotch, and Irish, but the first and last the most numerous."† The north side of Orange county, Smith states, was inhabited by Scotch, Irish, and English Presbyterians; and he mentions a settlement of Scotch-Irish in Albany county.

The Quakers having made extensive settlements in West Jersey, became desirous of extending their influence through the eastern portion of the State. This induced Wm. Penn, and eleven other members of the Society of Friends, in 1682, to purchase East Jersey from the devisees of Sir George Carteret. In order to avoid exciting the jealousy of other denominations, these new proprietors connected with themselves twelve associates, many of whom were natives of Scotland, "from which country the greatest emigration was expected." To induce the Scotch to emigrate, a favourable account of the province was circulated among them, and the assurance given that they should enjoy that religious liberty which was denied them in their own country. "'It is judged the interest of the government,' said George Scot of Pitlochie, apparently with the sanction of men in power, 'to suppress Presbyterian principles altogether: the whole force of the law of this kingdom is levelled at the effectual bearing them down. The rigorous putting these laws in execution, has, in a great part, ruined many of those who, notwithstanding hereof, find themselves in conscience obliged to retain these principles. A retreat where, by law, a toleration is allowed, doth at present offer itself in America, and is no where else to be found in his majesty's dominions.' This is the era at which East New Jersey, till now chiefly colonized from New England, became

* Annals, vol. ii. p. 145.

† Smith's History, p. 218.

the asylum of Scottish Presbyterians."* "Is it strange," asks the author just quoted, "that many Scottish Presbyterians of virtue, education, and courage, blending a love of popular liberty with religious enthusiasm, came to East New Jersey in such numbers, as to give to the rising commonwealth a character which a century and a half has not effaced?"† "The more wealthy of the Scotch emigrants were noted for bringing with them a great number of servants, and, in some instances, for transporting whole families of poor labourers, whom they established on their lands."‡ In a letter from the deputy-governor, dated Elizabethtown, 1st month 2, 1684, it is said, "the Scots, and William Dockwras people, coming now and settling, advance the province more than it hath advanced these ten years."§

It is evident from these and similar testimonies which might be collected, that the emigrants from Scotland to East Jersey were numerous and influential. In some places they united with the Dutch and Puritan settlers in the formation of churches, in others they were sufficiently numerous to organize congregations by themselves. The church in Freehold, one of the largest in the State, was formed chiefly by them. It was organized about 1692.|| Their first pastor was the Rev. John Boyd, from Scotland; who died, as appears from his tombstone, in 1708. Subsequently the Rev. William Tennent became their minister, and continued with them forty-four years.

It was, however, to Pennsylvania, that the largest emigrations of the Scotch and Irish, particularly of the latter, though at a somewhat later period, took place. Early in the last century they

* Bancroft, vol. ii. p. 411. † Ibid. p. 414. ‡ Gordon, p. 51.

§ Smith, p. 177.

|| "The church was formed about an hundred years ago, chiefly by persons from Scotland." MS letter, dated, April 23, 1792. The building was long called the Scotch meeting-house. "Through the influence of Gov. Belchior, a charter of incorporation was obtained for this church, including those of Allentown and Shrewsbury; but since the independency of America, Freehold has given up said charter, and is incorporated under the authority of the State." MS.

began to arrive in large numbers. Near six thousand Irish are reported as having come in 1729;* and before the middle of the century, near twelve thousand arrived annually for several years.† Speaking of a later period, Proud says, "they have flowed in of late years from the north of Ireland in very large numbers." Cumberland county, he says, is settled by them, and they abound through the whole province. From Pennsylvania they spread themselves into Virginia, and thence into North Carolina. A thousand families arrived in that State from the northern colonies in the single year 1764.‡ Their descendants occupy the western portion of the State, with a dense and homogeneous population, distinguished by the strict morals and rigid principles of their ancestors. In 1749, five or six hundred Scotch settled near Fayetteville; there was a second importation in 1754; and "there was an annual importation, from that time, of those hardy and industrious people."§

A considerable number of Scotch also settled in Maryland. Col. Ninian Beall, a native of Fifeshire, having become implicated in the troubles arising out of the conflict with Episcopacy, fled first to Barbadoes, and thence removed to Maryland, where he made an extensive purchase of land, covering much of the present site of Washington and Georgetown. He sent home to urge his friends and neighbours to join him in his exile, and had influence enough to induce about two hundred to come over. They arrived about 1690, bringing with them their pastor, the Rev. Nathaniel Taylor, and formed the church and congregation of Upper Marlborough.||

* Holmes, vol. ii. p. 123.

† Proud's History of Pennsylvania, vol. ii. p. 273–4. This emigration continued for a long time. Holmes states that "in the first fortnight of August 1773, three thousand five hundred passengers arrived in Pennsylvania from Ireland. In October a ship arrived from Galway in the north of Ireland, with eighty passengers; and a ship from Belfast with a hundred and seventy passengers. Vol. ii. p. 305.

The Irish emigrants, of whom mention is made above, were almost all Presbyterians. The flow of the catholic Irish to this country did not take place until a comparatively recent period.

‡ Holmes, vol. ii. p. 268.

§ Williamson's History of North Carolina, vol. ii. p. 80.

|| MS. by the late Dr. Balch of Georgetown.

As early as 1684, a small colony of persecuted Scotch, under Lord Cardross, settled in South Carolina, and a colony of Irish under Ferguson.* In 1737, it is said, "multitudes of labourers and husbandmen" from Ireland embarked for Carolina.† In 1764, "besides foreign Protestants, several persons from England and Scotland, and great multitudes from Ireland, settled"‡ in that State. Within three years before 1773, sixteen hundred emigrants from the north of Ireland, settled in Carolina.§ Dr. Ramsay says, "of all other countries, none has furnished the province so many inhabitants as Ireland. Scarcely a ship sailed from any of its ports for Charleston that was not crowded with men, women, and children."‖ These were almost entirely Presbyterians. There was no Catholic place of worship in Charleston before 1791. In another place the same author says, "the Scotch and Dutch were the most useful emigrants. . . . . to the former South Carolina is indebted for much of its early literature. A great proportion of its physicians, clergymen, lawyers and schoolmasters were from North Britain."¶ Edisto Island was settled by emigrants from Scotland and Wales.** The inhabitants were either Presbyterians or Episcopalians; the former were the more numerous. The time of the organization of the Presbyterian church there, is not known. But in 1705, Henry Brown obtained a grant for three hundred acres of land, which in 1717 he conveyed to certain persons in "trust for the benefit of a Presbyterian clergyman in Edisto Island." In 1732, another donation was made for the benefit of a minister "who owns the Holy Scriptures as his only rule of faith and practice, and who, agreeably to the Holy Scriptures of the Old and New Testaments, shall own the Westminster Confession of Faith, with the Larger and Shorter Catechisms as a test of his orthodoxy, and that before the church session for the time being, before his settlement there as the

* Bancroft, vol. ii. p. 173. † Holmes, vol. ii. p. 145. ‡ Ibid. vol. ii. p. 268.

§ Ibid. vol. ii. p. 305. Holmes says, America, but the context shows that Carolina is intended, since in the same note he mentions the arrival of thirty-five hundred Irish in Pennsylvania.

‖ Ramsay's History of South Carolina, vol. i. p. 20.

¶ Ibid. vol. ii. p. 23. ** Ibid. vol. ii. p. 548.

rightful minister of the aforesaid church or congregation." (Vol. ii. p. 558.) The Scotch and Irish were also among the early settlers of Georgia.*

From this slight and imperfect view of the several classes of people by whom our country was settled, it is evident that a broad foundation for the Presbyterian Church was laid from the beginning. The English Puritans were all Calvinists and many of them Presbyterians. The Dutch were Calvinists and Presbyterians; a moiety, at least, of the Germans were of the same class. All the French Protestants were Calvinists and Presbyterians, and so, of course, were the Scotch and Irish. Of the several classes, the Dutch and Germans formed distinct ecclesiastical organizations, and subsist as such to the present time. In a multitude of cases, however, their descendants mingled with the descendants of other Presbyterians, and have entered largely into the materials of which our church is composed. The same remark applies to the descendants of the French Protestants, who have generally joined either the Episcopal or Presbyterian church. The early influence of the New England Puritans was, as has been seen, nearly confined to Long Island and East Jersey. Of those who settled in Jersey, a portion were, no doubt, inclined to Congregationalism, others of them were Presbyterians. All the ministers, according to Mr. Andrews, were of the latter class. The strict Presbyterian emigrants, Scotch, Irish, Dutch and French, laid the foundation of our church in New York, East Jersey, Pennsylvania, Maryland, Virginia, and the Carolinas, through which provinces, as has been shown, they were early extended in very great numbers.

This review accounts for the rapid increase of the Presbyterian church in this country. In about a century and a quarter, it has risen from two or three ministers to between two and three thousand. This is no matter of surprise, when it is seen that so large a portion of the emigrants were Presbyterians. As they merged their diversities of national character into that of American citizens, so the Scotch, Irish, French, English, Dutch, and German Presbyterians became united in thousands of instances in the Ameri-

* Holmes, vol. ii. pp. 131, 142.

can Presbyterian Church. Having the same views of civil government, our population, so diversified as to its origin, forms a harmonious civil society, and agreeing in opinion on the government of the Church, the various classes above specified formed a religious society, in which the difference of their origin was as little regarded as it was in the State.

The review given above of the settlement of the country shows also, that nothing but a sectional vanity little less than insane, could lead to the assertion that Congregationalism was the basis of Presbyterianism in this country, and that the Presbyterian church never would have had an existence, except in name, had not the Congregationalists come among us from New England. The number of Puritans who settled in New England, was about twenty-one thousand. If it be admitted that three-fourths of these were Congregationalists, (which is a large admission,) it gives between fifteen and sixteen thousand. The Presbyterian emigrants who came to this country by the middle of the last century, were between one and two hundred thousand. Those from Ireland alone, imperfect as are the records of emigration, could not have been less than fifty thousand, and probably were far more numerous. Yet the whole Presbyterian Church owes its existence to the mere overflowings of New England! It would be much nearer the truth to say, that Presbyterians have been the basis of several denominations. Half the population of the country would now be Presbyterian, had the descendants of Presbyterians, in all cases, adhered to the faith of their fathers.

It is to be remembered, that the emigration of New England men westward, did not take place, to any great extent, until after the revolutionary war; that is, until nearly three-fourths of a century after the Presbyterian Church was founded and widely extended. At that time western New York, Ohio, and the still more remote west was a wilderness. Leaving that region out of view, what would be even now, the influence of New England men in the Presbyterian Church? Yet it is very common to hear those, who formed a mere handful of the original materials of the Church, speaking of all others as foreigners and intruders. Such representations would be offensive from their injustice, were it not for their absurdity. Suppose the few (and they were comparatively very few) Congregationalists of East Jersey had refused to associate with their Dutch and Scotch Presbyterian neighbours, what great difference would it have made? Must the thousands of Presbyterians already in the country, and the still more numerous thousands annually arriving, have ceased to exist? Are those few Congregationalists the fathers of us all? The truth is, it was not until a much later period that the great influx of Congregationalists into our church took place, though they are now disposed to regard the descendants of its founders as holding their places in the church of their fathers only by sufferance.

Sectional jealousies are beginning to threaten the safety of our country. They surely ought not to be brought into the church. They cannot be avoided, however, if arrogant and injurious assumptions on either side are allowed. The above remarks are made with the view of suppressing such prejudices. This can be effected in no other way, than by preventing unjust and irritating claims. Justice is the only stable foundation of peace. It is the peculiar characteristic of America, that it is the asylum of all nations. The blood of the Huguenots, of the Puritans, of the Dutch, of the Germans, of the Scotch, and of the Irish, here flows in one common stream.* A man, therefore, must fight against himself who would contend for any one of these classes against all others.

* There is more than one child in this village in whose veins is mingled the blood of Puritans, Huguenots, English, Irish, and Germans. Such instances, it is to be presumed, are to be found every where.

CHAPTER II.

PRESBYTERIAN CHURCH FROM 1705 TO 1729.

Introductory remarks.—Design of the chapter to exhibit the character of the Church during this period.—Origin of the congregations connected with the Presbytery of Philadelphia at the time of its organization.—Origin of the ministers who constituted that Presbytery.—Ministers connected with the church at the formation of the Synod.—Ministers who joined the Synod from 1717 to 1729.—Standard of doctrines assumed by the Presbytery.—Form of government established by the Presbytery.—Government of the individual congregations.—Powers exercised by the Presbytery over the churches.—Its authority over its own members.—Peculiarities in its modes of action.—The powers of the Synod.—Its peculiarities.—Examination of Mr. Gillespie's overture respecting acts of Synod; and of president Dickinson's four articles relating to church government.—Conclusion.

In the preceding chapter, it was shown that the materials of the Presbyterian Church were, towards the close of the seventeenth and beginning of the eighteenth centuries, widely scattered over the middle and southern States; and that these materials increased with great rapidity for a long series of years. It was shown also that a large proportion of all the emigrants who arrived in this country during that period, from Great Britain and the continent of Europe, were Calvinists in doctrine and Presbyterians in discipline. It was natural that the Puritans from New England who settled in the middle provinces should unite in ecclesiastical connections with these European emigrants. These Puritans were all Calvinists; many of them were Presbyterians, and those who were Congregationalists were accustomed to a far different Platform from any now in force. They were familiar with the government of churches, by elders, differing little in their functions from those in the Presbyterian Church. Their Synods, especially in Connecticut, were clothed with the power, which at present would be considered as little short of Presbyterianism. That the early Puritans were rigid Calvinists, no one has ventured to deny. Cotton Mather informs us, that a gentleman in New England having published a book in which he attempted to prove "that Christ bore not our sins by God's imputation, and therefore also did not bear the curse of the law for them, the General Court of Massachusetts, (the supreme civil authority,) concerned that the glorious truths of the Gospel might be rescued from the confusion whereinto the essay of this gentleman had thrown them, and afraid lest the church of God abroad should suspect that New England allowed such exorbitant aberrations, appointed Mr. Norton to draw up an answer to that erroneous treatise. This work he performed with a most elaborate and judicious pen, in a book afterwards published under the title, 'A discussion of that great point in divinity, the sufferings of Christ; and the questions about his active and passive obedience, and the imputation thereof.' In that book the true principles of the Gospel are stated, with so much demonstration, as is indeed unanswerable. The great assertion therein explained and maintained is, according to the express words of the reverend author, 'that the Lord Jesus Christ, as God-man, and Mediator, according to the will of the Father, and his own voluntary consent, fully obeyed the law, doing the command in the way of works, and suffering the essential punishment of the curse, in the way of satisfaction unto Divine justice, thereby exactly fulfilling the first Covenant; which active and passive obedience of his, together with his original righteousness, as a surety, God, of his rich grace, actually imputeth unto believers; whom by the receipt thereof by the grace of faith, he declareth and accepteth as perfectly righteous, and acknowledgeth them to have a right unto eternal life.' And in every clause of this position, the author expressed, not his own sense alone, but the sense of all the churches in the country; in testimony whereof there was published at the end of the book, an instrument signed by five considerable names, Cotton, Wilson, Mather, Symmes, and Thompson, who, in the name of others declare, 'As they believe, they also profess, that the obedience of Christ to the whole law, which is the law of righteousness, is the matter of our justification; and the imputation of our sins to Christ, and thereupon his suffering the sense of the wrath of God upon him for our sins, and the imputation of his obedience to us, are the formal cause of our justification, and that they who deny this, do now take away both of these, both the matter and form of our justification, which is the life of our souls and of our religion, and therefore called the justification of life.'"* With men holding such opinions, Presbyterians might well unite. To what extent these doctrines have become obsolete in New England, it is not for us to say. Dr. Beecher, in relation to a cognate doctrine says, "our Puritan fathers adhered to the doctrine of original sin, as consisting in the imputation of Adam's sin, and in a hereditary depravity; and this continued to be the received doctrine of the churches of New England until after the time of Edwards. He adopted the views of the Reformers on the subject of original sin, as consisting in the imputation of Adam's sin, and a depraved nature transmitted by descent. But after him, this mode of stating the subject was gradually changed, until long since, the prevailing doctrine in New England has been, that men are not guilty of Adam's sin, and that depravity is not of the substance of the soul, nor an inherent physical quality, but is wholly voluntary, and consists in the transgression of the law, in such circumstances as constitutes accountability and desert of punishment."† It is not to be presumed that all the New England clergy would assent to the correctness of this representation of their rejecting the doctrines of the Puritans and of Edwards, any more than the advocates of those doctrines would assent to the correctness of the exposition here given of the doctrine of depravity. Still no one doubts, that there has been an extensive change of views in New England upon all these subjects; and that the doctrines which the early Puritans declared to be the life of their souls and of religion, are by very many rejected.

The change has been equally marked as it regards discipline. Elders have been long discarded from their churches. No Synod has been held in Massachusetts for more than a century. The

* Magnalia, vol. i. p. 266. † Spirit of the Pilgrims, vol. i. p. 158.

Cambridge Platform has become a dead letter; and a system differing but little from independency, has taken the place of the original discipline of their churches.* It would, therefore, be a great mistake to suppose that the New England people, who before the middle of the last century associated themselves with the Presbyterian Church, brought with them the views on doctrine and discipline, which, to so great an extent, now distinguish the church in that part of our country.

It is the object of the present chapter to ascertain and exhibit the character of the Presbyterian Church in the United States, during its forming period; that is from 1704 or 1705 to 1729. For this purpose it will be necessary to ascertain, as far as possible, the origin of the several congregations of which the church was originally composed; and the origin and character of the members of the first Presbytery; to learn what standard of doctrine was assumed by them, and what form of government they instituted and administered. This latter point can, of course, best be learned from the record of their proceedings, by ascertaining what powers the Presbytery exercised over the churches, and over its own members; and what relation the Synod, after its formation, assumed to the Presbyteries and churches.

The first subject of investigation, then, is the origin of the early Presbyterian churches. It might be inferred from the statements in the preceding chapter, that Presbyterian churches would be formed nearly cotemporaneously in various parts of the country. And such in fact was the case. In a letter written by the Presbytery of Philadelphia to that of Dublin, and dated 1710, it is said, "In all Virginia we have one small congregation on Elizabeth river, and some few families favouring our way in Rappahannoc and York; in Maryland four, in Pennsylvania five, in the Jerseys two, which bounds with some places in New York, make up all the bounds

* In a MS. letter to Mr. Hazard, dated Boston, Nov. 20, 1807, the writer says, "our people are so jealous of rule and authority, that even the Cambridge Platform is a dead letter, and I don't see wherein we differ from the Baptists; we are alike Independent."

which we have any members from, and at present some of these are vacant."*

Of the church on Elizabeth river little is known. It seems from commissary Blair's report on the state of the church in Virginia, that it existed before the commencement of the last century.† From the fact of Mr. Makemie's directing in his will, that his dwelling-house and lot on Elizabeth river should be sold, it has been inferred that he had resided there before he moved to the opposite side of the Chesapeake, and that the church in question was gathered by him. If so, it must have been formed before 1690; for at that time Mr. Makemie was residing on the eastern shore. Others have supposed that the congregation was composed of a small company of Scotch emigrants, whose descendants are still to be found in the neighbourhood of Norfolk. Though reported by the Presbytery, they seem to have had little connection with that body. The name of their pastor, the Rev. Mr. Macky, never appears on the minutes as a member.‡

It is not easy to reconcile altogether the statements given in the Presbyterial letter quoted above, with the facts recorded on the minutes. For example, it is said there were four churches in Maryland in connection with the Presbytery in 1710, whereas the minutes mention at least five. It is probable, however, that when two congregations were under the care of the same pastor, they were not counted separately. These congregations were Upper Marlborough,

* Letter-book of the Presbytery.

† Dr. Hill's Sketches, No. 5.

‡ In the minutes for 1712, there is a record to the following effect: — "A complaint of the melancholy circumstances that the Rev. John Macky, on Elizabeth river, Virginia, labours under, [being made] by Mr. Henry, the Presbytery was concerned; and Mr. John Hampton saying, he designed to write to him on an affair of his own, Presbytery desired him to signify their regard to, and concern for him." Dr. Hill supposes, from the interest taken by Mr. Henry in Mr. Macky's case, that they came over from Ireland together at the instance of Mr. Makemie. His name, however, would rather lead to the conjecture that he came from Scotland, whence it is known Mr. Makemie endeavoured to procure ministers for this country.

Snowhill, Rehoboth, Monokin, and Wicomico.* The first of these was formed by a company of Scotch emigrants, who came to this country with their pastor, Rev. Nathaniel Taylor, about the year 1690.† The other four churches were in Somerset county, on the eastern shore, and were the fruits of Mr. Makemie's labours. Of this there can be no reasonable doubt, as his memory is still cherished among them, and as there is neither tradition nor record of any other Presbyterian minister in that district at the date of their formation.‡ Of Snowhill, Mr. Spence gives the following account: "A town to be called Snowhill, was established in Somerset, now Worcester county, by an act of the provincial legislature, passed in 1684, and I believe," he adds, "that the Presbyterian church in that place is nearly or quite as old as the town. Snowhill was settled by English Episcopalians, and Scotch and Irish Presbyterians; and it is certain that persons resided there at the time, or soon after the time in which the town was laid out, who were afterwards members of the Presbyterian church. My ancestor, to whom I have already alluded, was a ruling elder in that church."§ Of this family of churches Rehoboth is commonly considered to be the eldest. It consisted originally of English dissenters. Their first pastor was the Rev. Mr. Makemie, who, in his will, directs his executrix "to make over and alienate the lot on which the meeting-house is built, in an ample manner, to all intents and purposes, as shall be required for the ends and uses of a Presbyterian congregation, as if I were personally present, and to their successors for ever, and to none else but to such as are of the same persuasion in matters of religion."‖ It may be inferred from the terms of this

* According to Mr. Spence, "there is record evidence of the fact, that there were five church edifices, and as many organized Presbyterian churches in Somerset county, on the 13th of March, 1705."— Spence's Letters, p. 82. This evidence, which is given in the appendix to the Letters, consists in an extract from the records of the court which names four meeting-houses in which Mr. Hampton and Mr. McNish were authorized to preach. To these are to be added Rehoboth and Upper Marlborough, making six congregations.

† See above, p. 48. ‡ Spence's Letters. § Spence's Letters, p. 80.

‖ Spence, p. 89, and also Letter xiii.

bequest, and from the character of its founder, that this church was strictly Presbyterian; a point which, it is believed, has never been disputed.* The congregations of Monokin and Wicomico were under the pastoral care of Mr. McNish, and were organized before 1705, the date of his application to the court for permission to preach. It can hardly be presumed that these five Presbyterian congregations with distinct church edifices, some of them within fifteen miles of each other, could, at so early a period, and in so thinly settled a part of the country, have been formed in a few years. And as they all existed prior to 1705, and as Mr. Makemie had resided and laboured in that district for near twenty years before that date, it is altogether probable that several of them were formed before the commencement of the last century. That they were all Presbyterian churches never has been questioned. As early as 1723, as appears from a recorded deed, the church at Monokin had eight elders.†

The Presbytery state in their letter that they had five congregations in Pennsylvania, in 1710. The minutes, however, furnish the names of the following places, viz. Philadelphia, Neshaminy, Welsh Tract, New Castle, White Clay, Apoquinimi, and Lewes.

* Dr. Hill, after saying of Mr. Makemie, that "he was in principle and from conviction a thorough Presbyterian, and wished others to become so as fast as they could be brought to bear it, and until that time, was willing to exercise lenity and forbearance," quotes the passage from his will relating to Rehoboth, and adds: "Here he is upon his own ground; ground which he had regained from the world's wide waste; he had trained and got together this congregation, and had organized them upon consistent Presbyterian principles. So that I have no doubt but there were ruling elders, regularly inducted into office in Rehoboth and Accomac congregations, under the pastoral care of Mr. Makemie; and at Monokin and Wicomico congregations, in Somerset, Maryland, and also in Snowhill, and the meeting-house on Venable's land. The two former under the care of Mr. McNish, and the two latter under Mr. Hampton." — Sketches, No. 6.

† Spence's Let. Ap. E. That deed is to the Rev. William Steward and others, the elders "and their successors for ever, for the use, support, and continuance of a meeting-house, for the worship and service of Almighty God, according to the Presbyterian persuasion, and for no other use whatever." The number of the elders is mentioned on p. 193.

Welsh Tract is first mentioned in the following minute, 1710: "Upon information that David Evans, a lay-person, had taken upon himself publicly to teach or preach among the Welsh in the Great Valley, Chester county, it was unanimously agreed that the said Evans had done very ill, and acted irregularly, in thus invading the work of the ministry, and was thereupon censured." It may be inferred from this, that Mr. Evans was in some way connected with the Presbytery, but not that there was a church already organized among the Welsh. White Clay Creek, New Castle, and Apoquinimi were associated, as appears from the following record made in 1709: "Ordered that Mr. Wilson, (pastor of New Castle,) preach at Apoquinimi once a month upon a week-day, and one Sabbath in a quarter till the aforesaid meeting, provided always that the Sabbath-day's sermon be taken from the White Clay Creek people their time." These three places of preaching, therefore, were probably numbered as one congregation in the Presbytery's letter.

The first church in Philadelphia was organized about 1698. A number of English and Welsh dissenters, together with some French Protestants, had for some time been accustomed to assemble for religious worship, in connection with a few Baptists, in a storehouse at the corner of Chestnut and Second streets, belonging to the Barbadoes Company. Neither party had a settled pastor, but the Rev. Mr. Watts, a Baptist minister of Pennepek, had agreed to preach for them every other Lord's day. This gentleman says in his narrative, "that divers of the persons who came to that assembly were Presbyterians in judgment; they having no minister of their own, and we having hitherto made no scruple of holding communion with them in the public worship of God."* The Presbyterians, probably finding themselves unpleasantly situated, determined upon calling a minister, and invited the Rev. Jedediah Andrews, from Boston, who accepted their invitation, and arrived in Philadelphia in 1698. Shortly after his arrival, dissensions arose between the Baptists and Presbyterians, which resulted in

* Edwards's Materials for a History of the Baptists, vol. i. p. 104; quoted by Mr. Hazard, MS. History.

their separation. The former withdrew, leaving the latter in possession of the store-house, where they continued to worship until 1704, when they removed to a new meeting-house on Market street.*

* Hazard's MS. History. Dr. Jackson, who, thirty years ago, was one of the oldest members of the Market street congregation, gave Mr. Hazard the following account of the origin of the First Church. "A number of English dissenters, Welsh people, and French Huguenots, that had been banished for their attachment to what were called Puritanical principles, not being satisfied with the Episcopal persuasion (of which denomination there was already a congregation in the city), united in calling the Rev. Jedediah Andrews, from Boston, or some part of New England. Accordingly, in 1701, the Rev. Mr. Andrews settled in Philadelphia. In 1704, a small Presbyterian church was raised in Market street between Second and Third streets. Mr. John Snowden, tanner, and Mr. Wm. Gray, baker, were elders connected with Mr. Andrews. In process of time the society was greatly augmented as to numbers by emigrants from Ireland." Mr. Andrews's elder, as given in the minutes of Presbytery, was Mr. Joseph Yard, whose name appears without intermission for ten years.

Dr. Hill says, "That the records of the First Church in Philadelphia, which Mr. Andrews organized in 1701, and served to his death, in the year 1747, and even after that time till 1770, show that the church was managed by the minister and committee-men alone, without what we would call an eldership or a session at all. In the year 1770, they chose a bench of elders, who were to serve but one year, and to sit and act conjointly with the committee in managing their ecclesiastical affairs." Sketches No. 8. Mr. Spence, whose Letters are repeatedly and strongly recommended by Dr. Hill, is unwilling to allow the First Church in Philadelphia to have been Presbyterian at all. He says, "it was an association of Congregationalists, Baptists, and Presbyterians, and their minister was a preacher of the Baptist persuasion. Was that a regularly constituted Presbyterian church? I cannot consider any congregation organized as regularly Presbyterian, unless constituted according to the principles of that form of government adopted by an act of the General Assembly of the Kirk of Scotland, on the 10th day of February, 1645. . . . . The Kirk of Scotland, so far as human arrangement is concerned, is certainly the mother of the Irish and American churches, and to be a Presbyterian church, her principles of government must be adopted." p. 87. Mr. Spence's zeal for the priority of the Maryland churches carries him too far. The First Church in Philadelphia was not a motley collection of Presbyterians and Baptists. The two parties separated and formed distinct congregations after Mr. Andrews's arrival. Irish Presbyterians soon constituted a large, if not a predomi-

The congregation at Neshaminy was a Dutch Presbyterian church. Their pastor was the Rev. Mr. Van Cleck, from Holland, and the letter addressed to them by the Presbytery is directed to the "Dutch people." That they were regularly organized is evident from a minute recorded in 1711, which states that Mr. Van Cleck's absence from Presbytery was accounted for "by one of his elders, sent for that purpose."

In the manuscript history of the church in New Castle, it is stated, that the first account of a Presbyterian congregation in that town is about 1704, at which time the Rev. Mr. Wilson was the pastor. August 15, 1707, a deed for a lot of land was made to certain persons in trust "for the use of the Presbyterian congregation in New Castle, on which they were to build a house for public worship." The church at Lewes was organized about the same time, though no record goes further back than 1708.

The two congregations in Jersey, were Freehold and Woodbridge. The former was constituted, principally by emigrants from Scotland, about 1692. Their place of worship was long known as the "Scotch meeting-house." It was mentioned in the preceding chapter, that Woodbridge was settled partly by the Scotch, and partly by emigrants from New England. The congregation is first mentioned as in connexion with the Presbytery, in a letter dated May 1708. In that letter, which is addressed to several New England clergymen, the Presbytery say, "We find by divers letters which have passed between you and sundry persons in Woodbridge, that you are not unacquainted with the confusions and distractions arising from the accession of Mr. Wade to be the minister of that town, and the aversion of a considerable part of the people to the accepting of him as such." It is probable that it was the Scottish portion of the congregation that was opposed to Mr. Wade, as the first healing measure proposed by the Presbytery was that Mr. Boyd, the Scotch clergyman of Freehold, should

nant part of the congregation, and the people, and all their early pastors, Andrews, Cross, and Ewing, especially the two latter, were through evil and through good report, 'old-side' men, strenuous to a fault.

preach every third Sabbath in Woodbridge; and Mr. Wade's accession to the Presbytery in 1710, was with the view of reconciling the disaffected portion of his people. Whatever may have been the ground of the opposition, it came from the majority of the congregation.*

Besides the churches in connection with the Presbytery of Philadelphia, there were several others organized at an early date in various parts of the country. In his History of South Carolina, Dr. Ramsay says, "the Presbyterians formed congregations, not only in Charleston, but in three of the maritime islands, and at Wilton, Jacksonborough, Indian-land, Port-royal, and Williams-

* In the letter just quoted it is said, "a considerable part of the people" were opposed to Mr. Wade. In another letter they speak of "a great part of the people" as being opposed to him; and in the minutes for 1712, it is said that he acted in opposition "to the greatest part of the people."

Besides the two congregations in New Jersey, mentioned in the text, there was a third which had some connection with the Presbytery as early as 1708. In that year a request was presented from the people of Cohanzy that Mr. Smith should be ordained as their pastor. This request was granted; and in 1709, Mr. Smith appears as a member of the Presbytery. In the same year, however, he is spoken of as going to New England. The congregation is not mentioned again until 1712, when they presented another petition to the Presbytery, and a letter was written to them. In 1714, the Rev. Howell Powell, a member of the Presbytery, became their pastor, and their connection with that body was thus established. The whole country before the Revolution, about the Cohanzy river, Cumberland county, New Jersey, was called by that name; but the congregation so designated upon our minutes must have been the one which is now called Fairfield; as what is called Cohanzy in the early minutes is called Fairfield in the minute relating to their pastor, Rev. Henry Hook, made in 1722. This congregation had its origin from Connecticut, as appears from a law passed in 1697, which enacts, "that the tract of land in Cohanzy, purchased by several people lately inhabitants from Fairfield in New England, from and after the date hereof, be erected into a township and be called Fairfield." For this fact the writer is indebted to L. Q. C. Elmer, Esq. of Bridgeton, New Jersey.

The people of Maidenhead and Hopewell, West Jersey, are also mentioned in the minutes as early as 1709, when Mr. Smith was directed to preach to them on his way to or from New England. In 1711, they applied to the Presbytery for assistance in obtaining a pastor.

burg."* And again, "the Presbyterians were among the first settlers, and were always numerous in South Carolina. Their ministers in the maritime districts were mostly from Scotland and Ireland, men of good education, orderly in their conduct, and devoted to the systems of doctrine and government established in Scotland. In conjunction with them the Independents or Congregationalists were formed into a church in Charleston about the year 1690, and after being about forty years united, they separated and formed different churches. Rev. Archibald Stobs took charge of the church in the autumn of 1700, and the Rev. William Livingston in 1704."† The Presbytery of Charleston, he says, "was constituted at an early period of the 18th century, agreeably to the principles and practice of the Church of Scotland."‡ The distance of these southern churches from those about Philadelphia, and the difficulty of communication, sufficiently account for there being no connection between them. A union did not take place until the year 1800, when the Presbytery of Charleston connected itself with the Synod of Carolina.

What "the some places in New York" were, whence the Presbytery had members, as stated in their letter of 1710, does not appear from the minutes. No minister, congregation, or elder, is

* Ramsay's History, vol. ii. p. 16. † Ibid. p. 25.

‡ Mr. Hazard's MSS. contain the following extract from a "Letter from South Carolina," published in London, 1732, (second edition,) but dated, "Charleston, June 1, 1710." "There are eight ministers of the Church of England; three French Protestant churches, whereof two of their ministers have lately proselyted to the church; five of British Presbyterians; one of Anabaptists, and a small number of Quakers. The ministers of the Church of England have each £100 paid out of the public treasury, besides contributions and perquisites from their parishioners. The other ministers are maintained by voluntary subscriptions. The proportions which the several parties in religion do bear to each other, and to the whole, are at present as follows:

Episcopal party to the whole	. . . .		as 4¼ to 10
Presbyterian party including the French who retain their own discipline, to the whole	. . .		as 4½ to 10
Anabaptists	do.	do.	as 1 to 10
Quakers	do.	do.	as ¼ to 10."

there spoken of as belonging to that province. There were indeed Presbyterians in the city of New York, as early as 1707, who had principally emigrated from Great Britain and Ireland, but they were so few that they had neither a church to worship in, nor a minister to lead their worship. The congregation was organized, and Mr. Anderson called as their pastor in 1717. The church in Jamaica appears to have become connected with the Presbytery in 1712; that of Newtown in 1715; that of Southampton in 1716.

Several of the churches mentioned as belonging to the Presbytery in 1710, were not in connection with that body at the time of its organization. This was the case in regard to Neshaminy, the Welsh Tract, and Woodbridge. Of the remainder, it appears from the preceding account, that the four or five in Maryland were strictly Presbyterian. Those in Pennsylvania were all composed predominantly of Scotch and Irish Presbyterians, except the first church in Philadelphia. This appears from the statement of Mr. Blair, that "all our congregations in Pennsylvania, except two or three, chiefly are made up of people from that kingdom," i. e. Ireland.* This was written in 1744, when the Dutch congregation of Neshaminy, two Welsh congregations in the valley, besides the mixed church in Philadelphia, had long been connected with the Presbytery. The two or three exceptions, therefore, are accounted for; the remainder, which includes all the original churches, except that of Philadelphia, were, according to Mr. Blair, composed principally of Irish Presbyterians.† There were, doubtless, a good many Dutch and Swedes included in the congregations in the lower counties on the Delaware, as they were the earliest and principal settlers of those counties, and as the names of church members occurring on the minutes, would also seem to intimate. In Jersey, the church

* Account of the revival in New Londonderry, by Samuel Blair, p. 11.

† Mr. Andrews seems to say the same thing in a letter, written in 1730. "Such a multitude of people coming in from Ireland of late years, our congregations are multiplied to the number of fifteen or sixteen, which are all, but two or three, furnished with ministers; all Scotch or Irish, but two or three." Whether this means that all the ministers, or all the congregations were Scotch or Irish, except two or three, it agrees with the statement of Mr. Blair, written fourteen years later.

in Freehold was the only one at first belonging to the Presbytery. As far as can be ascertained, therefore, the congregations connected with the Presbytery at the time of its formation were all strictly Presbyterian, unless the First Church in Philadelphia be considered an exception. Up to 1710, the only Presbyterian church in which there was an appreciable number of New England men, was Woodbridge, and that, unfortunately, gave the Presbytery more trouble than all the rest put together. This, however, appears to have arisen quite as much, to say the least, from the character of the minister, as from that of the people.* As far then as the character of the original congregations is concerned, it would be difficult to find any church more homogeneous in its materials than our own; certainly not the church of Scotland; and certainly not the churches of New England. The former contained, proportionably, more members inclined to Episcopacy, and the latter more inclined to

* It is evident that the opposition to Mr. W. was not made on ecclesiastical grounds exclusively. The Presbytery in their letter to the people in Woodbridge, announcing his accession to their body, say, "nothing appearing against him sufficiently attested, we judged it unjust to deny his desire." In the following year, 1711, they say," diverses of the people of Woodbridge appeared, some for and some against Mr. Wade, and grievous scandals were charged against him, against which he made the best vindication he could, but not so good but that we thought it convenient to advise him to demit his pastoral relation to the whole people of Woodbridge."—See Letter to Cotton Mather. In the same letter the Presbytery accused him of having violated his promise to them. Wearied out by these contentions and misconduct, they at last, in 1712, authoritatively dismissed him, and appointed Mr. Gillespie to supply the congregation. There was every prospect of the people uniting in him, when Mr. Wade returned from Boston, bringing a letter from Dr. Mather, in which he recommended a Mr. Wiswall for their pastor. This renewed the contention, some declaring for that gentleman, and some for Mr. Gillespie. It was to remonstrate with Dr. Mather for this unfortunate interference, and to beg him to use his influence with the New England portion of the people, to unite in settling Mr. Gillespie, that the above quoted letter was written. This the Doctor appears to have done, though not with much effect, as Mr. Gillespie soon left the place. Within a year or two, Mr. John Pierson took charge of the congregation, and things went on smoothly, which seems to show that the opposition to Mr. Wade was something more than opposition to New England men.

Presbyterianism, than were to be found in our church inclined to Congregationalism.

The next subject of inquiry is the character of the ministers of which the Presbytery was at first composed. The original members, as far as can be ascertained from the minutes, were Messrs. Francis Makemie, Jedediah Andrews, George McNish, John Wilson, Nathaniel Taylor, and Samuel Davis. To these may be added John Boyd, who became a member by ordination in 1706. Of the original members of the Presbytery, Mr. Hazard says, "It is probable that all, except Mr. Andrews, were foreigners by birth, and that they were ordained to the gospel ministry in Scotland and Ireland."* The correctness of this statement can be proved by documentary evidence in regard to most of these gentlemen, and by the strongest circumstantial evidence with regard to the others.

The Rev. Francis Makemie, who is often spoken of as the father of our church, was settled in Accomac county, Virginia, anterior to the year 1690, when his name first appears upon the county records. According to some accounts he was a native of Scotland; according to Mr. Spence, of the North of Ireland. Mr. Spence thinks that he was ordained by the Presbytery of Donegal. It is certain, however, that he came to this country an ordained minister, and was "in principle and upon conviction, a thorough Presbyterian." He is represented as having been "a venerable and imposing character, distinguished for piety, learning, and much steady resolution and perseverance." His successful labours in the eastern shore of Maryland, his imprisonment in New York for preaching in that city, and his able defence upon his trial, are familiarly known to the public. He died in 1708, leaving a large estate.† In 1704, he went to Europe and returned the following year, accompanied by two Presbyterian ministers from Ireland, Messrs. Hamp-

* MS. History. As this statement was written perhaps thirty years ago, it must be regarded as impartial.

† Spence's Letters contain much information relating to Mr. Makemie. In Smith's History of New York may be found an instructive account of his imprisonment and trial; and the most interesting portion of Dr. Hill's sketches relate to his character and labours.

ton and McNish.* The former became the pastor of Snowhill; the latter of Monokin and Wicomico, in the first instance, but removed in 1712, to Jamaica, upon Long Island.

It is probable that the Rev. Samuel Davis was another of the ministers, whom Mr. Makemie, during his last visit to Europe, induced to come to this country. The scene of his labours, from 1705 or 1706, onwards, was the churches planted by Mr. Makemie, or those in their immediate vicinity. He was appointed to take part in the installation of Mr. Hampton, at Snowhill, in connection with Mr. McNish. And subsequently he was associated in another service with Mr. Hampton and Mr. Henry. It appears from the minutes of 1715, that he had for some time been fixed at Lewes or its neighbourhood, as the people applied to have another minister, as Mr. Davis could not take the pastoral charge of the congregation. He finally succeeded Mr. Hampton as minister of Snowhill. All these circumstances connect him with the churches in the peninsula, all whose ministers, Makemie, Hampton, McNish, Henry, Clement, Steward, Thompson, were from Scotland or Ireland. If Davis was not, he is the only exception. In the absence of all evidence to the contrary, or of any circumstance connecting him with New England, it is in the highest degree probable that he had the same origin with his associates.

Mr. Nathaniel Taylor, as stated in the preceding chapter, was a minister from Scotland, who came to this country with his congregation and settled in Upper Marlborough, about 1690. Mr. John Wilson was the pastor of the church in New Castle. As he died in 1708, there are few memorials of him now preserved. That he was from Scotland may be inferred not only from the place of his labours and his associates, but from his being appointed to conduct the correspondence with that country. It was natural that those members of the Presbytery, who came from Scotland or Ireland, should be designated to write, as occasion required, to the places whence they came. This natural rule, it is evident from the minutes, was

* Spence, p. 70. This writer speaks of Mr. Hampton as coming from Ireland; but Dr. Rodgers of New York, and other ministers of our church of the last generation, always spoke of him as a Scotchman.

actually adopted. Mr. Andrews was the great penman of the Presbytery, and as he lived in Philadelphia, and kept the books, a great part of the burden of conducting the correspondence of the body, which was no slight matter, was devolved upon him. Yet it is believed there is no instance in the early minutes of his being appointed to write to either Scotland or Ireland. This duty was assigned to Makemie, Wilson, Anderson, Gillespie, Henry.* As all these are known to have been Scotch or Irish, it is hardly to be doubted, as there is not the slightest evidence to the contrary, that Mr. Wilson was also. Mr. John Boyd, the minister of Freehold, who became a member of the Presbytery in 1706, was also a native of Scotland.†

As far then as can be ascertained, all the original members of the Presbytery were either Scotch or Irish, except Mr. Andrews. As this gentleman was among the first, so he was one of the most laborious and useful members of the Presbytery. All the minutes, both of the Presbytery and Synod, for a long series of years, are in his handwriting. He was also the treasurer of the Synod, and seems to have been one of its most punctual and active members.‡ He was probably a moderate man. His name never appears attached to any protest or counter-protest, and he says he was often instrumental in healing differences between the brethren of conflicting views. He did not join in the protest excluding the New

* "Ordered that Mr. Makemie write to Scotland, to Mr. Alexander Colden, minister at Oxam, about coming to this country." p. 4. "Ordered that Mr. Henry write to the Presbytery of Dublin." p. 8. "Ordered that Mr. Wilson and Mr. Anderson write to the Synod of Glasgow." p. 8. "Ordered that Mr. Gillespie write to the Synod of Glasgow." p. 22. "Ordered that Mr. Magill, and Mr. Young write to the Synod of Glasgow and Air, and to Principal Stirling." p. 55.

† MS. History of Freehold, quoted above.

‡ His name occurs in the list of ministers as present at Presbytery in 1706. From that time it is never missed until his death in 1746. He, therefore, attended every meeting of Presbytery before the formation of the Synod, and every meeting of the Synod until '46, when his name appears for the last time. He seems also to have kept the records from 1708, to 1747. The minutes for that year appear in a new handwriting.

Brunswick Presbytery from the Synod, at the time of the schism, though he adhered to the 'old-side' throughout, and took part in all their ulterior measures.

So much stress has been laid upon the origin of the founders of our church, and is in reality due to it, that the preceding investigation cannot be deemed superfluous. If all, or any large proportion of them, had been previously Congregationalists, the presumption would undoubtedly be, that the form of government which they instituted was more or less allied to Congregationalism. And, on the other hand, if they were all, with one exception, Scotch or Irish Presbyterians,* the presumption is equally strong, that the system which they adopted was in accordance with that to which they had been accustomed. It is, however, but a presumption in either case. The decisive evidence must be sought in their declarations and acts.

The increase of the church after the organization of the Presbytery was rapid, and arose principally from the constant immigration of Presbyterians, ministers as well as people, from abroad, and from the organization of those already scattered through the country. In 1707, the number of ministers was eight, all but one from Scotland or Ireland. In 1716, the whole number was twenty-five, of whom seventeen were still living and in connection with the Presbytery.† In that year it was determined to form four Pres-

* Dr. Hill admits that, "if this could be satisfactorily proved, it would go far in settling this controversy."—Sketches, No. 7. The controversy to which he particularly refers, is about the standard of doctrine adopted by the first Presbytery.

† Of the eight members whose names do not appear on the minutes, in 1716, Messrs. Makemie, Wilson, Taylor, Boyd, and Lawson, were dead; Messrs. Smith, Wade, and Van Cleck, had withdrawn. Mr. Smith was probably from New England, as he was settled over the Cohanzy people for a short time, and as he was directed to preach at a certain place in New Jersey, on "his way to New England." These are slight circumstances whence to infer his origin, but they are all the minutes afford. He never met the Presbytery but once, and that was in 1709. Mr. Wade was also from New England; he was admitted in 1710, met the Presbytery in 1711, and was dismissed in 1712. Mr. Van Cleck was from Holland, as appears from the correspondence

byteries; the first to consist of the following members: viz. Messrs. Andrews, Jones, Powell, Orr, Bradner, and Morgan, and to meet at Philadelphia or elsewhere; the second of Messrs. Anderson, Magill, Gillespie, Wotherspoon, Evans, and Conn, to meet at New Castle; the third to consist of Messrs. Davis, Hampton, and Henry, to meet at Snowhill; and the fourth of Messrs. McNish and Pumry, on Long Island, who were directed to endeavour to induce some of the neighbouring ministers to associate with them in forming a Presbytery. The Presbytery of Snowhill does not appear ever to have met. Most of its members became attached to that of New Castle. Of the above seventeen ministers, Mr. Andrews and Mr. Pumry are the only two of whom there is any evidence that they were from New England, and the latter had joined the Presbytery the preceding year. Almost the whole amount of New England influence, therefore, in the Presbytery, from the time it was formed until after the constitution of the Synod, rests with Mr. Andrews. Of the two other New England members, Mr. Smith never met the Presbytery but once, and Mr. Wade but twice.*

respecting him. He was an unworthy member, and absconded while under process in 1715.

* It is very difficult, after such a lapse of time, to ascertain the origin of the different members of the Presbytery. The following notices contain all the information which the writer, after a good deal of search, has been able to obtain.

The Presbytery of Philadelphia.—Mr. Andrews, known to have been from Boston, a graduate of Harvard College and pastor of the First Church, Philadelphia.

Rev. Malachi Jones, pastor of the church at Abingdon, admitted to the Presbytery as an ordained minister in 1714. He was from Wales, as appears from a letter of Mr. Andrews to Dr. Colman of Boston.

Rev. Howell Powell, pastor of the Cohanzy church, was received as an ordained minister in 1713, and was directed to obtain further testimonials from his friends in England. He therefore was, probably, English or Welsh.

Rev. Robert Orr, pastor of the congregations of Maidenhead and Hopewell, New Jersey; afterwards a member of the Presbytery of Donegal, was received as a licentiate, and ordained by the Presbytery in 1715.

Rev. John Bradner, pastor, first of Cape May, afterwards of Goshen, New

From 1716 to 1729, the proportion of New England ministers was considerably increased; several of the most prominent and useful members of the Synod were from that section of the country. They formed, in 1728, from a fourth to a third of the whole

York, was ordained by the Presbytery in 1714. It is stated in MS. history of Goshen, that he was from Scotland.

Rev. Joseph Morgan, settled first at Freehold, and then at Maidenhead and Hopewell, was admitted as an ordained minister in 1710. He was, probably, from Great Britain.

Presbytery of New Castle (and Snowhill.)—Rev. James Anderson, settled first in New Castle, afterwards in New York, and finally in Donegal, was an ordained minister from the Presbytery of Irvine in Scotland; came to this country in 1709, and was received into the Presbytery in 1710. See Dr. Miller's Life of Dr. Rodgers.

Rev. Daniel Magill, in the first instance pastor of the church at Patuxent or Upper Marlborough, was sent out at their request by one of the Presbyteries in Scotland, as is stated in the MS. history of that church, and received into the Presbytery in 1710.

Rev. George Gillespie, first settled at White Clay creek near New Castle, was received as a licentiate from the Presbytery of Glasgow in 1712.

Rev. David Evans, pastor of the congregation on the Welsh Tract, ordained by the Presbytery in 1714.

Rev. Robert Wotherspoon, first settled at Apoquinimi, near New Castle, was received as a licentiate and ordained by the Presbytery in 1714. He was probably from Scotland.

Rev. Hugh Conn, settled in Baltimore county, Maryland, received as a licentiate and ordained by the Presbytery in 1715. He was probably from Ireland.

Rev. Samuel Davis, settled in the peninsula, was one of the original members of the Presbytery. Believed to have been from Ireland.

Rev. John Hampton, pastor of Snowhill, was one of the original members of the Presbytery, and came from Scotland or Ireland.

Rev. John Henry, successor of Mr. Makemie at Rehoboth, was received as an ordained minister in 1710. He came from Ireland.

Long Island Presbytery.—Rev. George McNish, pastor first of Monokin, Maryland, afterwards of Jamaica, was one of the original members of the Presbytery of Philadelphia, and came from Scotland or Ireland. See Spence's Letters.

Rev. Samuel Pumry, minister of Newtown, was received as an ordained minister in 1715. He was from Connecticut, as the writer learns from Rev. John Goldsmith, pastor of the church in Newtown.

The following list contains the names, residence, and origin of the several

body. This review shows the great injustice of representing the Scotch and Irish members as mere intruders, and the New England or Congregational portion as the true original Presbyterian Church. As far as the character of the body may be inferred

members who joined the Synod from 1717 to 1729, as far as the writer has been able to ascertain the facts. It is hoped that others may be able to correct its mistakes, or supply its deficiencies.

Rev. John Thompson, settled first at Lewes, afterwards at Chestnut Level, was received as a probationer, and ordained by the Presbytery in 1717. His arrival in the country and first application to the Presbytery, took place in 1715. He was from Ireland.

Rev. John Pierson, settled at Woodbridge. He was ordained by the Presbytery in 1717. He was from New England.

Rev. Jonathan Dickinson, pastor of Elizabethtown, appears as a member of the Synod, for the first time in 1717. He was a native of Massachusetts.

Rev. Samuel Gelston, settled first at Southampton, afterwards near Elk river, was ordained 1717. His first application to the Presbytery as a licentiate was in 1715. He was, it is believed, from Long Island.

Rev. Henry Hook, settled at Cohanzy, was received in 1718. He was from Ireland, as appears from the minutes for 1722.

Rev. William Tennent, settled at Neshaminy, was received as an ordained minister of the established church of Ireland in 1718.

Rev. Samuel Young, settled ——— was received as an ordained minister from the Presbytery of Armagh in 1718.

Rev. John Clement, settled at Rehoboth, was received as a probationer from Britain in 1718.

Rev. William Steward, settled at Monokin, received as a probationer from Britain in 1718, and ordained by order of Synod, together with Mr. Clement.

Rev. George Philips, ——— Long Island, first mentioned as a member of Synod in 1718.

Rev. Joseph Lamb, ——— Long Island, first mentioned as a member in 1718. These two gentlemen were associated with Messrs. McNish and Pumry, in the Presbytery of Long Island. Their names are very rarely mentioned on the minutes, except in the list of absent members.

Rev. Robert Cross, settled first at New Castle, afterwards at Jamaica, Long Island, and finally over the First Church, Philadelphia, received as a licentiate and ordained by the Presbytery of New Castle in 1719. He was a native of Ireland, as is stated on his tomb-stone.

Rev. Joseph Webb, pastor of the church in Newark, is first mentioned as a member of Synod in 1720. He was from New England.

Rev. John Orme, pastor of the church of Upper Marlborough, is first men-

from that of its founders, it was a purely Presbyterian church from the beginning. It was not founded upon Congregationalism, nor by Congregationalists. It was founded by Presbyterians, and upon Presbyterian principles, and those who subsequently joined

tioned as a member of Synod in 1720. He was from Devonshire, England, as is stated in the history of his congregation.

Rev. Moses Dickinson, ——— mentioned as a member of Synod in 1722; brother of President Dickinson. He was settled, after leaving the Presbyterian church, in Norwalk, Connecticut.

Rev. Thomas Evans, Welsh Tract, (Penkader,) licensed by the Presbytery of New Castle in 1720, and stated in their minutes to have presented credentials from the Presbytery of Carmarthenshire, South Wales. Belonged to the Presbytery of New Castle.

Rev. Alexander Hucheson, pastor of Bohemia and Broad Creek, received as a probationer from the Presbytery of Glasgow in 1722. Belonged to the Presbytery of New Castle.

Rev. Robert Laing, Somerset county, Maryland, received as a minister from Great Britain in 1722, and referred to the Presbytery of New Castle.

Rev. Thomas Creaghead, White Clay creek, received by the Presbytery of New Castle, in 1724. It is recorded on their minutes, p. 77, that he had "lately come from New England." Whether a native of that part of the country or of Ireland is not known.

Rev. Joseph Houston, Elk river, received by the New Castle Presbytery, as a probationer, "lately from New England" in 1724, and ordained by them.

Rev. Adam Boyd, settled in Octarara, received by the New Castle Presbytery as probationer, "lately from New England," in 1724, and ordained by them.

Mr. William McMillan. The minutes of the New Castle Presbytery contain the record of his licensure in 1724, and he was directed to labour among the people in Virginia, where he resided.

Rev. Noyes Parris, settled for a time at Cohanzy, mentioned as a member of Synod in 1725. He was probably from New England, as his name would indicate, (Mr. Noyes was one of the early ministers of Massachusetts. Mather's Magnalia, vol. i. p. 436,) and when he left the Synod in 1727 or 1728, he is reported as having gone to New England.

Rev. Archibald Cook, Kent county in Delaware, received by the New Castle Presbytery, "as late from Ireland," and ordained by them in 1726.

Rev. Hugh Stevenson, Snowhill, received by the New Castle Presbytery, "as late from Ireland," in 1726, and ordained by them in 1728.

Rev. Gilbert Tennent, New Brunswick, afterwards pastor of the Second Church, Philadelphia. He is mentioned in the New Castle book, as a licen-

it, joined it as a Presbyterian body. Mr. Andrews was the only minister from New England who had any permanent connection with the church before 1715, and he so far from being a Congregationalist, was an "old-side" Presbyterian. Of the six or seven additional New England members who joined the Synod before 1729, some were among the strictest Presbyterians of the whole body; and not one of them was either a Congregationalist, or inclined to Congregationalism, if any dependence is to be placed upon their declarations or acts.

Having taken this view of the origin of the Presbyterian Church, during its forming period, in order to ascertain its character, as far as it may be inferred from the materials of which it was composed, it is time to inquire more particularly into its doctrines and discipline, during the same period. As it regards doctrines, the point to be ascertained is, whether the Presbyterian church was a Calvinistic body, and required adherence to that system of doctrine as a condition of ministerial communion, or whether it demanded nothing more than assent to the essential doctrines of the gospel. The latter position, as was shown in the introductory chapter, has been unequivocally assumed. That this assumption is incorrect, and that our church has from the beginning required adherence to Calvinism as a condition of ministerial communion, can be made very clearly to appear. It is admitted that the Presbytery required of its members what it considered soundness in the faith, or orthodoxy. The only question then is, what was orthodoxy, in the estimation of the founders of our church? Was it faith in the essential doctrines of the gospel? or was it faith in that system of doctrines, which, for convenience' sake, has obtained the name of Calvinism? This is the only important question. The method which they adopted to decide upon the orthodoxy of a member, is of very subordinate consequence. Whether it was by personal examination; by satisfactory

tiate in 1725. His name first appears as a member of Synod in 1727. He was from Ireland.

Rev. Nathaniel Hubbell, Westfield, New Jersey, first appears as a member of Synod in 1728. He was from Massachusetts, as is stated in the MS. History of Westfield.

testimonials; or by assent to a prescribed formula of doctrines, is comparatively of but little moment. The question is, what they did require? Not, how did they satisfy themselves? It seems a matter of supererogation to prove that men educated towards the close of the seventeenth, or the beginning of the eighteenth century, in Scotland, Ireland, or New England, regarded Calvinism as the true doctrine of the Scriptures, and considered any essential deviation from it as a disqualification for the work of the ministry. Is the faith of the church of Scotland at that period a matter of doubt? Was she not still reeking with the blood of her children, martyrs for her faith and discipline? Were men who had suffered so much in their own persons, or in those of their friends, for Presbyterianism, likely to cast it away, the moment they got to a place of perfect security? It has never yet been made a question, what was the faith of the Puritans who first settled New England, or what was the standard of orthodoxy among her churches. No one has ventured to assert that Christianity, in the general adherence to doctrines absolutely fundamental, was all that was there required of ministers of the gospel. And why not? Not because there is documentary evidence that every candidate for ordination was required to sign a particular formula, but because the opinions of those Puritans are a matter of notoriety. Their opinions, however, were neither more pronounced, nor more notorious than those of the churches of Scotland or Ireland. Why then should it be assumed that the ministers of the latter were so latitudinarian, as soon as they reached this country, when no such assumption is made with regard to the former?

It is to be remembered that the great majority of the early ministers of our church were either ordained or licensed before they became connected with it. The very testimonials which they brought with them, if they came from Scotland or Ireland, stated explicitly that they had adopted the Westminster Confession of Faith; if they came from New England, they brought evidence of their Calvinism just as unequivocal. No doubt could be entertained what was meant by 'orthodoxy,' in certificates given by men who expressed so much alarm lest 'the churches of God should suspect that New England allowed such exorbitant aberrations' as the denial that Christ bore the penalty of the law. It was just as natural, and as much a matter of course, for the Presbytery of Philadelphia to receive with confidence men coming from the Scotch and Irish Presbyteries, as it is for one of our Presbyteries to receive the members of another. The moment, however, it was discovered that these certificates deceived them, they began to adopt other methods to ascertain the Calvinism of those whom they admitted.*

The single consideration, then, that all the early ministers of our church came from places where Calvinism not only prevailed, but where it was strenuously insisted upon, is, in the absence of all evidence to the contrary, sufficient to prove that they were not so singular, or so much in advance of the spirit of their age, as to bring down their demands to the low standard of absolutely essential doctrines. It is not, however, merely the origin, but the known opinions of these ministers, which are relied upon to prove the Calvinistic character of our church. There is not a single minister, whose sentiments are known at all, who was admitted to the church, or allowed to remain in it during the period under review, who is not known to have been not only a Calvinist, but a rigid one. This was the case with the members of the strict Presbytery of New Castle, the men who are now reproached for sectarian bigotry for their zeal for this very subject. It was the case with Jonathan Dickinson, Gilbert Tennent, and every other minister connected with the church, before 1729, who has left any memorials of his opinions. It is contrary to all experience, and to the principles of human nature, that men, who have been accustomed to one standard of doctrines, should suddenly lower their demands, unless they themselves were disaffected towards those doctrines.

Another evidence of the Calvinistic character of our church, may be found in the circumstances attending the reception of the Rev. William Tennent in 1718. That gentleman had been episcopally ordained in Ireland; but on coming to this country, applied to be received as a member of the Synod of Philadelphia. That body

* The correctness of this statement will appear, when the 'adopting act' comes under consideration.

required him to state in writing the reasons of his dissent from the Episcopal church. One of the most prominent of those reasons was, that the church of Ireland connived "at Arminian doctrines." Are we then to believe that Mr. Tennent left one church because it connived at Arminianism, to join another which tolerated Pelagianism; nay, that required nothing more than assent to the absolutely essential doctrines of the Gospel? Surely the Synod would have had too much self-respect to insert in their minutes a document charging it as a crime upon a sister church, that she connived at Arminianism, if they themselves did the same, and more.

The Calvinistic character of our church is further evident from the fact, that as soon as some other means than personal examination, or the testimonials of ecclesiastical bodies, became necessary to ascertain the orthodoxy of its members, subscription to the Westminster Confession of Faith was demanded and universally submitted to. As long as the church was small, and all, or a large portion of its members could be present at the admission of every new applicant, the most natural and the most effectual method to obtain a knowledge of his opinions, was personal examination. And as long as the churches with which the Synod corresponded were faithful to their own standards, their testimony was received as sufficient evidence of the soundness of the men whom they recommended. But when from the multiplication of Presbyteries, the first method became impossible, and when the second was found to be unworthy of confidence, another plan was adopted. On the supposition that the church was to remain one, and that it had any zeal for its own doctrines, it was necessary that the several Presbyteries should understand each other, and unite in adopting a common standard of orthodoxy. Hence arose the call for a general agreement, to make the adoption of the Westminster Confession a condition of ministerial communion. There can be no stronger evidence of the Calvinistic character of the church, than that this new test of orthodoxy was universally admitted, and that there was not a single member of the Synod who objected to any one article in the Confession of Faith, except that which related to the power of the civil magistrates in matters of religion. That article was, by common consent, discarded; all the others were cordially adopted.* It is inconceivable that a body of men should have unanimously adopted this measure, had it been the fixing a new and higher standard of orthodoxy, and not merely a new method for ascertaining the adherence of the ministry to what had always been demanded.

Some portions of the church felt the necessity for the adoption of this measure before others. One method, as already remarked, which had been relied upon to secure the church from unsound ministers, was the demand of testimonials of orthodoxy from all applicants for admission. So long as confidence was felt in those giving such testimonials, the church was satisfied; but when suspicion arose on this point, something more was demanded. The earliest and most serious suspicions were felt with regard to the Presbyteries in the north of Ireland; and hence the New Castle Presbytery, within whose bounds most of the ministers from Ireland came, was the first that insisted on something more than clean papers from the applicants for membership. As early at least as 1724, they began to require the adoption of the Westminster Confession of Faith.†

It has been made a question, whether the Presbytery of Philadelphia did from the beginning, regularly and formally adopt the Westminster Confession, or not. As the first leaf of the book of records is lost, it is impossible that this question should be satisfactorily answered. Dr. Green has argued for the affirmative with a great deal of force, and has rendered it highly probable that the first page contained some statement of the principles, both as to doctrine and discipline, on which the Presbytery was formed. It is certain they had "a constitution" to which they could appeal, and to which their members promised subjection. In a letter written by the Presbytery to the people of Woodbridge, in 1712, they say

* The correctness of this statement shall be proved in the next chapter.

† "I do own the Westminster Confession of Faith as the confession of my faith." This formula was subscribed by Wm. McMillan in 1724, by Archibald W. Cook and Hugh Stevenson, in 1726. John Tennent, September 18, 1729, subscribed the following declaration: "I do own the Westminster Confession of Faith, before God and these witnesses, together with the Larger and Shorter Catechisms, with the Directory thereto annexed, to be the confession of my faith, and rule of faith and manners, according to the word of God.

that Mr. Wade "submitted himself willingly to our constitution." Whether this constitution was a written document, or a formal recognition of the standards of the church of Scotland; or whether the passage quoted merely means that Mr. Wade had submitted himself to the acknowledged principles of Presbyterianism, cannot be certainly determined. The *a priori* probability is in favour of the supposition that the first page of the minutes contained some general recognition of the standards of the church of Scotland, as all the original members of the Presbytery, as we have every reason to believe, except Mr. Andrews, had already adopted those standards at the time of their ordination.

What was on the first page of the minutes, however, is a very different question from another, with which it appears sometimes to be confounded. It may be admitted that the Presbytery, at the time of its organization, commenced its records with some preamble stating the principles upon which it was organized; but was it customary to require a formal assent to the Westminster Confession as a condition of membership? That this question must be answered in the negative, appears plain from two considerations. The first is, that from 1706 to 1729, there is no mention, either in the minutes of the Presbytery before 1716, or in those of the Synod after that date, of such assent having been demanded or given. Whereas, after the adopting act in 1729, the record is uniformly made that the new members had adopted the Confession of Faith. This certainly seems to show that a change of custom was effected by that act; that, however, some Presbyteries, for their own satisfaction, had made the demand before, the original Presbytery and Synod had not been in the habit of making it. In the second place, the history of the adopting act itself establishes the same point. It appears that the church had hitherto relied upon other means for securing orthodoxy in its ministers, but as new dangers arose, new means of guarding against them were devised. The overture which led to the adopting act, though of considerable length, and though reciting the reasons which called for that measure, makes no allusion to its having been previously the custom to exact assent to the Westminster Confession, but speaks of it as a new measure, designed to meet a new difficulty.

The question whether the Westminster Confession was uniformly adopted by new members, as before remarked, is one of subordinate importance. The church did not become Calvinistic by adopting that Confession; but adopted it because it already was so, and always had been. Its demands were in no respects altered, much less were they raised, by the act of 1729. That act was nothing more than a measure, arising out of the altered circumstances of the church, designed to accomplish a purpose which had hitherto been attained by other means. The New England Puritans were not stricter Calvinists in 1640, when they adopted the Cambridge Platform, than they were in 1620; nor had they become more rigid in 1688, when they recognized the Westminster Confession. No historical fact of the same kind admits of clearer proof, from their origin, declarations and acts, than that the founders of our church were Calvinists, and that they demanded Calvinism, and not merely faith in the absolutely essential doctrines of the gospel, as the condition of ministerial communion.

The next subject of inquiry is the form of discipline adopted during the period under review. If, as has been proved, all the original members of the Presbytery, except one, were Presbyterian ministers from Scotland or Ireland, and if all the congregations, unless the First Church in Philadelphia be partially an exception, were composed of Presbyterians, as has also been shown,* then there can be little doubt that, at least at the beginning, whatever it may have become afterwards, our church was a Presbyterian Church. These considerations, however, are merely presumptive. They are of great weight, if confirmed by other kinds of evidence, but of very little, if contradicted by the conduct or avowals of those concerned. The real question then is, what, in point of fact, was the form of government on which the founders of our church acted? Was it Presbyterianism? or was it Congregationalism? or was it some anomalous system partaking of the features of both, yet belonging to neither? This point must be settled by an inspection of the records.

It is plain that, whatever these men really were, they thought

* The church at Woodbridge was not one of the original congregations.

themselves Presbyterians. It is the name which they adopted. They called their judicatory, not an association or council, but a Presbytery; they always speak of Presbyterians as being "of our persuasion." In corresponding with the judicatories of Ireland and Scotland, they called themselves Presbyterians, to those who were accustomed to affix a definite meaning to the term. When writing to the governor of Virginia, in order to inform him of their principles, they tell him they were "of the same persuasion as the church of Scotland." * In 1721, the Synod declare in the preamble to an overture which they adopted, that they had "been for many years in the exercise of Presbyterian government and discipline, as exercised by Presbyterians in the best reformed churches, as far as the nature and constitution of this country would allow." † By "Presbyterians in the best reformed churches," must be understood those of Scotland, Ireland, France, and Holland; and what the Presbyterianism of those countries was, is not a matter to be disputed. It is only asking then that the founders of our church should be regarded as sane and honest men, when it is asked

* The date of this letter is 1738, and therefore subsequent to the period under consideration. But as it states what the character of the church was, and always had been, its citation is not out of place.

† "As far as the nature and constitution of this country would allow." This is a limitation, and it is the only one of the analogy between American Presbyterianism and that of the best reformed churches. How did the nature or constitution of this country prevent the carrying out the Presbyterian form of government? Did it forbid the government of the church by Sessions, Presbyteries, and Synods? Did it prevent a subordination of one of these courts to another? Did it forbid the church to form rules for the management of its own affairs? It clearly did none of these things. As the Synod declare they conformed to the Presbyterianism of Europe, so far as the constitution of the country would allow, they do thereby declare that they conformed in every thing which did not arise out of the peculiar local circumstances of the foreign churches, either as civil establishments, or as controlled and fettered by the state. This is all the difference which, in 1721, a man educated in Scotland, and who had been for nine years a member of the Synod, declared he could see between our Presbyterianism and that of his native country. Surely he is a better judge, and a more competent witness than those who, at a distance of more than a century, pronounce so confidently on the early character of our church.

that they should be regarded as a Presbyterian, and not as a Congregational or nondescript body.

Still, as actions speak louder than words, it is best to see how these men acted; how the individual congregations were organized and governed; how the Presbyteries were constituted; what authority they exercised over their churches and members; and what relation subsisted between them and the Synod. Presbyterianism is a mode of church government as definite and as well understood as any other form of ecclesiastical polity. Its fundamental principle is, that the government of the church rests upon the Presbyteries; that is, the clerical and lay elders. It demands, therefore, congregational, classical, and provincial assemblies of such elders, i. e. Sessions, Presbyteries, and Synods. It establishes a regular subordination of the lower of these judicatories to the higher, giving to the latter the right of review and control over the former. And, finally, it declares the determinations and decisions of these several judicatories, relating to matters of government and discipline, to be binding upon all under their authority, when not inconsistent with the word of God, or some previous constitutional stipulation. Such is the Presbyterianism of Scotland, Ireland, France, and Holland. This is the whole system, and every feature of it is found in the form of discipline of the churches of those countries. The question is, are they all found in our system as at first established? If they are, it is a mere waste of time to dispute further about the nature of the system. It is what, in all ages and countries, has been called Presbyterianism, and it may safely be called so still.

How then were the individual congregations governed? It has already been shown that all the churches *originally* belonging to the Presbytery were regularly organized, unless the First Church in Philadelphia be an exception. This is admitted to have been the case with the four or five Maryland churches organized by Mr. Makemie before 1705. There is no doubt it was the case with the Scotch church of Upper Marlborough. Of the fifteen or sixteen churches in Pennsylvania in 1730, all were Scotch or Irish but two or three; and of these three, the one in Philadelphia was the only one connected from the beginning with the Presbytery. Of the remaining two, one was a regular Dutch Presbyterian church. Of those in New Jersey, Freehold was Scotch; Newark was settled by English Presbyterians, and had elders from the beginning, according to the best information and belief of Dr. McWhorter. Elizabethtown also must have had them under President Dickinson, unless he acted in opposition to his avowed principles. With regard to Cohanzy, and the united congregations of Maidenhead and Hopewell, the facts are not known. Woodbridge is the only church of which there is satisfactory evidence that it was managed on the Congregational plan, and it is very doubtful whether this was the case even there, before the settlement of Mr. Pierson in 1714.

It is, however, highly probable, that there were several churches connected with the Presbytery before 1715, which were but imperfectly organized. This could hardly have been otherwise under the circumstances of the country. Perfect order and regularity are not to be expected in any rising community, whether civil or ecclesiastical. The wonder is, even on the assumption that the ministers were the strictest Presbyterians, that there is so little indication of imperfect organization in the churches. The existence of such churches may be inferred from the language of Mr. Andrews in 1730. In a letter of that date, he says: "In the Jerseys there are some Congregational assemblies, that is, some of the people are inclined that way, being originally from New England, yet they all submit to the Presbyteries readily enough; and the ministers are all Presbyterians, though most from New England." This moderate language is indeed very far from being decisive. He does not speak of Congregational churches, but merely says, that "some of the people are inclined" to Congregationalism. This is just what might be expected from all other contemporary accounts. The churches there were composed of Dutch, Scotch, and New England people, and hence the moderate and correct mode adopted by Mr. Andrews of stating the amount of Congregationalism among them.

A more decisive proof that there were churches imperfectly organized, in connection with the first Presbytery, upon its formation, is to be found in the following minute, adopted in 1714: "For the better establishing and settling of congregations, it is ordered and appointed, that in every congregation there be a sufficient number of assistants chosen, to aid the minister in the management of congregational affairs; and that there be a book of records kept for that effect, and that the same be annually brought here to be revised by Presbytery." p. 25. The next year, there is the following minute on this subject: "In pursuance of an act made last Presbytery, appointing every minister to appoint assistants and session book, &c. and in regard divers of the ministers have not complied with the designs of said act, it was therefore ordered, that the several ministers come with said books, and perform the other ends of the said act, as it is specified therein." p. 28. Again, in 1716, when the Presbytery was divided, it is said: "With respect to session books, mentioned in our last year's minutes, it is ordered that they be brought into, and revised by the respective Presbyteries, to which they shall after this time, according to our preceding appointment, belong." p. 34.

It is certainly to be inferred from these minutes, that there were some congregations in 1714, which had no regular sessions. From the second minute, however, it would appear, that the difficulty related more to session books than to the sessions themselves. It is surprising that any one should attempt to prove from this order of 1714, that there were no elders appointed in our churches before that date, when the reverse is perfectly notorious.* It is

* "Ruling elders," says the Cincinnati Journal, July 30, 1838, "are frequently called assistants, and this settles the question, that Dr. Hill is right in supposing that the order of the mother Presbytery in 1715, to their churches to choose assistants, meant elders, and that elders had not been elected previously." A statement so much at variance with notorious facts, ought not to be imposed upon Dr. Hill. The Doctor so far from saying that elders were not elected before 1715, says the very reverse: "The impression has been taken up by some, that I denied that there were any such officers as ruling elders in those early times. I never meant to convey this idea."—Sketches No. 6. In the same No. he says, "I have no doubt there were ruling elders regularly inducted into office in Rehoboth and Accomac congregations under the pastoral care of Mr. Makemie, and at Monokin and Wicomico, in Somer-

not only known and admitted, that the Maryland and many of the Pennsylvania churches had elders from the beginning, but they are constantly recorded as present, as members of the Presbytery. The first record is a fragment containing the minutes of an afternoon session, of December 27, 1706, when no elders are mentioned;

set, Maryland, and also in Snowhill, and the meeting-house on Venable's land." All these congregations were formed before 1705. If there is no doubt that there were ruling elders in these churches, what reason is there to doubt that there were similar officers in the other Scotch and Irish churches, i. e. in all originally connected with the Presbytery, with one exception?

Dr. Hill makes a great mistake, when he says that "these elders are no where spoken of as elders, under that distinctive title but in the opening minute at the commencement of each session." This is very far from being correct. See the memorandum quoted on the next page of the admission of three additional elders, after the commencement of the meeting in 1709. In 1710, there is this minute: "Ordered that the ministers and elders of this meeting come prepared," &c. In 1711, Mr. Van Cleck's absence was excused "by one of his elders sent for that purpose." In the same year, "inquiry was made of the ministers . . . . then of the several elders," &c. These are only examples. Dr. Hill, adds, "whenever they are spoken of or alluded to afterwards, they are called representatives of the people, and sometimes the minister's assistants." That this is incorrect as far as it asserts that the elders are always so called, has just been shown. They are sometimes so called. And are not our elders the representatives of the people, and minister's assistants? and are they not so called? Every one knows that these were common designations for elders, but no one has supposed that they were thereby proved not to be elders. These forms of expression are sometimes interchanged on the same page. For example, on page 30, it is said, "Mr. Henry's representative of his congregation being absent," &c. and then in the next sentence, "The reasons of Pumry's elder's absence were inquired into and sustained." It may be supposed that this diversity of form was intentional, and that some congregations sent representatives, and some elders. It happens unfortunately for this hypothesis, that Mr. Henry, whose elder is called a representative, was the pastor of Mr. Makemie's favourite church of Rehoboth, where Dr. Hill says he doubts not there were regular ruling elders; and that Mr. Pumry was minister of Newtown, Long Island, where, if any where, we should expect committee-men. Besides, on p. 29, we find Mr. Edmunson mentioned "as the representative of the church at Patuxent." This was the Scotch congregation, elsewhere called Upper Marlborough. Nothing can be gained, therefore, from this source, to prove that representatives were not elders.

an occurrence far too frequent, even now, to excite surprise. At the next meeting, 1707, there were present four ministers and four elders, and from that time onward there is no meeting, either of the Presbytery or Synod, of which elders are not mentioned as constituting a part. In 1710, three ministers were admitted as new members, and it is immediately recorded: "Memorandum upon the admission of those ministers above mentioned, three more elders sat in Presbytery, namely, Mr. Pierce Bray, Mr. John Foord, Mr. Leonard Van Degrift." p. 9. There is, therefore, just as much evidence that there were elders from the beginning of the Presbytery, as that there were preachers. While this is an undeniable fact, it is freely admitted there were churches in which elders were not to be found. The wonder is that such churches were not more numerous. Perfect organization, as before remarked, is not to be expected at the beginning of any community. The Presbyterian Church in this country has never pretended to be more strict than that of Scotland. According to the theory of that church, every congregation should have its own elders. Yet knowing it was vain to try to make bricks without straw, it wisely ordered that this should not be attempted, and hence in the early period of the history of that church, there were multitudes of congregations without a session. "When we speak of the eldership of particular congregations," says the book of policy of 1581, "we mean not that every particular parish kirk can or may have their own particular eldership, specially inlandward, but we think that three, four, more or fewer, particular kirks, may have one eldership common to them all." The Presbyterianism, therefore, of the Scotch and Irish ministers who came to this country, need not be very violently questioned, if, after the example of their fathers, they appointed elders when they could obtain suitable persons, and where they could not, did the best they could without them.*

* It is somewhere noticed as a great departure from Scottish Presbyterianism, that in one or more of our early churches, elders were elected annually. In the Scotch church, however, this was originally the rule. "The election of elders and deacons ought to be made every year once, which we judge most convenient to be done the first of August yearly, lest men by long

After all, the really important question respects the principles of the founders of our church. What form of government did they aim at introducing? What were their demands? Most of the churches were regularly organized, some few were not. Was the Presbytery satisfied with this? Were they willing that things should remain in this state, or that the Congregational plan should be introduced? Far from it. They "ordered" those churches which, as yet, had no sessions, to choose them, to keep regular records, and to produce them annually to be revised by the Presbytery. When this "act" was, in some instances, disregarded, the order was repeated again and again. It is hard to see what a set of men, though just from Scotland, could have done more. Had they been as indifferent on this subject as the church has been for the last forty or fifty years, they would have let it alone, and allowed the several congregations to take their own course in relation to it. It is, therefore, very evident, that the original Presbytery was far more strict in regard to this point than the church has been, at least since 1801.

There is one record on the minutes which presents the opinions of the early members of our church, on this subject, in so clear a light that it must not be passed over. In 1722, Mr. Dickinson and some others introduced four articles into Synod, explanatory of their principles of church government. The first of these declares, "that the power of the keys is committed to church officers and to them only." By the power of the keys is, of course, meant the power of discipline; the right to open or shut the door of the church. This right, according to Congregationalism, belongs to the brotherhood; according to Presbyterianism, to church officers, and to them only. This article, then, contains an explicit condemnation of the Congregational method of conducting the discipline of the church, and of consequence of those churches (connected with the Synod) that acted upon that plan. Yet these articles came from what may be called the New England side of the house. They were introduced in opposition to a measure proposed by one of the Scotch members,

continuance in those offices, presume on the liberty of the church."—Spotswood's History of the Church of Scotland, p. 167.

and were unanimously adopted. There was, therefore, as to this point, no diversity of opinion. Whatever irregularity in practice might, in some cases, exist, it was never sanctioned, but condemned by all parties and on all suitable occasions.

The next subject of investigation is the organization and power of the original Presbytery. A Presbytery, according to our present constitution, is a convention of bishops and elders within a certain district. It has "power to receive and issue appeals from church sessions, and references brought before them in an orderly manner; to examine and license candidates for the holy ministry; to ordain, install, remove, and judge ministers; to examine, and approve or censure the records of church sessions; to resolve questions of doctrine and discipline seriously and reasonably proposed; to condemn erroneous opinions which injure the peace or purity of the church; to visit particular churches for the purpose of inquiring into their state and redressing the evils that may have arisen in them; to unite or divide congregations at the request of the people, or to form or to receive new congregations, and, in general, to order whatever pertains to the spiritual welfare of the churches under their care." That the first Presbytery was a convention of ministers and elders, has already been satisfactorily shown. And it is really remarkable, considering the circumstances, how large and regular an attendance of elders was obtained. In 1707, there were four ministers and four elders present; in 1708, six ministers and three elders; in 1709, seven ministers and five elders; in 1710, at first four ministers and four elders, afterwards seven of each class. Thus it continued until the formation of the Synod, when the proportion of elders in attendance is generally less.

That this Presbytery exercised all the powers above specified in their fullest latitude, is evident from every page of their records. With regard to the powers of ecclesiastical bodies, much confusion and misapprehension have arisen by pressing too far the analogy between them and those of similar names in civil society. Our judicatories are neither courts nor legislatures, properly speaking. They are the governing bodies in the church, and are invested with the general authority to administer its affairs. This authority no more admits of being reduced to distinct categories, than that of a parent. It is that of general direction and control; limited, as in the case of a parent, by the nature of the relation, by the word of God, and by mutual stipulations.

It is precisely such a general authority, as above stated, that we find the first Presbytery exercising over the churches under its care. No congregation could either settle or dismiss a pastor without its permission. All calls then, as now, were presented to the Presbytery, and if approved, were handed to the persons for whom they were designed. Thus, in 1710, the call from Monokin for Mr. McNish was presented to him by the Presbytery. In the same year, Mr. Wade, having resigned his charge, it is said, "the Presbytery do henceforth allow the good people of Woodbridge to supply themselves with another pastor." In 1712, a call was presented from one of the Maryland churches for the Rev. Thomas Bratten, and forwarded to him; and he having died before his settlement, another was presented the following year from the same church to the Rev. Robert Lawson. Similar records occur in the minutes of almost every year. In 1715, we find the following: "Mr. Philip Ringo having presented a call from the people of Maidenhead and Hopewell, in West Jersey, unto Mr. Robert Orr, the Presbytery called for, considered of, and approved the said Mr. Orr his [Mr. Orr's] credentials as a preacher of the gospel, and likewise considered of and approved the call, which being presented by the moderator unto the said Mr. Orr, he accepted of it." On the same page there is a record of precisely the same character, respecting a call from Baltimore county, for Mr. Hugh Conn. In the minutes for 1716, it is stated: "A call from the people of South Hampton, on Long Island, to Mr. Gelston, wherein the said people do subject themselves to us in the Lord, as a Presbytery, being presented to us in the name of their representatives, we did tender it to the said Mr. Gelston, and he accepted it."

In like manner we find the Presbytery dismissing pastors, with or without their consent. Mr. Wade's case is an example of the latter kind. He resigned his charge in Woodbridge in 1711, but immediately retracted his resignation, and insisted upon continuing to act as the pastor of the church. Whereupon, in 1712, the Presbytery, after a recital of the grounds of their dissatisfaction with him, say, "We, therefore, in the fear and in the name of our great Master, do appoint and ordain that the said Mr. Wade do no longer exercise his ministerial office in the town of Woodbridge, or among the people thereof, unless allowed by the Presbytery hereafter, but that he forthwith, and without resistance directly or indirectly, give place to some other, whom God in his providence may send, and the good people of Woodbridge, or the major part of them, call and agree about." An example of an opposite kind occurred in 1718, when the Synod acting in a Presbyterial capacity, say: "Rev. John Hampton having petitioned for a dismission from his pastoral relation to the people of Snowhill, they considering that the said Mr. Hampton was not able to perform the office of a pastor to that people, without manifest hazard to his life, through bodily indisposition, the Synod upon mature deliberation having put the matter to vote, it was carried *nemine contradicente* to accept of his resignation, and to declare his congregation vacant; to the great regret of Synod." In 1726, in consequence of a reference from the Presbytery of Long Island, the Synod determined *inter alia*, "That Mr. Anderson, according to his desire, be left at liberty to remove from New York, and to accept of a call from any other people, as Providence may determine, and that the people of New York be at liberty to call another minister, in an orderly way, as soon as they shall pay up what arrears appear justly due to Mr. Anderson." In the following year, Mr. Pemberton having been called without the intervention of the Presbytery of Long Island, the Synod made the following minute: "As to the call and settlement of the Rev. Mr. Pemberton at New York, the Synod do determine that the rules of our Presbyterian constitution were not observed, in several respects, by the congregation in that matter. This also passed *nemine contradicente.* And it was put to vote, receive or delay the receiving of Mr. Pemberton as a member of this Synod, and it was carried for delaying, which delay did not flow from disrespect to Mr. Pemberton or any fault or objection to him, but from other reasons." These examples, which are only a few of those which might be selected from the minutes for the period under consideration, illustrate the kind of authority exercised by the Presbytery in relation to the calling and settling of ministers.

Similar instances might be adduced of every other power ever exercised at the present day by a Presbytery over a congregation; as that of erecting new churches; dividing congregations; appointing supplies, &c. &c. These, however, are so familiar as to render any thing more than this general reference unnecessary. It will be more interesting to notice a few examples of a somewhat different character. As early as 1708, the people of New Castle petitioned "that the people of White Clay Creek be not suffered to set up a new meeting-house." These early Presbyterians must have had high ideas of the authority of Presbytery, or they never would have presented such a request. In consequence of this petition it was "ordered that the people of New Castle, and of the country, should not be divided by setting up two separate meetings." This appears to have been not merely a refusal to divide an ecclesiastical body, but to allow the same church to have two places of worship. A similar case occurred at a somewhat later period. The Presbytery of New Castle had refused to sanction a portion of Mr. Houston's congregation on Elk river having a new meeting-house. An appeal was taken from this decision to the Synod, which in 1726, unanimously approved of the conduct of the Presbytery. In the meantime the meeting-house was built, and the matter coming up the following year, the Synod, "desirous of taking healing as well as just measures in determining that affair," judged, "First, that that party be allowed to have a new meeting-house in some part of their side of the congregation, yet still remain a part of the congregation, until the Synod or Presbytery have more encouragement for a new erection. Secondly, that in order to this the new meeting-house be removed to any place above six miles distant in a direct line from the old meeting-house, which said supplicants shall agree upon, and that it shall be seven miles from any other," &c. At a subsequent meeting, the Synod agreed to abate one half mile of the specified distance. It is not often that we see ecclesiastical bodies quite so authoritative, in such matters, at the present day.

Again it was very common for the Presbytery to see that the congregations paid their pastors' salaries. Thus in 1708, it was ordered that a letter be written to Snowhill, "requiring their faithfulness and care" in collecting Mr. Hampton's salary. A similar order was made the next year in relation to Mr. McNish. In like manner, as mentioned above, the New York congregation were allowed to call another minister, when they had paid what was due to Mr. Anderson. And, in 1733, (though this is rather beyond our present limits,) when the church in Philadelphia wished to call an assistant minister, they were not allowed to do it, until they had pledged themselves not to diminish Mr. Andrews's salary on that account.

Another prerogative of a Presbytery is the right to review and correct the proceedings of church sessions. That the original Presbytery exercised this power has been already shown, from the order made in 1714, and twice repeated, that the sessional records should be regularly produced for examination. The authority to sit in judgment on the decisions of the lower courts, is involved in this general right of review. To the original Presbytery, therefore, appeals were regularly made from church sessions. Thus in 1711, a censure inflicted upon two members of Mr. Wade's church was reversed by the Presbytery, and the precise form of words prescribed, in which their decision was to be announced. There are, happily, but few cases of appeal upon record before the formation of the Synod. When the church was enlarged they became more numerous. Though these cases, in one aspect, belong to the exhibition of the relation in which the Synod stood to the Presbyteries, yet as they serve, at the same time, to illustrate the nature of the control exercised by the Presbyteries over the congregations, they may be properly referred to in this place. In 1717, Mr. Wotherspoon presented to the Presbytery of New Castle the case of one of his members who had married the widow of his brother. "The Presbytery considering some circumstances in regard of different sentiments, between us and the Dutch ministers in this affair, thinks fit," as it is recorded, "to defer further consideration upon it till our next meeting; against which time we may have occasion to hear more from the Dutch ministers about this case."* At the next meeting, it is said, that as the Dutch ministers were expected to be at Synod, which was to meet the following week in Philadelphia, the whole matter was referred to that body. The Synod decided, *nem. con.* that the marriage was unlawful, and that as long as the parties lived together, "they be debarred from all sealing ordinances, and that Mr. Wotherspoon make intimation hereof to his congregation in what time and manner he shall think convenient." The following year it was reported, "that Mr. Wotherspoon had, in due time, observed the order of the Synod concerning" this affair. In 1728, six persons who had been excommunicated by the Rev. Mr. Jones, appealed to the Presbytery of Philadelphia, who referred the matter to Synod. That body decided that as the appellants confessed they had done wrong in breaking away from the communion of Mr. Jones's church, they should, on a public acknowledgment of their error, "be absolved from the aforesaid censure, and so be free to join with what congregation they please."

These few examples are sufficient to show the regular operation of the system of appeals, and the supervision of the higher judicatories over the acts of church sessions, which is one of the leading features of Presbyterianism. Another illustration of the nature of this general supervision over congregations may be found in the standing rule adopted in 1710, when it was "ordered that the ministers and elders of this meeting come prepared for the future, to give a true and impartial account how matters are mutually betwixt them, both with regard to spirituals and temporals." It was accordingly the custom, after this, to call first upon the ministers to give an account of the state of their congregations; and then upon the elders to say how their ministers were supported, and how they discharged their duties. Thus, in 1711, we find the

* Presbytery Book of New Castle, p. 2.—The individual concerned in this case was, as is evident from his name, of Dutch origin, and hence the deference paid to the opinion of the Dutch ministers. This record is interesting, as it seems to prove the existence of Dutch churches, at this early period, in what is now the State of Delaware.

following record: "Inquiry was made of the several ministers, touching the state of their congregations and of themselves in relation thereto; and also of the several elders, not only of the measures taken to support the ministers, but of the life, conversation, and doctrine of their several pastors, and report was given to our satisfaction for this time." This custom was long continued as appears from the records.

As this is an illustration, not only of the superintendence exercised by the Presbytery over the churches, but also of the "watch and care" which they extended over the ministers, it naturally introduces the consideration of the authority of that body over its own members. That it exercised the right of examining, licensing, ordaining, suspending, and deposing ministers, is what might be expected from its name, as these are ordinary and acknowledged Presbyterial functions. The examples of the exercise of this power are so numerous that they need not be adduced. It will be more instructive to refer to some illustrations of a more general character. When a new member joined the Presbytery, it was customary to make him promise subjection to them in the Lord. This much at least was included in Mr. Wade's voluntary submission to "our constitution," as the Presbytery expressed themselves, because it was disobedience to a decision of the Presbytery in continuing to preach in Woodbridge after his resignation, that led to their censure upon him. In like manner, when the Rev. Mr. Pumry was received in 1715, it is stated that "he was heartily and unanimously accepted, he promising subjection to the Presbytery in the Lord." The same formula is used upon other similar occasions. When the Rev. Mr. Powell was received in 1713, the Presbytery being satisfied as to his ordination, &c., admitted him as a member, but advised him to obtain from England more ample testimonials within a year, and "that till then it shall be free to him to exercise his ministry in all its parts, where Providence shall call him, but not fully to settle until the expiration of the said time." In the following year the Presbytery resolved, "that having considered that their brother Mr. Powell had used diligence to procure further credentials, according to last year's minutes, but not having received answers from England, and we being further satisfied by such long trial and personal acquaintance, together with other considerable circumstances, and now a unanimous call being presented to us for him from the people of Cohanzy, the Presbytery, after mature deliberation, did sustain the call, but withal did recommend him, as formerly, that he should procure letters from England." Such cases illustrate, both the watchfulness of the Presbytery, and the authority which they exercised over their own members. Mr. Powell was admitted a member, but was forbidden to settle for a year; and at the expiration of that period it was a matter of deliberation whether he should be allowed to accept a call or not.

It appears then, that there is no one of the functions of a Presbytery, as now understood, which the original Presbytery of our church did not exercise from the beginning. It claimed the same supervision and control over churches; the same authority over its own members; and was in all respects as thoroughly Presbyterian in its powers as any similar body at the present day. It may be asked, however, whether there were not some modes of action adopted by that body, more allied to Congregationalism than any thing which now occurs. So it has been said. Proof of this point has been sought in the fact, that the Presbytery performed so much of its appropriate business by committees. It was very common, for example, for the Presbytery to appoint a committee to examine a candidate for the ministry, and if satisfied with his qualifications, to license, ordain, or install him. Mr. Gillespie was thus ordained by a committee in 1712; Mr. Wotherspoon in 1713; Mr. Bradner in 1714; Mr. Thompson in 1716. Indeed this was the method commonly pursued.* Should it even be admitted that there was a departure in this mode of procedure, from strict Presbyterianism, a sufficient explanation might be found in the circumstances of the church, without assuming any tendency to Congregationalism on the part of the Presbytery. It is to be

* Dr. Hill, after referring to some of these cases, asks, "Does this resemble a Presbytery, or a Congregational council matter?"— Sketches, No. 8.

remembered that the members of that body were scattered over the country at distant intervals, from the mouth of the Chesapeake to Long Island Sound. There were then no such facilities for travelling as those which we have long enjoyed. On this account the Presbytery met but once a year. As it was deemed important that the candidate should be ordained in the presence of the congregation which he was called to serve, such ordinations could seldom be performed at the stated meetings of Presbytery. Is it a matter of surprise then, that instead of requiring all their scattered members to be present, at a great expense of time and money, they should devolve this duty upon three or four of the neighbouring ministers, and authorize them to act in their name? Do we not constantly install by committee? And is not installation as much a Presbyterial act as ordination? The founders of our Church must have been formalists indeed, had they not acted as they did.

There is, however, no need of any apology in the case. The course in question is not only consistent with the strictest Presbyterianism, but arose out of its strictness. The idea of inherent, in opposition to delegated power in the Presbytery, is involved in this assumption of the right to delegate its authority to a committee of its own appointment. So far from such a committee resembling a Congregational council, it is the opposite extreme. There is some analogy between such a council and a Presbytery, considered as a convention of ministers and elders, who are representatives of the churches; but none at all between a council and a committee appointed, not by the churches but by Presbytery, and by them clothed with authority to exercise one of its most important functions. It is in perfect accordance with this idea that the Synod were accustomed to appoint a commission invested with all Synodical powers, and to nominate committees to visit particular places and decide cases of discipline, or to adjust difficulties with the full authority of the appointing body. It was on the same principle also, that the Synod would name some half dozen of its members, and bid them retire, and examine and ordain a candidate; or that in matters of difficulty, they would direct two or three experienced ministers to meet with a particular Presbytery as members, and assist in adjudicating a given case. All these modes of proceeding were borrowed from Scotland, and they all continued in our church as long as its original character lasted. It is rather singular that the very circumstance should be fixed upon, to prove the Congregationalism of the early members of our church, which most distinctly proves the reverse. It was certainly not Congregationalism which induced the General Assembly in Scotland to appoint committees, with full powers to visit different parts of the kingdom, "to plant kirks with qualified ministers, and to depose and deprive such as be unqualified either in life or doctrine;" * or to designate the Presbytery of Edinburgh with eight other ministers, to summon certain Earls, Lords, Barons, and freeholders, and institute process against them;† or to give a commission "to certain brethren to visit and try the doctrine, life, conversation, diligence, and fidelity of the pastors within the said (i. e. all) Presbyteries." ‡ Things analogous to these we find in the early history of our church, and they savour of any thing rather than of Congregationalism. This acting then, by committees clothed with plenary powers, should never be referred to in proof of the lax Presbyterianism of the founders of our Church.

What renders this reference in the present case the more surprising is, that in ordaining by committee, the Presbytery acted in obedience to the very letter of the Westminster Directory. It is therein ordered that, "upon the day appointed for the ordination, which is to be performed in the church where he that is to be ordained is to serve, a solemn fast shall be kept by the congregation, that they may more earnestly join in prayer for a blessing upon the ordinance of Christ, and the labours of his servant for their good. The Presbytery shall come to the place, or *at least three or four ministers of the word shall be sent thither from the Presbytery*, of which one appointed by the Presbytery shall preach to the people concerning the office and duties of the ministers of Christ, and how the people ought to receive them for their work's

* Calderwood, p. 220. † Ibid. p. 258. ‡ Ibid. p. 286.

sake." In this point, therefore, the original Presbytery must stand acquitted of any want of fidelity to their own system.

There is, however, one case, and as far as is known, one only, which is not accounted for by what has now been said. The people of Cape May were without a pastor. Mr. Bradner, a candidate for the ministry, was willing to serve them, but had no authority to preach. In this emergency, three of the nearest ministers, Messrs. Davis, Hampton, and Henry, on their own responsibility examined and licensed him. This was in March; and in September the matter was reported to Presbytery and received their sanction. That is, as a *pro re nata* meeting of the Presbytery was out of the question, these gentlemen thought it better that they should act informally, than that a people should be deprived of the preaching of the gospel for six months. The Presbytery said they did right; John Knox or Andrew Melville would have said the same. It is difficult to see what this case can prove, beyond what every one must be ready to admit, that though consistent Presbyterians, the founders of our church were not bigots for matters of form. Nothing can more clearly show the character of the members of the first Presbytery, than the fact that the above mentioned case is the only one, as it is believed, which can be produced from their minutes, of departure from even the forms of Presbyterianism.

The preceding review will serve to exhibit with sufficient clearness, the nature of the ecclesiastical system introduced by the first ministers of our church. It was Presbyterianism; for there is no function of a Presbytery which they did not claim and exercise as fully as is done by any similar body at the present day. There is no evidence of indifference with regard either to doctrine or order, and no relaxation of discipline for moral offences. The minutes abound with evidence of the diligence, punctuality, and zeal of the members; and of their earnest desire to promote the spiritual welfare of the people and their own improvement.

It has already been stated that in 1716, three Presbyteries were constituted, who agreed to meet annually as a Synod. It is therefore necessary, in order to understand the character of American

Presbyterianism, to ascertain the relation which this Synod sustained to the Presbyteries and to the churches under their care. In order to illustrate this subject, it must be stated that the first Synod not only exercised all the powers which, at the present day, are claimed by such bodies, but several others which our present Synods are not in the habit of assuming. To the former class belongs, first, the general power of review and control of Presbyteries. This, as far as the review of records is concerned, was provided for at the time the Synod was constituted. It was then "ordered that a book be kept by each Presbytery containing a record of their proceedings, and that it be brought every year to our anniversary Synod to be revised." Accordingly, it is regularly noticed what Presbyterial books were presented at each meeting, and who were appointed to examine them. Thus in 1719, it is stated, "that the Presbytery book of New Castle was revised and approved by the Synod unto the end of sessio septima in page 19, as is to be seen in the margin of the said book, in the above said page. Ordered, that the Presbytery of Long Island get a new, well-ordered book against the next Synod, and that they leave marginal room for Synodical corrections." Secondly, to the class of ordinary powers belongs also that of receiving and deciding appeals and references from the lower judicatories. Examples of the exercise of this power have already been given; as the reference by the New Castle Presbytery, of the case of the church member who had married his brother's widow; and of the appeal of the members of Mr. Jones's congregation, who had been excommunicated. In 1722, the Presbytery of New Castle rebuked, suspended, and deposed the Rev. Mr. Laing, "for violating the Lord's day by washing himself in a creek; and for his indiscreet carriage before the Presbytery at the time of his rebuke." When the matter was brought before the Synod in 1723, that body decided that, "they do judge those censures of suspension and deposition were too severe, and do therefore reverse them." The rebuke, they decided, was merited. In 1720, an appeal by certain members of Mr. Houston's congregation from a decision of the Presbytery of New Castle was tried, and the Presbytery unanimously sustained. There is one order of the Synod connected with this appeal, which, whether it is to be referred to the head of ordinary, or extraordinary powers, the reader must judge. The matter in dispute, as stated upon a preceding page, was the erection of a new meeting-house by a portion of Mr. Houston's congregation. The Synod at last decided that they might have a new house, provided they removed it to a distance of six miles from the old one. This, it appears, they neglected to do. Whereupon the Synod "ordered, that no minister preach in the said new meeting-house while in that place, where it now is." * That this order was not a dead letter, appears from the following minute in the records of the Presbytery of New Castle: "The Presbytery having inquired into Mr. Gelston's conduct, with respect to his violation of the Synod's act relating to the new erection at New London, by his preaching within the forbidden bounds of the said act, and in the prohibited house; the Presbytery having heard and considered his reasons, do judge them invalid; and that Mr. Gelston's conduct in that affair is highly offensive and irregular. Mr. Gelston being called in, and interrogated with respect to his resolution of receding from the said practice, he acknowledged his transgression, and promised absolutely not to preach in the said house, nor elsewhere within the prohibited bounds, till either the Synod or Presbytery opened the door for him." † This, it might be supposed, is Presbyterianism sufficiently rigid to satisfy the most sceptical as to the character both of the Synod and Presbytery.

To the class of ordinary powers belongs also the right "to take effectual care that the Presbyteries observe the constitution of the church." This is illustrated by such cases as the following. It seems that some doubt had arisen whether the Presbytery of Long Island had proceeded regularly in the settlement of Mr. Anderson in New York. When the matter came before Synod, the following record was made: "After a full hearing and long reasoning upon the case represented by Messrs. Livingston and Smith, touching Mr. Anderson's settlement in New York, the question was put,

* Minutes, vol. ii. p. 3.

† Minutes of the Presbytery of New Castle, vol. i. p. 143.

whether the proceedings of the Presbytery of Long Island, in the settlement of Mr. Anderson at New York, were regular; and it was decided in the affirmative by a great majority."* On the other hand, as stated above, when the question came up respecting the settlement of Mr. Pemberton, it was decided that, "the rules of our Presbyterian constitution" had not been observed in his case, and the Synod decline to recognize him as a member.

Finally, the Synod exercised a general supervision over the churches, warning them of improper or irregular preachers, receiving and answering their petitions or complaints. Especially did it concern itself for the supply of destitute places, which was one of the principal items of its business. To select but two cases out of a multitude: in 1719, a letter was received "from the people of Potomac in Virginia, requesting the Synod's care and diligence in providing them an able gospel minister." The Synod accordingly directed the Rev. Mr. Magill to visit them; who reported the next year that he went to Virginia, and after some months' continuance, "put the people into church order." This must have been one of the earliest Presbyterian organizations in that part of the State. In 1723, a representation having been made of the earnest desire of some Protestant dissenting families in Virginia for preaching, the Synod appointed "that Messrs. Conn, Orme, and Steward do each of them severally visit said people, and preach four Lord's days before next Synod to that people; and it is recommended to Mr. Jonathan Dickinson, to preach to the said people some Sabbath-days before next Synod; and in case he goes thither, that then Mr. Pierson, Mr. Webb, and Mr. Moses Dickinson, do supply his congregation with preaching. . . . And it is further ordered, that Mr. Hucheson supply Mr. Steward's congregation during his absence in Virginia." It need hardly be remarked that the Synod exercised constantly the general authority over its members of sending them to supply particular congregations or destitute places, and that an account was always demanded how the duty had been performed; and neglect was uniformly censured.

It thus appears that the original Synod of our church exercised

* Minutes, p. 53.

the power of review and control over Presbyteries and congregations, of receiving and deciding appeals, references and complaints, and of general supervision and direction. It exhibits as perfect an example of regular Presbyterian discipline, as is presented by any body of Christians at the present day. There are, however, several respects in which that Synod differed, in its modes of action, from what is now common among us. In the first place, it had a commission annually appointed, which was clothed with all the powers of the Synod. To this commission all items of business which could not be despatched during the sessions of Synod, were referred. To them all applications were made, which required immediate attention. They could suspend, censure, or dismiss ministers; decide appeals and references; and, in short, do all that the Synod itself could do; and from their decisions there was no appeal. Their records were regularly presented to Synod, and that body could correct any thing which they thought had been done amiss. Every one knows that this was in imitation of the commission of the General Assembly in Scotland, as it continues to the present time. Whatever may be thought of the wisdom of this arrangement, there can be but one opinion as to the tone of Presbyterianism which it indicates. If Congregationalists refuse to a whole Synod a definitive voice in their ecclesiastical affairs, how much less would they grant such authority to a mere committee of such a body! The fact that no such commission has been appointed since the adoption of our present constitution, is one of the many proofs that the Presbyterianism of the present day is much less strict and European than that of our fathers. They had no objection to this feature of the Scottish system. It continued uninterruptedly from 1720 to 1788. It was adopted by the old Synod before the schism; by both parties during the separation; and by the Synod of New York and Philadelphia after the union. The original minute on this subject, as adopted in 1720, is in these words: "Overtured that a commission of Synod be appointed to act in the name, and with the whole authority of the Synod in all affairs that come before them; and especially that the whole affair of the fund be left to their conduct, and that they be accountable to Synod. Which overture was approved by the Synod. Masters Jones, Andrews, McNish, Anderson, Dickinson, and Evans, appointed for said commission; any three whereof to be a quorum." *

A second particular in which the first Synod differed from ours, was the frequent appointment of plenipotentiary committees. In 1717, when the call from New York was presented to the Presbytery of New Castle for Mr. Anderson, it was referred by that body to the Synod, who appointed a committee to meet at New Castle, to receive and consider the reasons of that people against the removal of their pastor, and "to fully determine in that affair." The following year that committee reported "that they had transported him (Mr. Anderson) to New York, having had power lodged in them by the Synod to determine that affair." In 1720, some of the elders of the church of Rehoboth having forwarded a complaint against their pastor, it was determined, *nem. con.* "that a committee be sent to Rehoboth, with full powers from the Synod to act in their name and by their authority, in the affair between Mr. Clement and that people, and that Mr. Clement be suspended from the exercise of his ministry until the determination of that committee." On the same page there is a record of a committee's being appointed to proceed to Snowhill, "with full powers to hear, examine, and determine about the complaints" made against the pastor.

In 1722, the Presbytery had suspended a Mr. Walton, a licentiate, who thereupon complained to Synod. The Synod in consequence of his concessions modified the sentence, suspending him for three Sabbaths, and directing his acknowledgments to be read, at the expiration of that time, before the congregation of Newark. If Mr. Walton should then "own" those acknowledgments, Mr. Pumry, who was appointed for the purpose, was to remove the suspension.

* The fund mentioned in this minute was designed for "pious uses;" for aiding feeble congregations, relieving the widows of ministers, or ministers themselves when sick or in want. It arose from collections from the several congregations, and from contributions from abroad. One of the earliest contributors was the Synod of Glasgow and Ayr, as appears from the minutes of 1719, which mention the appointment of a committee to receive the collection of that Synod "if it arrive safe in goods," with directions to have the proceeds safely invested.

As the gentleman, however, seemed rather refractory, it was resolved: "That the Synod do appoint Messrs. George McNish, James Anderson, and Samuel Pumry, or any two of them, do, in the Synod's name, judicially deal with him upon information, as they shall see proper." It appears from the minutes of the following year that Mr. Pumry was prevented by illness from attending at Newark at the appointed time; and that Mr. Walton read his own acknowledgment "and absolved himself." Whereupon the Synod determined that the suspension was not thereby removed, and appointed "the Presbytery of Long Island, together with Mr. J. Dickinson, Mr. Morgan, and Mr. Pierson, to be a committee to transact in the whole affair relating to Mr. Walton, and to remove or continue the suspension, as they shall see cause." This committee, as appears from their report, met according to appointment, and unanimously decided that the suspension should not be removed. This is an instructive record, as it shows not only the authority of the Synod in modifying the sentence of a Presbytery, but the peculiarity of their mode of proceeding, in appointing, in the first instance, a committee of three to proceed judicially, should occasion require it; and then naming several ministers to be associated with a Presbytery in deciding the whole affair.

In 1727, "Messrs. Andrews, Morgan, Jon. Dickinson, Pierson, and Webb, were appointed a committee to meet in New York, to accommodate matters of difference between that congregation and the Presbytery of Long Island, and also any other differences that may be among themselves about their church settlements, and especially to receive Mr. Pemberton as a member of the Synod or not, as they shall see cause." The following year that committee reported among other things, "That Mr. Pemberton appearing before this committee, and desiring admission as a member of the Synod of Philadelphia, promised upon such admission, all subjection to the Synod in the Lord, the committee can see no cause why such admission should be refused or delayed, and do therefore admit him as a member of the said Synod." There seems to have been some misapprehensions as to the authority meant to be conferred on this committee; for when their report was presented, the following questions were proposed to the vote of Synod.

"1. Whether the committee had authority from the Synod to consider the admission of Mr. Pemberton as a member of the Synod, without previously considering what the Presbytery of Long Island had to offer in that affair. Carried in the negative by a great majority.

"2. Whether the Synod approve of the conduct of the committee with relation to the divisions of the said congregation. Carried in the affirmative, *nem. con.**

"3. Whether Mr. Pemberton be allowed as a member of this Synod, by virtue of what the committee has done. Carried in the negative.

"4. Whether, notwithstanding of all the irregularity that was in the accession of Mr. Pemberton to New York, the Synod do now accept him as a member. Carried in the affirmative, *nem. con.* And it is left to Mr. Pemberton and the congregation to join what Presbytery they shall think fit.

These instances of plenipotentiary committees are all selected from

* The substance of the arrangement effected by the committee, in reference to the difficulties in the congregation, was as follows;

1. Messrs. Liddel, Blake, and Inglis, were to make over all their interest in the meeting-house, &c., to certain ministers in Edinburgh, and to Dr. Nicoll, "for the use of the Presbyterian Church in New York;" and they were to empower the Presbytery of Edinburgh to supply the vacancies in the above-named trustees, as they might occur. Dr. Nicoll was to cancel all bonds given by Messrs. Liddel, Blake, and Inglis, on account of the said meeting-house.

2. Dr. Nicoll was to give a bond for two thousand pounds, to the ministers of Edinburgh, that neither he nor his heir would ever alienate their interest in the above-mentioned property; and that, as soon as he was paid what was due to him, he would make over to those ministers all his interest in the property.

3. No repairs were to be made or expenses incurred without the consent of the majority of the congregation.

4. It was agreed that the congregation might choose five men as public managers or representatives. And Dr. Nicoll agreed, that whoever wished might have copies at their own expense, of any of the papers in his hands relating to the congregation.

These articles were signed by John Nicoll, John Blake, Thomas Inglis, and Joseph Liddel.

the minutes of the years 1717 to 1728, the limit of the period now under consideration. Many examples of a similar kind might be taken from the records of subsequent years. It has already been shown that this mode of proceeding, though so different from our method of conducting Synodical business, is in perfect accordance with that in vogue in Scotland.

The great distinction, however, between the original Synod and ours, is, that the former exercised all Presbyterial powers. They examined and received new members; ordained, dismissed, suspended, or deposed ministers; regulated the affairs of congregations, and in short did every thing within their whole limits, that any Presbytery might properly do within its own. Thus in 1718, it is recorded that, "Mr. Wm. Tennent's affair being transmitted from the committee [of bills and overtures] to the Synod, was by them fully considered; being well satisfied with his credentials, and the testimony of some brethren here present, as also they were satisfied with the material reasons which he offered concerning his dissenting from the established church in Ireland; being put to a vote, it was carried in the affirmative to admit him a member of Synod." On the following page it is stated, that "Mr. Samuel Young, minister of the gospel, presenting his credentials from the Presbytery of Armagh, met at Donaghmore, in the county Down, in the kingdom of Ireland, to this Synod, they were cordially approved, and he admitted a member, *nem. con.*" In the same year Messrs. Clement and Steward, probationers, presented their credentials, which were approved; and calls having been handed in for them from the Eastern Shore of Maryland, the Synod appointed Messrs. Davis, Hampton, and Thompson, and such members of the Presbytery of New Castle as they might choose to call to their aid, to ordain them. The same year Mr. Hampton petitioned to be dismissed from his pastoral charge, which was granted, and his church declared vacant by the Synod. In 1720, Mr. Orme presented his testimonials, and was admitted a member of Synod; Mr. John Morehead applied for admission, and was refused. The complaints made by the elders of the church of Rehoboth against their pastor, were entertained, and he suspended by the Synod *ad interim*, and the whole matter referred to a committee of their own body. In 1726, a call from Donegal for Mr. Anderson was presented to the Synod, and by them handed to him for his acceptance. In 1728, various charges were presented by a people against their pastor, which were examined; from most of them he was acquitted, while others were referred to his Presbytery for further examination. These are only a few of the examples which might be selected of the exercise of Presbyterial powers by the Synod. All this is very different from any thing we are accustomed to, but it is in perfect accordance with the Scotch system. The explanation is to be found in the following provision of the Book of Policy: "These assemblies, (viz. Synods,) have the whole power of the particular elderships, (Presbyteries,) of which they are collected."* It appears, then, that the original Synod of our church not only exercised all the powers which are now recognized as belonging to such bodies, but that it went much further, conforming in various respects to the Scottish model, in points in which we have long differed from it.

There is still one very important record belonging to the period under review, which remains to be considered. In 1721, the Rev. Mr. Gillespie, who had been nine years a member of the Synod, and was not, therefore, a young man just from Scotland, as has been represented, brought forward the following overture: "As we have been for many years in the exercise of Presbyterian government and church discipline, as exercised by the Presbyterians in the best reformed churches, as far as the nature and constitution of this country will allow, our opinion is, that if any brother have any overture to offer to be formed into an act of Synod, for the better carrying on the matters of our government and discipline, he may bring it in against next Synod." This overture was carried by a majority of votes, and ordered to be recorded.

"Mr. Jon. Dickinson, Mr. Malachi Jones, Mr. Joseph Morgan, Mr. John Pierson, Mr. David Evans, and Mr. Joseph Webb, entered their protestations against the above-mentioned act, and the record-

* Calderwood, p. 109. Eldership is the old Scotch name for Presbytery, and is described as consisting "of pastors, doctors, and such as we call elders, that labour not in word or doctrine."

ing of it, and gave the reasons of their protest, which are *in retentis*. Ordered, that Mr. Magill and Mr. McNish draw up answers to the above said protest."

At this meeting of Synod there were twenty-one ministers present, viz. Messrs. Magill, Andrews, Gillespie, Anderson, Orme, Wm. Tennent, Thompson, Hook, Pumry, Davis, Cross, Steward, Gelston, McNish, Conn; and the six protesting brethren just mentioned. Of these six, Messrs. Dickinson, Pierson, and Webb, were from New England; and Messrs. Morgan, Evans, and Jones, were probably all of Welsh origin. Though it cannot be certainly inferred that all who did not join in the protest, voted for the overture, yet it is highly probable that the above division gives a fair view of the state of parties, so to speak, in the Synod. This was a subject which evidently excited much interest, with regard to which there were not likely to be many *non liquets;* and in the following year, we find no additional names attached to Mr. Dickinson's articles relating to this subject.

No one at all familiar with the history either of our own church, or of that of Scotland, can be at a loss as to the meaning of the phrase, "an act of Synod," as used in Mr. Gillespie's overture. Any proposition containing a rule of action, enacted by an ecclesiastical body, obligatory on its members or inferior judicatories, is called an *act*. The records of the church of Scotland are full of such acts, which are rules remaining in force until properly repealed. The records of our own church abound with similar rules, which, especially in the earlier periods of our history, are called acts. The rule that ministers and elders should regularly report on the state of their congregations, was such an act; the rule that every church should keep sessional records, and present them annually for revision, was such an act, and is so called in the minutes already quoted. Such also was the order that Presbyteries should bring their minutes to be examined in Synod. All these were adopted prior to the year 1717. Even the order that no minister should preach in a particular church, is called, as we have seen, "an act of Synod." Mr. Gillespie's proposition, therefore, was in strict accordance, not only with the usage of other Presbyterian churches, but with the customs of our own.

It was, moreover, perfectly reasonable. The church was now divided into several Presbyteries. If it was to remain one body, it was evidently desirable that it should have some common rules of action with regard to the qualifications of candidates, the admission of members, &c. such as we have now embodied in our written constitution, and such as not only Episcopalians and Methodists have in their canons and books of discipline, but even Congregationalists possess in the Cambridge and Saybrook Platforms. The propriety and even necessity of this measure were so obvious, that, after a little temporary opposition, arising as is evident from misapprehension, it was cordially acquiesced in by all parties, and has been from that day to this the common understanding of the church.

It seems, however, that some members of the Synod were startled at the assertion of a power in the abstract, which they had themselves already exercised,* and were afraid of its being carried to an extent to which they could not willingly submit. They therefore protested. The minutes of the next year contain the following record relating to this subject: "The brethren who entered their protestation against the act for allowing any brother or member of this Synod to bring in any overture to be formed into an act by the Synod, for the better carrying on in the matters of our government and discipline, &c. The said brethren protestants brought in a paper of four articles, testifying in writing their sentiments and judgment concerning church government, which was approved by the Synod, and ordered by the Synod to be recorded in the Synod-book. Likewise the said brethren being willing to take back their protestation against said act, together with their reasons given in defence of said protest, the Synod doth hereby order the protest, together with the reasons of it, as also the answers at the appointment of the Synod given to the reasons alleged by Mr. Daniel Magill and Mr. George McNish, be all withdrawn, and that the said act remain and be in all respects as if no such protest had been made. The articles are as followeth:

* This is believed to be true of all the protestants, unless Mr. Webb be an exception. As he had but just entered the Synod, he may have never voted for any such rule, as Mr. Gillespie contemplated. Mr. Dickinson and Mr. Pierson had been four years members.

"1. We freely grant that there is full executive power of church government in Presbyteries and Synods, and that they may authoritatively, in the name of Christ, use the keys of church discipline to all proper intents and purposes, and that the keys of the church are committed to the church officers and them only.

"2. We also grant that the mere circumstantials of church discipline, such as the time, place, and mode of carrying on the government of the church, belong to ecclesiastical judicatories to determine as occasions occur, conformable to the general rules in the word of God, that require all things to be done decently and in order. And if these things are called *acts*, we will take no offence at the word, provided that these acts be not imposed on those who conscientiously dissent from them.

"3. We also grant that Synod may compose directories, and recommend them to all their members respecting all the parts of discipline, provided that all subordinate judicatories may decline from such directories, when they conscientiously think they have just reason so to do.

"4. We freely allow that appeals may be made from all inferior to superior judicatories, and that superior judicatories have authority to consider and determine such appeals.

MALACHI JONES,
JOSEPH MORGAN,
JONATHAN DICKINSON,
DAVID EVANS."

"The Synod was so universally pleased with the above said composure of their difference, that they unanimously joined together in a thanksgiving prayer, and joyful singing the 133d Psalm." *

* The reader cannot fail to notice that these four articles contain the whole system of Presbyterianism. They assert, 1. That the government and discipline of individual churches belong to the church officers, and not to the church members. 2. That full executive power of church government belongs to Presbyteries and Synods. 3. That the higher judicatories have the right to review and control the decisions of the lower. The only other feature of the system is the right of Synods to make acts, or "to set down rules for the government of the church." How far their authors denied this, remains to be

It is evident from this record that these brethren, who the year before supposed themselves to differ widely in their views, found, upon mutual explanations, that they perfectly agreed. It is to be remarked that the friends of Mr. Gillespie's overture did not relinquish the ground which they had assumed. On the contrary, it was expressly stipulated, "that the said act (Mr. Gillespie's) remain and be in all respects as if no such protest had been made." The protestation and the reasons for it were withdrawn, and the matter left where it was, as though no objection had ever been urged against it. There was, therefore, no concession inconsistent with the assertion of the principle contained in the overture. There is no reason to suppose that either party was overreached in this matter. It would be a gratuitous and ungracious assumption, that there was, on either side, a wish to hoodwink or cajole the other. These brethren, from all that appears or is known of their character, were honest men, and had confidence in each other. This must be presumed, unless we suppose them capable of the basest hypocrisy in thanking God for the success of a stratagem. This is not to be credited of such men as President Dickinson, and Mr. Pierson. Besides, the brethren on the other side were not likely to be easily deceived. Most of the oldest, shrewdest, and most strenuous of the Scotch and Irish members of the Synod were present at this meeting, concurred in all that was done, and joined in giving thanks to God for the result.* Two things, therefore, are evident; first, that there must have been some misapprehension, on the part of Mr. Dickinson and his friends, of the design of Mr. Gillespie's overture, against which they at first protested, but subsequently allowed to stand as it was; and secondly, that Mr. Dickinson's four articles must admit of an interpretation consistent with that overture, and satisfactory to its advocates.

seen. This record is the more interesting, as these articles proceeded from the least Presbyterian part of the Synod, and therefore conclusively prove how little there was of Congregationalism in that body, or rather that there was none at all.

* There were nineteen ministers present at Synod this year; among whom were Messrs. Anderson, Gillespie, Thompson and Cross.

Otherwise they never would have insisted on the overture's remaining, and yet have adopted the articles. The protesting brethren seem to have considered the proposition of Mr. Gillespie, asserting as it does in general terms and with little limitation, the right of the Synod to form acts obligatory on all its members, as assuming the power "to make laws to bind the conscience." The right to make rules for the discipline and government of the church, and to frame directories, they admitted; provided these rules did not trespass on the domain of conscience. With this the friends of the overture were perfectly satisfied. It was all they ever intended or wished. Thus both parties united in letting the overture stand, in ordering the articles to be recorded, and in praising God for their agreement.

That this is the true solution of this problem in our history, is evident, in the first place, from the very facts of the case as they appear on the record. A proposition is introduced asserting the right of the Synod to make rules for the government of the church. This proposition is adopted. Certain members protest; but the following year they withdraw their opposition, and acknowledge that Synod may make such rules, "provided such acts be not imposed upon those who conscientiously dissent from them." The question is, what is the meaning of this proviso? It is certainly ambiguous. It admits of one interpretation, which involves both parties to this transaction in glaring contradictions; but also of another, which makes them both act consistently. If by 'conscientious dissent' is meant dissent on conscientious grounds, all is plain and satisfactory. The Synod never pretended to the right to impose any thing upon any man contrary to his conscience. But if by conscientious dissent is meant merely honest dissent, in opposition to what is feigned or factious, then the whole history is a riddle. The Synod declare their right to make rules, and yet admit they may be regarded or disregarded at every man's pleasure! Is it to be credited that a set of Scotch and Irish Presbyterians would have assented to such an exposition of a Synod's power, or have joined in thanking God for its acknowledgment? It is not to be believed that any sane men would have insisted that the assertion of this right of the Synod should stand uncontradicted upon the minutes, and upon the next page admit that Synodical rules had no binding force: the two assertions are contradictory, and could not have received the assent of the same men. The record itself, therefore, forces us to understand, by conscientious dissent, dissent on conscientious grounds. This interpretation does no violence to the words, and renders the different parts of the minutes perfectly consistent.

That this is the true meaning of these articles is further proved by the uniform action of the church under them. This argument can be fully appreciated by those only who are aware of the fact that our records abound with rules, or acts of Synod, many of them passed by mere majorities, to which the minorities uniformly submitted, except when they could plead conscientious scruples. To take a single example. What was the famous adopting act of 1729? Was this a mere recommendation on the part of the Synod that the reception of the Westminster Confession of Faith should be demanded by the Presbyteries from all candidates for the ministry? Far from it. It was an obligatory act; so regarded at the time, and so regarded, by friends and foes of the measure, from that day to this. This indeed is evident from the very form of it, as well as from the contention about it, and from the uniformity with which it was enforced. An act of Synod, therefore, in the view of those who assented to these articles, was not a mere recommendation, but an authoritative rule.

This interpretation of these articles is confirmed by what took place at the time of the schism. This question was involved in that controversy. The ostensible occasion of the whole difficulty was an act of Synod. That body had passed an order that candidates for the ministry, before being taken on trial by a Presbytery, should be furnished with a diploma from some European university, or from some college in New England, or, wanting these, that they should be provided with a certificate of competent scholarship by a committee of the Synod. This act the Presbytery of New Brunswick disregarded. Their reason was not the denial of the right of the Synod to make such rules, but the plea that they could not conscientiously obey that particular rule.* Their conscientious dissent was a dissent for conscience' sake.

And finally, the true interpretation of these articles, or the manner in which they were understood, is manifest from the manner in which this matter was arranged upon the re-union of the two Synods. As the right of the Synod to make such acts had been drawn into the controversy, it was necessary that there should be some distinct agreement on the subject. Though the negotiations for a union were protracted through several years, and though much difficulty was experienced in arranging other points, that respecting the power of Synod seems to have been settled at once. The reason was, there was no real difference of opinion on the subject. Both parties agreed, "that when any matter is determined by a major vote, every member shall either actively concur with, or passively submit to such determination; or, if his conscience permit him to do neither, he shall, after sufficient liberty modestly to reason and remonstrate, peaceably withdraw from our communion, without attempting to make any schism. Provided always that this shall be understood to extend to such determinations only as the body shall judge indispensable in doctrine or Presbyterian government."† This is precisely the meaning of Mr. Dickinson's article on the same subject. The decisions of Synod were to be binding on all those who could obey them with a good conscience.‡ This interpretation is

* Their opponents, indeed, charged them with going further, and with taking the general ground; but this they denied. And well they might, for they were the greatest rule-makers in the whole Synod.

† Article second of the Terms of Union; see minutes of the Synod of New York. Appendix.

‡ A still more decisive proof that this is the true meaning of these articles, is to be found in the second of the articles agreed upon by the Synod of New York, as "the plan and foundation of their Synodical union." This Synod was formed in 1745, a few years after the schism. President Dickinson was present when these articles were adopted, and was in all probability the framer of them. The members of that body say: "They agree that in matters of discipline, and those things which relate to the peace and good order of our churches, they shall be determined according to the major vote of ministers and elders, with which vote every member shall actively concur, or passively acquiesce; but if any member cannot in conscience agree to the deter-

the only one consistent with the facts in the case; with the known and vowed opinions of those who assented to the articles; with the uniform practice of the church after their adoption; and with the more explicit declarations of the Synod relating to the same subject. On the opposite interpretation these articles are completely isolated; inconsistent with all that precedes and with all that follows them, like a dead tree in a long avenue of living ones.

Such then was American Presbyterianism during the forming period of our Church, from 1705 or 1706 to 1728. When the Presbytery was organized, there was but one congregation in New Jersey, the Scotch church at Freehold, in connection with it. Those in Pennsylvania and Maryland were strictly Presbyterian, unless the church in Philadelphia was an exception. All the original members, except Mr. Andrews, were, as far as can be ascertained, educated and ordained in Scotland or Ireland. Such was the original body around which, as a nucleus, other churches and ministers were rapidly collected. This Presbytery exercised all Presbyterial functions as fully as any similar body at the present day; reviewing and controlling the exercise of discipline in the several

mination of the majority, but supposes himself obliged to act contrary thereunto, and the Synod think themselves obliged to insist upon it as essentially necessary to the well-being of our churches, in that case such dissenting member promises peaceably to withdraw from the body, without endeavouring to raise any dispute or contention upon the debated point, or any unjust alienation of affection from them.—Minutes of Synod of New York, p. 2. There were twenty-two ministers present when this Synod was constituted and these articles were adopted; among whom, besides President Dickinson, were Messrs. Pierson, Pemberton, Burr, G. Tennent, W. Tennent, Samuel Blair, John Blair, and Samuel Finley. When the circumstances are considered under which these gentlemen met, the above article, which goes the whole length of what was contended for by the friends of Mr. Gillespie's overture, will appear the more decisive. A schism had just occurred in the church, from a refusal of the New Brunswick Presbytery to submit to the determination of the Synod respecting the examination of candidates. To prevent any such disastrous occurrence in future, the members pledged themselves, if they could not conscientiously submit to the majority, peaceably to withdraw. The unanimous adoption of this principle shows how unfounded is the general impression of the lax Presbyterianism of the Synod of New York.

churches; examining, ordaining, installing, and dismissing pastors, and judging their own members. The Synod, after its formation, exercised a similar review and control over the Presbyteries and congregations; received and decided appeals, and references, and complaints from the lower judicatories, and not only exercised the various powers now recognized as belonging to Synods, but, in strict accordance with the Scottish system, all those which more immediately pertain to Presbyteries. In all the particulars in which the original Presbytery and Synod differed from such bodies among us, they conformed to the usages of the Church of Scotland. Our Church was, therefore, more strictly Presbyterian during the first five-and-twenty years of its history, than it has been at any period since the formation of the General Assembly.

CHAPTER III.

PRESBYTERIAN CHURCH FROM 1729 TO 1741.

Adopting act.— Its origin.— False assumptions as to its design.— Mr. Thompson's overture.— President Dickinson's objections.— The act itself.— The true interpretation of it, as determined by its own language and avowed design.— As determined by the action of the Synod.— As authoritatively declared in 1730 and in 1736.— How acted upon by the Presbyteries.— How explained by contemporary writers.— What has been the doctrinal standard in our church since 1729? — Bearing of the acts of 1730 and 1736 upon this question.—The standard assumed by the Synod of Philadelphia.— The standard adopted in the Synod of New York.— The standard assumed at the time of the union and ever since maintained.— Constitution of the Church during the period from 1729 to 1741.—Ordinary powers of the Synod. — Presbyterial powers of the Synod.— Its action by committees.—Acts and Overtures.

THE most prominent event during this period of our history is the passing of the adopting act, by which assent to the Westminster Confession of Faith was required of all members of the Synod, and of all candidates for admission to the Presbyteries. This event forms an era in our history, and has exerted an influence on our Church, which is still felt in all her borders. The origin, design, and import of this celebrated act deserve particular attention. It was stated in the preceding chapter, that the Presbytery of New Castle had begun, at least as early as 1724, to require the adoption of the Westminster Confession by their candidates for the ministry. The first record relating to this subject refers to Mr. William McMillan, who was licensed September 22, 1724, for distant service in Virginia. His subscription to the Confession of Faith bears the same date. What led to the adoption of this measure is not recorded; and there does not appear to have been any previous order of the Presbytery that such subscription should be demanded.* From this time, however, it seems to have been the common practice of the Presbytery.

It is obvious that the same reasons which induced the Presbytery of New Castle to adopt this measure themselves, would lead them to wish for the concurrence of the whole Church of which they were a part. No one will be surprised, therefore, to learn that the overture which led to the adopting act had its origin in this Presbytery. Under the date of March 27, 1728, it is recorded that, "an overture formerly read before Synod, but which was dropped, being now at the desire of the Presbytery produced by Mr. Thompson and read, the Presbytery defer their judgment concerning it until next meeting." At the subsequent meeting the subject was again deferred until the sessions of the Presbytery during the intervals of Synod. No further mention of it is made on the minutes; and it is therefore uncertain what was the decision of the Presbytery respecting it. It is probable that they referred the whole matter to the Synod, without any expression of their own opinion, as it is not reported as the overture of a Presbytery but of an individual, and as Mr. Thompson speaks in it, throughout, in his own name. This gentleman, who is thus prominently connected with this subject, was a native of Ireland. He came to this country as a probationer for the ministry in 1715, and was ordained over the congregation at Lewes in 1717. He had, therefore, been at this time eleven years a member of the Synod. He appears to have been a man of self-command, learning, and piety. He took indeed an active, and in some respects a very mistaken part in opposition to Mr. Whitefield and Mr. Tennent; yet no one can read his writings without being impressed with respect for his character and talents. And it is a gratifying fact, that Mr. Tennent himself, after the excitement of controversy had subsided, came to speak of him in terms of affectionate regard. Indeed, were nothing known of these men, but their controversial

* The only ministers present at that meeting of the Presbytery, were Messrs. Thomas Creaghead, George Gillespie, John Orme, Thomas Evans, and Alexander Hucheson.

writings, the reader could hardly fail to think, that in humility, candour, and Christian temper, Mr. Thompson was greatly superior to his opponent. It is, however, the weakest side of Mr. Tennent's ardent and impetuous character that appears in those writings, and they therefore would be a very unfair criterion of the man.*

When the overture respecting the adoption of the Confession of Faith was introduced into Synod in 1728, though it had been presented the year before, and though there were twenty-nine members present, of whom seventeen were ministers, it was deemed of so much importance that, by common consent, it was deferred to the next Synod. There was, therefore, no attempt, as has been ungenerously asserted, to take the Synod unawares. The record in relation to this point is as follows: "There being an overture presented to the Synod in writing, having reference to the subscribing the Confession of Faith, &c.; the Synod, judging this to be a very important affair, unanimously concluded to defer the consideration of it till the next Synod; withal recommending to the members of each Presbytery to give timeous notice to the absent members, and it is agreed that the next be a full Synod." †

It is strange that this measure, after the lapse of a century, should still be held up to reprobation by members of our own communion. As every other church has a creed, why should not the Presbyterians be allowed to have one? Why should motives the most improbable be attributed to the advocates of this measure, when reasons which the Christian world have, by their practice, pronounced sufficient, lie on the very surface of the transaction? If it was so sectarian in 1729, to adopt the Confession of Faith, why,

* In what is here said in relation to Mr. Thompson's controversial writings, reference is had to those which were published with his name, or in defence of the Synod. The writer is not aware that any of the scurrilous anonymous publications of that day were ever attributed to him.

† By a full Synod is meant a Synod at which all the members were expected to attend. In 1724, it had been agreed that the Presbyteries should appear by delegates, except every third year, when all the ministers were required to be present. It was provided, however, that if any important business arose, the commission was to give notice for a full meeting.

in the course of more than a hundred years, has the adopting act never been repealed? Why do those who impute such evil designs to its authors, reject as injurious all suspicion that they are in favour of such repeal, or of any modification of the Confession itself?

It has been said that the advocates of the adoption of the Westminster Confession designed to subject the church irrevocably to the power of the civil government, and that this design was successfully resisted by the sons of New England. This is a calumny which might safely be left to be refuted by its inherent absurdity. All sects, even the Popish, are said to be tolerant, when in the minority. Yet Presbyterians call upon us to believe that Presbyterians, when thinly scattered over the country, with some twenty or thirty ministers; when suffering oppression in Carolina, Virginia, and New York; when under an Episcopal government hostile to all their peculiarities, wished to subject the church more completely to the state, to justify their oppressors, and to deprive themselves of the poor consolation of petition and remonstrance. To make this aspersion the stronger, it is cast upon Scotchmen, upon the descendants of the men who had been struggling for two centuries for the independence of the church; who had included in their earliest confession the assertion of the right to resist unjust rulers, and whose great reproach is that they carried the liberty of the Church so far as to encroach on the just prerogatives of the State. Yet their descendants in one breath are said to have come to this country with all the prejudices and principles of their fathers, and in the next, to have been intent on establishing the doctrine their fathers had suffered the loss of all things in opposing. The authors of the overture in question had no such suicidal or insensate purpose, as to subject a feeble church to hostile magistrates, or to solicit injury from the hand of oppression. Presbyterians in this country have always been tolerant, from necessity, if not from principle. Mr. Makemie, when imprisoned in New York for preaching the gospel, must have delivered his eloquent defence with a very bad grace, had he suffered merely from the application of his own principles. It is not pretended that Presbyterians were so much in advance of their generation, that they would have been free from reproach in this matter, had they been in power. This however was nowhere the case, for even where they formed the majority of the people, they were subject to Episcopal rulers over whom they had no control. Had the case been otherwise, they might have been as intolerant as their neighbours, and have pushed their principles to the extreme to which they were carried in New England. There, not only all places of power and trust, but even the right of suffrage was confined to members of the church. The magistrates were clothed with power to punish for opinion's sake; a power which they frequently exercised. It is a poor service to the Puritans to deny their principles, or to vindicate their conduct on grounds which they themselves would have despised. The intolerance of the Puritans, such as it was, arose out of their most cherished opinions. They came to this country to establish a society in which God should reign; where his truth should be preserved and his laws enforced. Hence all power was to be kept in the hands of the people of God. Hence the denial of the truth, or any moral offence, was regarded as a violation of the law of the land, and to be punished accordingly. Hence, too, when Roger Williams broached his doctrine of liberty of conscience, not only was he banished, but his opinions were laboriously controverted. A state founded upon such a principle, must be intolerant. Had no strangers come among them, their own children would have been disfranchised. Yet the Puritans adhered to this principle, and gave it up in practice by slow and reluctant concessions. This is not said to cast a reproach upon the pious founders of New England. Far from it. Those who retain the great scriptural doctrines for whose sake they constructed their whole economy, honour their memory far more effectually than those who merely garnish their sepulchres. They were the people of God; they loved and honoured the Saviour; and this is enough to preserve them in everlasting remembrance, and to shield them from all unjust or unkind aspersions. They were not fanatical persecutors, or blinded enthusiasts, but sober-minded and devout men. They allowed themselves, however, to be fascinated with the idea of a Christian theocracy; which, beautiful as it is, cannot be carried out, in the present state of the world, without practical injustice. These men, therefore, good as they were, should not be honoured at the expense of truth, nor held up as the friends of religious liberty in contrast with the Presbyterians, in order to cast odium upon the latter. The assertion, that the advocates of the adoption of the Confession of Faith had the design of subjecting the Church to the State, and were only prevented by the sons of the Puritans, appears still more extraordinary when it is known that they unanimously declared their rejection of the doctrine that the civil magistrates had the right to control ecclesiastical bodies, or to persecute for the sake of religion. It is certainly a very strange expedient to enforce a doctrine, openly and unanimously to renounce it. A charge, however, which is so obviously unjust does not merit even this brief refutation.

Another assumption equally gratuitous is, that the overture in question had its origin in disaffection towards the New England portion of the Synod. Had such disaffection existed, this was a singular way to manifest it. The Westminster Confession had long before been adopted in New England; and the catechism was there taught as faithfully as in Scotland itself. Even had the excepted clauses, about the power of the civil magistrate, been insisted upon, what was there in those articles to startle men brought up under the Cambridge Platform? New England men were not to be excluded by the adoption of their own confession, nor by the avowal of their own principles. There is, however, no ground for this suspicion. The overture itself does not contain the slightest manifestation of this sectional feeling. The Presbytery of New Castle, from the bosom of which it proceeded, was not a homogeneous body of Scotch and Irish members. It had scarcely a majority of such members; five were either originally or immediately from New England, two were from Wales, and one from England. The overture itself tells a plain story. It avows distinctly the object aimed at, and the means for its accomplishment. It states that errors of various kinds, Arminianism, Socinianism, and Deism, had begun to prevail even in the reformed churches. This was true, to some extent, of Scotland, still more alarmingly true of the north of Ireland; true of the Dissenters in England, who, a few years later, looked askant at President Davies, because he came from a church which had adopted the Westminster Confession, and are now applauded as "the friends of religious liberty" for so doing. It was true also of New England, where the Arminian declension had already begun. Is it wonderful, under these circumstances, that men who loved the truth should feel some anxiety; that being members of a church whose doors were wide open, they should be desirous to place some bar at the entrance; to exact some pledge that those who were admitted to the ministry would not labour in the vocation of error? When motives so obvious are avowed for this measure, why should evil motives and sinister designs be raked up from the dark corners of a suspicious imagination, and gratuitously imputed to its authors?

It has been said also that the adoption of the Confession of Faith was the result of sectarian bigotry and heartless orthodoxy. It is very easy to excite the prejudices of the simple, by such assertions. But zeal for the truth is surely no evidence of indifference for religion. This unnatural connection does indeed sometimes occur; and where these two things are united they produce a most offensive form of human character. For any one such instance, however, the history of the church furnishes an hundred of the far more congenial union of indifference to the truth and disregard to religion. The strictest churches have been the most pious, laborious, and useful churches. And the strictest age of any particular church has almost always been its best age. Holland is not better now than when she demanded a strict adherence to her doctrinal standards. The Socinianised Presbyterians of England did not become better than Calamy, Reynolds, and other members of the Westminster Assembly, when they rejected all creeds but the Bible. The French Protestants are not better now than when their noble army of martyrs and confessors, whose blood still calls to heaven for a blessing on the remnant of their children, "swore" to live and die by their confession of faith. And it may well be doubted if New England is more religious at the present time than in the days of her rigid Calvinism, when the catechism was taught at every fire-side and in every district school.

The mere adoption of the Confession of Faith, therefore, is not in itself an evidence of heartless orthodoxy. And there is no evidence of any other kind that the advocates of this measure were less zealous in their religion than their opponents. It may be said it was the Scotch and Irish members who were in favour of the measure, and the English members who opposed it. To a certain extent this is true. But were not the Irish members the leaders in the great revival of 1740–1744? Were not many of those leaders members of the obnoxious Presbyteries of New Castle and Donegal? On the other hand, some of those who were most averse to the adoption of the Confession of Faith, were most bitter in their opposition to the revival. These facts are referred to, to show the injustice of imputing a mere lifeless orthodoxy to the advocates of Mr. Thompson's overture, and of the assumption that it was designed to get rid of the troublesome zeal of the better members of the Synod.

The design is clearly expressed in the overture itself; it was to guard against the inroads of error, which had begun to prevail upon every side. The chief apprehension was directed, not towards New England, but towards Ireland. The Synod had already rejected one ministerial applicant from that country, upon suspicion of unsoundness in the faith, and doubtful character. A few years later, they rejected another. And again, in a few years, they cast out a third, who had gained admittance upon deceptive testimonials of orthodoxy. That the chief immediate purpose of this overture was to keep out unsound men from the Irish Presbyteries, is distinctly avowed by its author, and avowed in such a way, as to leave no doubt of his sincerity. In the appendix to his work on the government of the church of Christ, published in 1741, he has some reflections on the state of the church, which were written at an earlier period. He there says: "When it pleased our glorious and almighty king Jesus, who has the hearts of the kings of the earth in his hands, that, as the rivers of water are turned, he can turn them whithersoever he pleaseth, to move the hearts of our

Synod, with such a remarkable degree of unanimity to adopt the Westminster Confession and Catechisms, &c., it was matter of very great satisfaction to most of us, and to myself in particular, who had been for some time before under no small fears and perplexities of mind, lest we should be corrupted with the new schemes of doctrine which for some time had prevailed in the north of Ireland, that being the part from whence we expected to be, in a great measure, supplied with new hands to fill our vacancies in the ministry, within the bounds of our Synod. And I hope still, that that very step not only hath been of good effect among us already, but also will still continue to be so while it continues in force, in pursuance of the end for which it was first intended." * To under-

* Government of the Church of Christ, by John Thompson, minister of the gospel, p. 116. As it has become common to speak in very disparaging terms of this gentleman, and as he seems to have been a really good man, it is a pleasure and honour to be allowed to vindicate his memory. This can best be done by letting the reader see how he spoke of the state of religion in our church, and of the duty of ministers, before the convulsion which unhappily tore the church asunder. In these reflections, after describing the confusions and divisions which had begun to prevail, he says to his brethren, "This matter belongeth unto us in a special manner — firstly, by virtue of our office and station; and again, because we have had a guilty hand in bringing in the evil; we should, therefore, strive and endeavour to have a prime and leading hand in healing and removing it. In order to this, I think these things are undoubtedly incumbent on us: First, that every one of us endeavour, with an impartial severity, to examine and look back upon our past conduct and behaviour, as Christians and as ministers of the gospel, calling and setting our consciences to work, to compare our past behaviour with the divine law, which is holy, spiritual, just, and good; weighing ourselves in the balances of the sanctuary, with the same exactness with which we expect to be weighed by our holy and impartial Judge, that we may be convinced how far we have come short of our duty, even of what we might have done, as Christians and ministers, for the glory of God, our own and others' salvation; and especially how far we have come short of that exemplary piety, circumspection, and tenderness of walk, and spiritualness of converse with others, which, as ministers of the gospel of Christ, we should have studied; as also, how far we have failed in degree of love, care, zeal, and tender concern for the souls of men.

"2. Another thing incumbent on us is, that whatever our consciences lay to our charge in these matters, we confess the same before the Lord, and be-

stand fully the design of the adopting act, the overture which led to it ought to be read, and it is therefore here inserted at length.

"An overture humbly offered to the consideration of the reverend Synod; wherein is proposed an expedient for preventing the

wail them with grief and sorrow of heart, in deep humiliation, earnestly praying for pardon; and resolving in the strength of divine grace, to amend and reform all we find wanting or amiss in these or any other particulars, resolving still to grow in the exercise of every grace and the practice of holiness.

"3. Another thing incumbent is, that we labour to be possessed with an earnest care and concern for the salvation of our own souls; and particularly to make sure of a work of grace and regeneration in our own hearts, so as never to be at ease and quiet without some comfortable evidence of it, in the discernible exercise of grace in our hearts, together with the suitable genuine fruits of holiness in our lives.

"4. Let us earnestly labour to get our affections weaned from the world and all sublunary things, and to set them on things above, that our love to God and to our Lord Jesus Christ, our concern for his glory in the faithful performance of duty and the promotion of the kingdom of grace, by the conversion and edification of souls, may so employ and take up our thoughts that all worldly interests may appear but empty trifles in comparison with these things. . . . There is a great difference between preaching the gospel that we may get a living, and to desire a living that we may be enabled to preach the gospel. And happy is that minister who is enabled cheerfully and resolutely to do the latter, and truly and effectually to avoid the former.

"5. Another thing to be endeavoured by us, is to strive to suit our gospel ministrations, not so much to the relish and taste as to the necessities of our people; and in order thereunto to endeavour, by all proper means, to be acquainted with their spiritual state, as far as practicable by us; that knowing their diseases and wants we may know how to suit our doctrine thereunto.— And particularly we should endeavour to bend our forces and to use our best skill, to suit the prevalent distemper of this carnal and secure age, striving with all our might to rouse secure sinners and awaken them out of their sleep, and drowsy saints from their slumber and carnal security.—For this purpose we should not only assert and maintain the necessity of regeneration and converting grace, and of a righteous and godly walk, and of increase and advancement therein, but also endeavour to press the same home upon their consciences with all earnestness, as if we saw them perishing and would gladly be the means of their deliverance.

"6. It would also contribute not a little to promote and revive a work of grace, if we could effectually revive congregational discipline, in order to con-

ingress and spreading of dangerous errors, among either ourselves or the flocks committed to our care.

"*Reverend Fathers and Brethren:*

"I would be heartily grieved if the following overture, or any thing in it, should, in the event, prove the occasion of any heat or contention among us. Sure I am that every thing of this kind is far from my intention, and I hope all my brethren will not only be persuaded of the peaceableness and sincerity of my intentions, but also to judge for the necessity of such an expedient, when they seriously ponder and consider these few particulars. First, that it is the unquestionable duty of every Christian, according to his station and talent, to maintain and defend the truths of the gospel against all opposition. Secondly, that this work or duty is in an especial manner incumbent on the ministers of the gospel in virtue of their office. Thirdly, that not only every Christian and minister, but also every church, as an organized body politic, methodised by order and government, is also obliged to act with Christian vigilance and sagacity in maintaining and defending gospel truth. Fourthly, that the parties aforesaid are not only obliged to maintain and defend the truth for themselves, but also to endeavour to perpetuate and propagate it unto posterity pure and uncorrupt. Fifthly, as the light of nature teaches all kingdoms, commonwealths, cities, &c., even in time of peace to prepare for war, so a principle of spiritual wisdom should direct the church of Christ to fortify itself against all the assaults and invasions that may be made upon the doctrine it professes, according to the word of God. Sixthly, that secret bosom enemies of the truth, (I mean those who being visible members of a church do not openly and violently

vince sinners and make them ashamed of their scandalous outbreakings. For I am afraid that most of us are too lax and remiss in this matter, so that the highest privileges of Christ's church, I mean external privileges, are too often given to such whose conversation is very unsuitable unto them."

These few extracts will show the spirit of the work, and the manner in which "the notorious" Thompson thought and wrote on these subjects. Such a man does not deserve to have his name cast out as evil.

oppose the truth professed therein, but in a secret covert way endeavour to undermine it,) are as dangerous as any whatever; and, therefore, the church should exercise her vigilance in a special manner against such, by searching them out, discovering them, and setting a mark upon them whereby they may be known, and so not have it in their power to deceive. The churches of Ephesus and Smyrna are commended for this, but Pergamos and Thyatira are reproved for the neglect of it. Seventhly, that we, the members of this Synod, together with the particular congregations of professors under our care, are a church which is one entire organized body or society of Christians united together by order and government, according to the institution of the word, and therefore ought (especially when apparent dangers call for it,) to exert ourselves and the authority with which we are invested, in vindication and defence of the truths which we profess, and for preventing the ingress and spreading of error. Eighthly, that we are so a particular church as not to be a part of any particular church in the world, with which we are united by the joint exercise of church government, and therefore we are not accountable to the judicial inquiry of any superior ecclesiastical judicature upon earth, and therefore if we do not exert the authority inherent in us for maintaining the purity of gospel truth, it is not in the power of any superior ecclesiastical judicature to call us in question for our neglect, or for our errors or heresies should we be corrupted with them. Ninthly, although, I hope, there are as yet few or none among us (especially of the ministers) who are infected with any gross errors or heresies in doctrine, yet I think I may say we are in no small danger of being corrupted in doctrinals, and that even as to fundamentals, which to me seems evident from the consideration of these few particulars of our present circumstances.

"First, it seems to me that we are too much like the people of Laish, in a careless defenceless condition, as a city without walls; (or perhaps my unacquaintedness with our records may cause me to mistake.) For as far as I know, though we be an entire particular church, as has been observed, and not a part of a particular church, yet we have not any particular system of doctrines, composed by ourselves, or others, which we, by any judicial act of our church, have adopted to be the articles or confession of our faith, &c. Now a church without a confession, what is it like? It is true, as I take it, we all generally acknowledge and look upon the Westminster Confession and Catechisms to be our confession, or what we own for such; but the most that can be said is, that the Westminster Confession of Faith is the confession of the faith of the generality of our members, ministers and people; but that it is our confession, as we are a united body politic, I cannot see, unless, First, it hath been received by a conjunct act of the representatives of our church; I mean by the Synod, either before or since it hath been *sub forma synodi.* Secondly, unless due care be, and hath been taken that all intrants into the ministry among us have subscribed the said confession, or by some equivalent solemn act, *coram auctoritate ecclesiastica,* testified their owning it as the confession of their faith; which how far it is observed within the bounds of our Synod, I am ignorant. Now, if this be so, (for upon this supposition I speak,) I think we are in a very defenceless condition. For if we have no confession which is ours by synodical act, or if any among us have not subscribed or acknowledged the confession, *ut supra,* then — First, there is no bar provided to keep out of the ministry those who are corrupt in doctrinals; they may be received into the ministry without renouncing their corrupt doctrines. Secondly, those that are in the ministry among us may propagate gross errors and corrupt many thereby without being discovered to preach any thing against the received truth, because (*supposito ut supra*) the truth was never publicly received among us.

"Secondly, another of our present circumstances is, that we are surrounded by so many pernicious and dangerous corruptions in doctrine, and these grown so much in vogue and fashion, even among those whose ancestors, at the beginning of the reformation, would have sealed the now despised truth with their blood. When Arminianism, Socinianism, Deism, Freethinking, &c., do like a deluge overflow even the reformed churches, both established and dissenting, to such a degree, have we not reason to consult our own safety?

Tum tua res agitur paries cum proximus ardet.

"A third circumstance we are in, which increaseth our danger of infection by error, is partly the infancy, and partly the poverty of our circumstances, which render us unable to plant a seminary of learning among ourselves, and so to see to the education of our young candidates for the ministry, and therefore we are under the necessity of depending upon other places for men to supply our vacancies in the church, and so are in danger of having our ministry corrupted by such as are leavened with false doctrine before they come among us.

"Fourthly, I am afraid there are too many among ourselves, who, though they may be sound in the faith themselves, yet have the edge of their zeal against the prevailing errors of the times very much blunted, partly by their being dispirited, and so by a kind of cowardice are afraid, boldly, openly, and zealously to appear against those errors that show themselves in the world under the patronage and protection of so many persons of note and figure; partly by a kind of indifference and mistaken charity, whereby they think they ought to bear with others, though differing from them in opinion about points which are mysterious and sublime, but not practical nor fundamental, such as predestination. Now, although I would grant that the precise point of election and reprobation be neither fundamental nor immediately practical, yet take predestination completely, as it takes in the other disputed points between Calvinists and Arminians, such as universal grace, the non-perseverance of the saints, foreseen faith, and good works, &c., and I think it such an article in my creed, such a fundamental of my faith, that I know not what any other articles would avail, that could be retained without it.

"Now the expedient which I would humbly propose you may take is as follows: First, that our Synod, as an ecclesiastical judicature of Christ, clothed with ministerial authority to act in concert in behalf of truth and opposition to error, would do something of this kind at such a juncture, when error seems to grow so fast, that unless we be well fortified, it is like to swallow us up. Secondly, that in pursuance hereof, the Synod would, by an act of its own, publicly and authoritatively adopt the Westminster Confession of Faith, Catechisms, &c., for the public confession of our faith, as we are a particular organized church. Thirdly, that further the Synod would make an act to oblige every Presbytery within their bounds, to oblige every candidate for the ministry, to subscribe, or otherwise acknowledge *coram presbyterio*, the said confession of theirs, &c. and to promise not to preach or teach contrary to it. Fourthly, to oblige every actual minister coming among us to do the like. Fifthly, to enact, that if any minister within our bounds shall take upon him to teach or preach any thing contrary to any of the said articles, unless, first, he propose the said point to the Presbytery or Synod to be by them discussed, he shall be censured so and so. Sixthly, let the Synod recommend it to all their members, and members to their flocks, to entertain the truth in love, to be zealous and fruitful, and to be earnest with God by prayer, to preserve their vine from being spoiled by those deluding foxes; which if the Synod shall see cause to do, I hope it may, through the divine blessing, prevent in a great measure, if not altogether, our being deluded with the damnable errors of our times; but if not, I am afraid we may be at last infected with the errors which so much prevail elsewhere.

"I will only add one argument to press this, viz.: It is to be feared if such an expedient be neglected, (now I hope it is in our power) ere many years pass over our heads, those, who now discern not the necessity thereof, may see it when it will be too late; when perhaps the number of truth's friends may be too few to carry such a point in the Synod. Thus, brethren, I have offered to your consideration some serious thoughts, in a coarse dress. May it please the Master of assemblies to preside among us, and direct and influence us in all things, for his glory, and the edification of his church. So prays your unworthy fellow labourer in Christ's vineyard." *

The wisdom of this proposal to adopt the Westminster Confession, has received the sanction of the church for more than a hundred years, during which time the only modifications which the

* This overture, though not inserted in the minutes of the Synod, was printed. The above transcript is taken from Mr. Hazard's MSS.

adopting act has received, were intended to render it more explicit and more binding. It is, therefore, a matter of surprise, that, at first, it should have met with so much opposition, and that this opposition should have come from the source it did. Mr. Andrews, in a letter, dated April, 1729, six months before the adopting act was passed, says, "I think all the Scotch are on one side, and all the English and Welsh on the other, to a man." * This he gives,

* As this letter of Mr. Andrews to Dr. Colman of Boston, dated Philadelphia, April, 7, 1729, is instructive and interesting, it is here inserted, as far as it is preserved in Mr. Hazard's MSS.

"As to affairs here, we are engaged in the enlargement of our house, and by the assistance we had from Boston, I hope we shall go on comfortably with that work. The stone-work at the foundation is laid, and all the materials are getting ready. We are now likely to fall into a great difference about subscribing the Westminster Confession of Faith. An overture for it, drawn up by Mr. Thompson of Lewes-town, was offered to our Synod the year before last, but not then read in the Synod. Measures were taken to stave it off, and I was in hopes we should have heard no more of it. But last Synod it was brought again, recommended by all the Scotch and Irish members present, and being read among us, a proposal was made, prosecuted, and agreed to, that it should be deferred till our next meeting, for further consideration. The proposal is, that all ministers and intrants should sign it, or else be disowned as members. Now what shall we do? They will certainly carry it by numbers; our countrymen say they are willing to join in a vote to make it the confession of our church, but to agree to making it a test of orthodoxy, and term of ministerial communion, they will not. I think all the Scotch are on one side, and all the English and Welsh on the other to a man. Nevertheless I am not so determined as to be uncapable to receive advice, and I give you this account, that I may have your judgment as to what I had best do in the matter. Supposing I do believe it, shall I, on the terms above mentioned, subscribe or not? I earnestly desire you by the first opportunity to send me your opinion. Our brethren have got the overture with a preface to it printed, and I intend to send you one for the better regulation of your thoughts about it. Some say the design of this motion is to spew out our countrymen, they being scarcely able to hold way with the other brethren in all their disciplinary and legislative notions. What truth there may be in this I know not. Some deny it, whereas others say there is something in it. I am satisfied some of us are an uneasiness to them, and are thought to be too much in their way sometimes, so that I think it would be no trouble to lose some of us. Yet I can't think this to be the thing ultimately designed, whatever smaller glances there may be at it. I have no thought that they have any design

as his impression, and it no doubt, in general, correctly indicates the dividing line between the friends and opposers of the measure. The expression, however, is certainly too strong. It is hardly possible that the English and Welsh members of the Presbytery of New Castle, who had been for several years in the habit of requiring the adoption of the confession by their candidates, should have opposed the Synod's doing the same thing. Besides, when dissatisfaction was manifested on account of some expressions in the adopting act, these members were among the first to render them more explicit. Still, it cannot be doubted, that the class of members to which Mr. Andrews refers, was at first opposed to the measure. How is this to be accounted for? The only reason applicable to them as a class that suggests itself is, that having been accustomed, especially those of them who came from New England, to act more as Independents, without any superior judicatory having the right to question their opinions, they felt that the proposed act would be an infringement of their liberty. Whereas the Scotch and Irish members, more accustomed to Presbyterianism, felt no such apprehensions. It is certain, from what followed, that the opposition did not arise from dislike of the doctrines taught in the Westminster Confession. The opposition was against all creeds, and not against that particular confession. Such at least was the ground taken by President Dickinson, the ablest

against me in particular; I have no reason for it. This business lies heavy on my mind, and I desire that we may be directed in it, that we may not bring a scandal on our profession. Though I have been sometimes the instrument of keeping them together, when they were like to fall to pieces, I have little hope of doing so now. If it were not for the scandal of a division, I should not be much against it, for the different countrymen seem to be most delighted with each other, and to do best when they are by themselves. My congregation being made up of divers nations of different sentiments, this brings me under greater difficulty in this contested business than any other minister of our number. I am afraid of the event. However, I will endeavour to do, as near as I can, what I understand to be duty, and leave the issue to Providence.

"P. S. Ten days ago was buried Mr. Malachi Jones, an old Welsh minister. He was a good man, and did good. He lived about eleven miles from this town."

and most influential member of the Synod, and the most strenuous opposer of his Scottish brethren. This appears from the following abstract of his objections to Mr. Thompson's overture. That "a joint acknowledgment of our Lord Jesus Christ for our common head, of the sacred Scriptures for our common standard both in faith and practice, with a joint agreement in the same essential and necessary articles of Christianity, and the same methods of worship and discipline, are a sufficient bond of union for the being or well-being of any church under heaven." That "we have already all the external bond of union that the Scriptures require of us. We have, all of us, for aught I know, one faith, one Lord, one baptism, and one discipline. Subscription to one confession is indeed required of us, but does our Lord Jesus Christ require this?" That "the requiring and enjoining any unscriptural terms of union or communion is a direct and natural means to procure rents and divisions in the church." That "we all of us know that the subscription under debate has been scrupled by many godly, learned, and faithful ministers of Christ, that it has made horrible divisions and confusions in other churches, and that it is like to have the same sad effects among ourselves." That "a subscription to any human composure as the test of our orthodoxy is to make it the standard of our faith, and thereby to give it the honour due only to the word of God." That imposing subscriptions on others, is "invading his royalty who is sole king and lawgiver to his church, and practising ourselves what we so loudly condemn in others." That imposing subscription on others, "must be done as a necessary duty, or as a thing in itself indifferent; not the former, till some Scripture can be found which requires subscription to human composures. If it be in itself indifferent, who gave the Synod authority to take away the liberty with which Christ has made us free?" That "in making this subscription the term of admitting candidates to the ministry," men may be kept "out of Christ's vineyard, whom he has sent to labour there, and qualified for glorious service in his church." *

* The above abstract is taken from Mr. Hazard's MSS. The writer has not been able to procure a copy either of Mr. Dickinson's Remarks upon the overture, or of Mr. Thompson's reply.

It is obvious from the nature of these objections, that President Dickinson belonged to that small class of persons who are opposed to all creeds of human composition. The sense of the Christian world on this point is against him, and it is not known that there is a single advocate of these views in the Presbyterian Church at the present time. How many of the members of the Synod agreed with him in these opinions, cannot now be ascertained. It is evident that his objections had not a very firm hold even of his own mind; for he joined in the adoption and imposition of the Westminster Confession, the very year these remarks were published. It matters not with what latitude he either received it himself or imposed it upon others. His objection was not to a long creed, or to a short one, but to any creed of human composition, and such is the Westminster Confession in all its parts, essential and non-essential.

When this subject was taken up by the Synod in 1729,* Mr. Thompson's overture was referred to a committee, who brought in a report "which, after long debate upon it, was agreed to *in haec verba:*

"Although the Synod do not claim or pretend to any authority of imposing our faith upon other men's consciences, but do profess our just dissatisfaction with, and abhorrence of, such impositions, and do utterly disclaim all legislative power and authority in the church, being willing to receive one another as Christ has received us to the glory of God, and to admit to fellowship in sacred ordinances all such as we have grounds to believe Christ will at last admit to the kingdom of heaven; yet we are undoubtedly obliged to take care that the faith once delivered to the saints, be kept pure and uncorrupt among us, and so handed down to our posterity;

* The ministers present at this meeting of the Synod, were Messrs. Andrews, Creaghead, Thompson, Anderson, Pierson, Gelston, Houston, G. Tennent, Boyd, Dickinson, Bradner, T. Evans, Hutchinson, Elmer, Stevenson, William Tennent, Conn, Orme, Gillespie, and Wilson. All these were old members of the Synod, except Mr. Elmer and Mr. Wilson. The former was pastor of Fairfield, Cohanzy, and was from New England, as is stated in a communication from L. Q. C. Elmer, Esq. quoted above. The latter was from Ireland, as appears from the minutes of the New Castle Presbytery.

and do therefore agree that all the ministers of this Synod, or that shall hereafter be admitted into this Synod, shall declare their agreement in and approbation of the Confession of Faith, with the Larger and Shorter Catechisms of the Assembly of Divines at Westminster, as being, in all the essential and necessary articles, good forms of sound words and systems of Christian doctrine; and do also adopt the said Confession and Catechisms as the Confession of our faith. And we do also agree, that all Presbyteries within our bounds shall take care not to admit any candidate for the ministry into the exercise of the sacred function, but what declares his agreement in opinion with all the essential and necessary articles of said Confession, either by subscribing the said Confession of Faith and Catechisms, or by a verbal declaration of his assent thereto, as such candidate or minister shall think best. And in case any minister of this Synod, or any candidate for the ministry, shall have any scruple with respect to any article or articles of said Confession or Catechisms, he shall, at the time of his making the said declaration, declare his sentiments to the Presbytery or Synod; who shall, notwithstanding, admit him to the exercise of the ministry within our bounds, and to ministerial communion, if the Synod or Presbytery shall judge his scruple or mistake to be only about articles not essential and necessary in doctrine, worship, or government. But if the Synod or Presbytery shall judge such minister or candidate erroneous in essential or necessary articles of faith, the Synod or Presbytery shall declare them incapable of communion with them. And the Synod solemnly agree, that none of us will traduce or use any opprobrious terms of those that differ from us in these extra-essentials, and not necessary points of doctrine, but treat them with the same friendship, kindness, and brotherly love, as if they had not differed from us in such sentiments."

The adopting act itself had reference only to the Confession of Faith and Catechisms; the same year, however, "a motion being made to know the Synod's judgment about the Directory, they gave their sense of that matter in the following words, viz.: The Synod do unanimously acknowledge and declare that they judge the Directory for worship, discipline, and government, commonly annexed to the Westminster Confession, to be agreeable in substance to the word of God, and founded thereupon, and therefore, do earnestly recommend the same to all their members, to be by them observed, as near as circumstances will allow, and Christian prudence direct." The "substance" of the Directory is of course its Presbyterianism. What is not substantial about it, is its numerous directions, having reference in many cases either to unimportant, or to local and temporary circumstances. A stricter adoption of the Westminster Directory, in this country, was impossible. It contemplated a very different state of things from that which then existed, or which now exists among us. It directs, for example, that the ministers of London should ordain ministers for the whole country, until Presbyteries were regularly established; that prayer be made for the queen of Bohemia, (sister of Charles I., a great friend of the Protestants, and therefore a great favourite with the Puritans;) that the candidates for the ministry, before being taken upon trial, should satisfy the Presbytery as to what degrees they had taken in the University, &c. &c.

Though the main subject now under consideration, is the standard of doctrine adopted by our church, reference is here made to the Directory for two reasons: First, it has a natural connexion with the adopting act; the one relating to the doctrines, the other to the order of the church. Secondly, it is generally united with the Confession of Faith in those declarations of the Synod to which reference must presently be made.

It will be observed that the Synod, in their preamble, "utterly disclaim all legislative power in the church." It need hardly be remarked, that this must be understood in a manner consistent with the passage of this act. It is not to be presumed that the Synod, in the preamble to a law, would disclaim all authority to make it. By legislative power in the church, was then understood the power to legislate about truth and duty, to make laws to bind the conscience. The disclaimer of such power is perfectly consistent with the assertion and the exercise of the right to make rules for the government of the church. To make the language above quoted include the denial of this latter right, reduces the act to so glaring an absurdity, that no set of rational men could have enacted it. There is not, in all the records of our church, a more striking example of a standing rule, or law, than this act. It was binding on all the members present or absent; it required of them the adoption of the Confession of Faith, in the manner prescribed, as a term of communion; it bound all the Presbyteries, prescribing a rule by which they were to regulate themselves in all their future licensures, ordinations, and admission of members. Its validity as a law of the church, though proceeding from the sole authority of the Synod, has never been questioned from that day to this. How can it then be made a matter of doubt, whether, according to our system, Synods have a right to make such rules? This act was passed unanimously, from which two things may be certainly inferred; the one, that the disclaimer of all legislative power was not understood by the Scotch members as a denial of the right of Synod to make rules for the government of the church; the other, that the New England members must have acknowledged this latter right, or they would not have joined in exercising it. That the expression, "legislative power," was always used in the sense of a power to make new laws in matters of faith or morals, is further evident from the fact that all the old-side writers at the time of the schism uniformly disclaim "all legislative power in the church," though they insisted so strenuously upon the binding character of the acts of Synod.* The more extended examination of the opinions of the two parties then

* This restricted use of the phrase in question has not been retained by ecclesiastical writers. Dr. Hill, in his Institutes, constantly speaks of the judicial, executive, and legislative powers of the General Assembly of the Church of Scotland. And the power to make rules, or binding enactments, is certainly, in the ordinary sense of the words, a legislative power. The restriction in the nature of the objects with regard to which it can be legitimately exercised, is not expressed by the word *legislative*, because a rule binding on a community and enforced by certain sanctions is a law, whether it relates to matter of duty or of government. Whatever it may be called, the power to make rules which the members and inferior judicatories were bound to obey, was not denied by either party, and was exercised without hesitation by the one as well as by the other.

in the church, in reference to this subject, belongs, however, to the next period of our history.

There are two questions of no small importance in relation to this adopting act which must be considered. The first is, what is its meaning? What were the terms of ministerial communion which it designed to establish? The second is, what are the terms of ministerial communion, as far as they relate to doctrine, in our church? These questions are very distinct from each other. For this act may have fixed one condition, and the Synod the very next year have prescribed a different.

What then is the meaning of this act? Did the Synod intend by the words "essential and necessary articles," articles essential to Christianity? or articles, in their estimation, essential to the system of doctrines contained in the Westminster Confession? If the former, they intended that every man, otherwise qualified, who held the fundamental doctrines of the gospel, might be admitted to the ministry in our church. If the latter, they intended that no man who was not a Calvinist, should be thus admitted. Apart from the language of the act itself, there are three sources of proof as to what was the intention of its authors; the history of the act; the subsequent declarations of the Synod as to their own meaning; and the testimony of cotemporary writers.

It must be admitted that the language of the act leaves the intention of its authors a matter of doubt. When they say that they adopt the Westminster Confession of Faith and Catechisms as the confession of their faith, their language admits of but one interpretation. This was the very form in which the subscription was made in the strict Presbytery of New Castle. To make this mean that they adopted only so much of the Confession as is essential to the gospel, would be to suppose a use of language such as never before was made, at least by honest men. If a man says he adopts the thirty-nine articles of the church of England as the articles of his faith; is he ever understood to mean that he adopts those portions of them merely which are essential to the gospel? Or, if another says, he adopts the Decrees of the Council of Trent, can he honestly mean that he adopts so much as is not inconsistent with the Augsburg Confession? Such a use of language would be inconsistent with the least confidence in the intercourse of life. It is not the meaning of the terms, and cannot honestly be made their meaning. Again, when the Synod say that every candidate must declare "his agreement in opinion with all the essential and necessary articles of the said confession," there is but one meaning that can be fairly put upon their language. The essential parts of a confession are those parts which are essential to its peculiar character. No man receives all the essential articles of a popish creed, who receives no more than is consistent with Protestantism. All such subscriptions are mockery and falsehood. If the Synod intended by the essential articles of the Confession, the essential articles of the gospel, why mention the Confession at all? The Presbyteries, surely, could pick out the necessary doctrines of the gospel from the Bible, as easily as from the Confession. The interpretation, therefore, which would make the Synod mean by the expressions just quoted, that they adopted, and required others to adopt, those articles merely of the Confession which are essential to the gospel, is inconsistent with all just and honest use of language. Thus far then this act admits of but one interpretation consistent with candour and fair dealing on the part of its authors.

What follows is more ambiguous. It is said that a candidate, at the time of his adopting the Confession, may state his scruples with regard to any article or articles, and that the Presbytery shall, notwithstanding, admit him if they judge that his scruples relate to "articles not essential and necessary in doctrine, worship, or government." Articles not essential in doctrine might well, in any other context, be understood to mean articles not essential to the gospel. But as the worship here spoken of is the Presbyterian mode of worship, and the government intended is Presbyterian government, so the doctrine referred to is the doctrine of the Presbyterian Church. It was not the intention of the Synod to exclude those only who denied every form of church government, but those also who rejected any essential feature of Presbyterianism. In like manner, they intended to reject all who denied any essential feature of the system of doctrine which they had adopted. It is not intended that this is the necessary meaning of the words, taken by themselves. But it is a natural interpretation, expressing a sense which the words will readily admit. And if it is the only interpretation which will save the act from the charge of direct contradiction, it must be assumed to be the true one. In the preceding clauses the Synod had declared that they adopted the Westminster Confession as the confession of their faith, and that every new member must, in like manner, adopt it, in all its essential and necessary articles. Did they then immediately declare that he might reject these articles, no matter how essential a part of the Confession they might be, provided they were not absolutely necessary to Christianity? If the sense of the former clauses is clear, it must determine the interpretation of the latter.

No impartial judge could hesitate to decide that this was the real meaning of the Synod, who took into view the history of the act and the character of the men who adopted it. It has already been shown that the act was introduced to guard against Arminianism, as well as Socinianism. This was its design. Its language, therefore, must be interpreted in reference to this design; especially as it is known that those who had this object in view were perfectly satisfied with it. Is it to be believed that Mr. Thompson, who had specified the doctrine of election as one which he would not venture to call fundamental, yet as one the denial of which ought not to be allowed, would have been contented with the act, had it made provision for the admission of ministers who not only denied that doctrine, but any and all others not absolutely essential to the gospel? Such an interpretation of the act would place its authors in a most extraordinary light. It must be remembered that the advocates of Mr. Thompson's overture were not thwarted; they were not voted down by their more liberal brethren, and forced to submit to a measure to which they were opposed. On the contrary, they had the power in their own hands. Mr. Andrews says he had no doubt of their ability to carry just what they wished. Yet they were satisfied with this act, and joined in praising God when it was passed. It must, therefore, be understood in a manner consistent with the avowed object of its introduction.

It is very evident, indeed, that the act was a compromise. Both parties were very desirous to avoid a schism; yet both were anxious that their own views should prevail. Their only expedient was to find some common ground on which they could stand. Mr. Dickinson had avowed his wish to establish the "essential and necessary doctrines of Christianity" as the condition of ministerial communion. Mr. Thompson wished the explicit adoption of the Westminster Confession, to be that condition. The common ground on which they met was the essential and necessary articles of that Confession. To make this mean exactly what Mr. Dickinson had proposed, is to present Mr. Thompson in a ridiculous position; and President Dickinson in one still less to be envied. When the Synod came to explain what they meant by the necessary articles of the Confession, they made them include so much that Mr. Thompson had nothing to wish for.

This is one hypothesis for accounting for the acknowledged ambiguity of this act, and supposes that both parties understood it in the same way. Another, and perhaps more probable one is, that in the mutual anxiety to have the act express their peculiar views, they at last got it into a shape in which each could adopt it, as being substantially what each desired. However this may be, it is perfectly clear, from subsequent events, that the Synod as such, never intended the act to fix as the condition of ministerial communion, the acknowledgment of the necessary doctrines of Christianity, whatever may have been the wishes of some few of its members.*

* How far President Dickinson adhered to the views expressed in his objections to Mr. Thompson's overture, is a matter of doubt. There is a pamphlet extant, published in 1735, entitled "Remarks on a Letter to a friend in the country, containing the substance of a sermon preached in Philadelphia in the congregation of the Rev. Mr. Hemphill," ascribed, no doubt correctly, to President Dickinson. In this pamphlet he says, Christian communion "should extend to all that we charitably suppose to be real Christians." "And as to ministerial communion, we should admit all to the exercise of the ministry among us, that we suppose qualified for the work, according to the instructions which Christ has given us in the gospel, and capable of doing service in the Church of Christ in that important character, how different soever in opin-

The first document explanatory of the intentions of the Synod in this measure, is found on the very same page with the act itself. In the morning the Synod had resolved that they would adopt the Confession of Faith; in the afternoon they carried their resolution into effect, and the result is thus recorded: "All the ministers of the Synod now present except one, who declared himself not prepared,* viz.: Messrs. Jedediah Andrews, Thomas Creaghead, John Thompson, James Anderson, John Pierson, Samuel Gelston, Joseph Houston, Gilbert Tennent, Adam Boyd, Jonathan Dickinson, John Bradner, Alexander Hucheson, Thomas Evans, Hugh Stevenson, William Tennent, Hugh Conn, George Gillespie, and John Wilson; after proposing all the scruples that any of them had to make against any articles and expressions in the Confession of Faith,

ion from us." This differs materially from what he had said in his remarks on Mr. Thompson's overture. There he demanded nothing more than agreement in the essential and necessary articles of Christianity. Here, this is what in so many words he makes necessary for Christian communion, saying, "we can't admit those to communion in sealing ordinances, whose errors we suppose inconsistent with the grace and favour of God." From this he expressly distinguishes ministerial communion, demanding for that all that was necessary, in our judgment, to qualify a man for the sacred office. "To admit others," he says, "were deliberately to send poison into Christ's household, instead of the portion of meat which he has provided." Mr. Thompson could have said all this, though he would doubtless have applied it very differently. On another page the writer says, "If a man be, in the society's opinion, qualified for the work of the ministry, and like to serve the interests of Christ's kingdom, they can with a good conscience admit him to the exercise of the ministry with them, notwithstanding lesser differences of opinion in extra-essential points. But then on the other hand, if he embrace such errors, as, in the judgment of the society, unqualify him for a faithful discharge of that important trust, they cannot admit him to the cure of souls, without unfaithfulness to God and their own consciences." Such is the view of this subject given in this pamphlet, which in the copy which belonged to the late Dr. Wilson, is stated to be from the pen of President Dickinson. That the writer considered his own views, as here given, to be in accordance with those expressed in the adopting act, is evident from his giving that act as an appendix, "to convince the reader," as he says, "that we govern ourselves according to the principles here asserted and pleaded for."

* This was the Rev. Mr. Elmer, who subsequently acceded.

and Larger and Shorter Catechisms of the Assembly of Divines at Westminster, have unanimously agreed in the solution of those scruples, and in declaring the said Confession and Catechisms to be the confession of their faith, excepting only some clauses in the twentieth and twenty-third chapters, concerning which clauses the Synod do unanimously declare that they do not receive those articles in any such sense as to suppose the civil magistrate hath a controlling power over Synods, with respect to the exercise of their ministerial authority, or power to persecute any for their religion, or in any sense contrary to the Protestant succession to the throne of Great Britain. The Synod observing that unanimity, peace, and unity which appeared in all their consultations and determinations in the affair of the Confession, did unanimously agree in giving thanks to God in solemn prayer and praise." * What gratulations would there be in the Church were there now the same unanimity, peace, and unity among her ministers! This then was what these fathers meant by adopting the Confession of Faith. They adopted all of it, except certain clauses in a certain sense, and as these clauses are no longer in the Confession, there is not an "article or expression" in that formula to which these men did not assent. Such was the latitudinarianism of those days! And it was in this sense and to this extent, that they required all new members to adopt the same Confession. That this is true, admits of proof that can neither be gainsaid or resisted.

Unfortunately, the adopting act had been printed and circulated among the churches without the minute just quoted, which might have served to explain its meaning. The question immediately arose, what do the Synod mean by essential and necessary articles? May the new members object to any and all articles not essential to Christianity? This ambiguity in the act excited immediate dissatisfaction, and the Synod were called upon to say explicitly how these expressions were to be understood. All this appears from the following record in the minutes for 1730. "Whereas some persons have been dissatisfied with the manner of wording our last year's agreement about the Confession, &c.; supposing some expres-

* Minutes, vol. ii. p. 12.

sions not sufficiently obligatory upon intrants; overtured, that the Synod do now declare that they understand those clauses that respect the admission of intrants in such a sense, as to oblige them to receive and adopt the Confession and Catechisms, at their admission, in the same manner and as fully as the members of the Synod that were then present. Which overture was unanimously agreed to by the Synod."* The design of this declaration was to state explicitly the meaning of the adopting act, to let the churches know what articles of the Confession the candidates for admission might object against. The Synod say that they intended, by the clauses in question, to bind the new members to adopt the Confession as fully as they themselves had done; that is, to adopt the whole of it, except certain clauses in the twentieth and twenty-third chapters. Here then is an authentic and official explanation of the act in question; proceeding from its authors, and of precisely the same authority as the act itself. Cases analogous to this frequently occur in civil governments. When an ambiguity is found to exist in an act of Congress, that body passes an explanatory act, declaring in what sense the doubtful expressions are to be taken. Who, after such explanation, ever ventures to assert that the interpretation given by Congress of their own act, is not the true interpretation? No candid man, therefore, in the face of this unanimous declaration of the Synod that they intended one thing, can assert that they meant the opposite. The case is the stronger on account of the unanimity with which this explanation was given; and because the composition of the Synod this year was, in the main, what it was the year before. What difference existed was much more favourable to a lax than to a strict interpretation of the act of 1729.† There can be no doubt, therefore, that the adopting

* Minutes, vol. ii. p. 16. It is worthy of remark, that the dissatisfaction which the above declaration was intended to allay, referred solely to the latter part of the adopting act which relates to the admission of new members. Against the former part no objection seems to have been made. This proves that the interpretation of that portion of the act given above, is the one which it received at the time of its first publication.

† The members who were present in 1729, but absent in 1730, when this explanatory declaration was passed, were Messrs. Dickinson, Bradner, Steven-

act, as understood and intended by its authors, bound every new member to receive the Confession of Faith and Catechisms, in all their parts, except certain specified clauses in chapters twentieth and twenty-third. Whether this was right or wrong, liberal or illiberal, it is what the Synod unanimously declared they intended.

This explanation, explicit as it is, did not put an end to the dissatisfaction. This, no doubt, arose from the fact that the original act continued to circulate unaccompanied by either the preceding explanation, or the minute of the afternoon session of September 19, 1729. New complaints were, therefore, made to the Synod, and a new demand for a public avowal of their meaning. This led, in 1736, to a declaration which seems, at least for the time, to have produced general satisfaction. In the minutes for that year it is recorded that, "an overture of the committee, upon the supplication of the people of Paxton and Derry, was brought in and is as followeth: That the Synod do declare that inasmuch as we understand that many persons of our persuasion, both more lately and formerly, have been offended with some expressions or distinctions in the first or preliminary act of our Synod for adopting the Westminster Confession and Catechisms, &c.; that in order to remove said offence and all jealousies that have arisen or may arise in any of our people's minds on occasion of said distinctions and expressions, the Synod doth declare that the Synod have adopted and still do adhere to the Westminster Confession, Catechisms, and Directory, without the least variation or alteration, and without any regard to said distinctions. And we do further declare this was our meaning and true intent in our first adopting of the said Confession, as may particularly appear by our adopting act, which is as followeth: "All the ministers of the Synod now present,

son, Conn, Orme, Gillespie, and Wilson. Mr. Dickinson is the only one of these who it can be presumed would have objected; and even he had adopted the Confession as fully as any of his brethren. Mr. Orme was a member of the Presbytery of New Castle, all the others were Scotch or Irish members. In place of these absentees we find the names of Messrs. David Evans, E. Pemberton, Joseph Morgan, Ebenezer Gould; all, it is believed, Welsh or English. The Synod of 1730, therefore, had not the advantage of that of 1729, in the number of strictly disposed members.

(which were eighteen in number,) except one who declared himself not prepared, after proposing all the scruples that any of them had to make against any articles and expressions in the Confession of Faith and Larger and Shorter Catechisms of the Assembly of Divines at Westminster, have unanimously agreed in the solution of those scruples, and in declaring the said Confession and Catechisms to be the confession of their faith, except only some clauses in the twentieth and twenty-third chapters, concerning which clauses the Synod do unanimously declare that they do not receive those articles in any such sense as to suppose the civil magistrate hath a controlling power over Synods with respect to the exercise of their ministerial authority, or power to persecute any for their religion, or in any sense contrary to the Protestant succession to the throne of Great Britain.' And we do hope and desire, that this our Synodical declaration and explanation may satisfy all our people as to our firm attachment to our good old received doctrines contained in the said Confession, without the least variation or alteration, and that they will lay aside their jealousies, that have been entertained through occasion of the above hinted expressions and declarations as groundless. This overture approved *nemine contradicente.*"*

* Minutes, vol. ii. p. 47. The ministers present at this meeting of Synod, were Messrs. Thomas Creaghead, J. Andrews, J. Thompson, J. Anderson, Richard Treat, J. Houston, Robert Cathcart, A. Boyd, Robert Cross, Robert Jamison, Ebenezer Gould, H. Stevenson, H. Carlisle, James Martin, William Bertram, Alexander Creaghead, John Paul, William Tennent, Sen., William Tennent, Jun., and David Evans. If to these be added those members who, though absent this year, were present when the explanatory declaration of 1730 was passed, viz.: Messrs. John Pierson, Samuel Gelston, Gilbert Tennent, Alexander Hucheson, Joseph Morgan, Daniel Elmer, Thomas Evans, and Ebenezer Pemberton, we shall have a formidable list of witnesses as to what was the true meaning and intent of the adopting act. We have the solemn official declaration of all these gentlemen as to the manner in which they understood their own acts and declarations. A man must have a good deal of courage who would contradict all these men, when the matter in debate is what they themselves intended. Of those members of the Synod, who were absent, both in 1730 and 1736, Messrs. Dickinson, Gillespie, Conn, Bradner, and Wilson had united in adopting all the articles and expressions in the Confession except the specified clauses. Of the few remaining members, the names of H. Hook and William Steward are subscribed to the strict and tho-

There is no inconsistency between this declaration and those of 1729. This is, indeed, in some respects more explicit, but it is not more comprehensive. The Synod adopted no more of the Confession in 1736, than they did in 1729. It is to be remarked that they call the overture adopted on the morning of September 19th, the preliminary act about adopting the Confession of Faith, and the minute of the afternoon of that day, their adopting act itself. In the former they determined that all their members shall declare first, their "agreement with the Confession, &c., in all the essential and necessary articles;" and secondly, that they "adopt the said Confession and Catechisms as the confession of their faith." When they came to carry this resolution into effect, they did actually adopt the whole of the Confession and Catechisms, "excepting only" the specified clauses in chapters twentieth and twenty-third. The act of 1736 does the same and no more. The preliminary act merely declared the purpose of the Synod to exact the adoption of the Confession in all its essential and necessary articles; the Synod not then knowing what exceptions they might choose to make, but subsequently they made no exception beyond what has just been stated. This, however, was not generally known to the churches, and hence the anxiety to ascertain what the Synod received and what they rejected. To satisfy this anxiety, the Synod tell the churches what they had done; that they had adopted the whole of the Confession, rejecting no part of it, but simply repudiating a certain specified interpretation of a few clauses. As far as our doctrinal standards, therefore, are concerned, this declaration of 1736 is nothing more than an announcement and repetition in full of what the Synod had done in 1729, by piecemeal, partly in the morning and partly in the afternoon.*

rough formula of subscription adopted by the Presbytery of New Castle in 1730. The other absentees were Messrs. Pumry, Webb, Hubbell, Horton, John Cross, Chalker, Blair, Wales, Glasgow, and Nutman; the record of their adoption of the Westminster Confession, &c. as the confession of their faith, is almost in every case found on the minutes of Synod. That body, therefore, cannot sustain its claims to any extraordinary liberality as it regards points of doctrine. It evidently belonged to the "most straitest sect of our religion."

* Dr. Hill, (Great Schism, No. 4,) says, in reference to this declaration, "A more fumbling *ex parte* statement can hardly any where be met with. They

It has been asserted that the ground of the dissatisfaction with the act of 1729, was the exception taken to the clauses respecting the power of the civil magistrate, and that the Synod was at last forced to restore those articles; and withdraw their objection. Neither of these assertions is correct. The dissatisfaction arose from the "printed paper" which contained merely the preliminary act, which says not one word about the clauses in question. The whole difficulty arose from the distinction between essential and unessential articles, which the people did not understand, or did not know how much was rejected as unessential. Accordingly this declaration is directed solely to that point. That the objection to the clauses in chapters twentieth and twenty-third were not withdrawn, is clear from the repetition of the minute which contains those objections, and which is here repeated to remove the dissatisfaction; a very clear proof that the difficulty did not relate to that point, and that the Synod had nothing to retract.

As these are official documents, emanating from the same authority as the adopting act itself, and expressly designed to declare its meaning, they must be regarded as decisive, and the question as to the true intention of that act might here be dismissed. Could it even be shown that individuals, or particular judicatories, took a different view of the subject, it would prove nothing, in opposition to the unanimous and repeated declarations of the Synod. Still as this is a subject of great historical interest to the members of our Church, it may not be amiss to gather what additional light we can from the records of the several Presbyteries, and the writings of contemporaries. How the Presbytery of New Castle regarded

(viz.: the adopting act and this declaration) are absolutely irreconcilable and contradictory to each other." But why *ex parte?* It was made by the whole Synod, without one dissenting voice; it contains nothing, as far as the Confession is concerned, that is not implied in the explanatory declaration of 1730. And as to this minute contradicting the adopting act, it merely contradicts Dr. Hill's interpretation of that act. It is certainly more probable that Dr. Hill should be mistaken, than that all these gentlemen should be guilty of direct and intentional falsehood, declaring that they meant one thing, when they really meant another; especially as they appeal to the records in proof of the correctness of their assertions.

this matter may be inferred from the two following extracts from their minutes. The first is dated September 2, 1730, and is as follows: "Whereas divers persons, belonging to several of our congregations, have been stumbled and offended with a certain minute of the proceedings of our last Synod, contained in a printed letter, because of some ambiguous words or expressions contained therein, being willing to remove, as far as in us lies, all causes and occasions of jealousies and offences in relation to that affair, and openly before God and the world to testify that we all with one accord firmly adhere to the same sound doctrine, which we and our fathers were trained up in; we, the ministers of the Presbytery of New Castle, whose names are underwritten, do, by this our act of subscribing our names to these presents, solemnly declare and testify, that we own and acknowledge the Westminster Confession and Catechisms to be the confession of our faith, being in all things agreeable to the word of God, so far as we are able to judge and discern, taking them in the true, genuine, and obvious sense of the words. Signed, Adam Boyd, Joseph Houston, H. Hook, Hugh Stevenson, James Anderson, William Steward, Thomas Creaghead, George Gillespie, John Thompson, Samuel Gelston, Thomas Evans, Alexander Hucheson." *

* Dr. Hill, after giving the above document with the names, says: "These were all foreigners from Scotland or Ireland, who, with their forefathers, had been trained up in swallowing the whole Confession, without change or diminution, in all its extent, embracing what is said respecting the power of the civil magistrate, contained in the twentieth and twenty-third chapters, &c., as agreeable in all things to the word of God. Although the Synod has made exception here, yet they would go the whole." Great Schism, No. 4. This is one of the many cases in which the venerable Dr.'s zeal has proved too strong for his discretion. These gentlemen were not "all foreigners from Scotland or Ireland." A good many of them were foreigners from New England and Wales. Of Mr. Boyd, for example, it is said on the minutes, p. 84: "The testimonials of Mr. Adam Boyd, lately come from New England, were read and approved." And of Mr. Houston, on the same page it is said, "Mr. Joseph Houston, who lately came from New England, his license, together with his other testimonials, were read and approved." Of Mr. Thomas Evans, it is said, "having showed to this Presbytery satisfying credentials from the Presbytery of Carmarthenshire in South Wales," &c. p. 24. Mr. Samuel Gel-

It is objected to these gentlemen, that they here adopt the whole Confession in the obvious sense of the words, without any reference to the clauses about the power of the civil magistrate. This is regarded as conclusive evidence that they were in favour of subjecting the Church to the power of the State. They must have been strange men if this were the case. Most of them as members of the Synod, in 1729, solemnly declared that they rejected and denied any controlling power in the civil magistrate over the Church, and all authority to persecute any one on account of his religion. In 1730, they declare that no new member should be obliged to profess any such doctrine. And in 1736, they repeat their own denial of it. Do they then here, in opposition to all their other professions, assert it? It is hardly to be believed. It is to be remembered that the Synod did not reject the clauses specified in chapters twentieth and twenty-third, absolutely, but "in any such sense" as taught the subjection of the Church to the power of the State; "a sense which, for my part," says the Rev. Samuel Blair, "I believe the reverend composers never intended in them." If then the signers of the above declaration were of the same opinion as Mr. Blair on this point, there is no inconsistency between this document and those to which they assented as members of Synod.

ston was received by the Presbytery of Philadelphia, as early as 1715 or 1716, from Long Island, where he first settled as pastor of the church at South Hampton. Of Mr. Thomas Creaghead it is said, in the minutes of the Presbytery of New Castle, p. 77: "This day several papers were produced by the Rev. Thomas Creaghead, who lately came from New England," &c. This form of expression is commonly used to indicate the origin of the members, as on p. 162, it is said of Mr. Wilson that he was late from Ireland. Still it is probable from his name, that Mr. Creaghead was of Irish origin. With regard to Mr. Boyd, there is another record, showing what kind of Puritans, at times, entered our Church in its early days. On p. 128, it is stated that "Mr. Boyd proposed an overture to the Presbytery that one of their members should be appointed to compose a short treatise on the divine right of Presbyterian church government." This overture was, at the next meeting, referred to the Synod, where the Scotch and Irish members let it sleep. Mr. Boyd's name also appears along with those of Robert Cross and John Thompson, attached to the protest against the New Brunswick Presbytery in 1741.

The second record in the minutes of the Presbytery of New Castle relating to this subject, occurs under the date of December 30, 1730, and is to the following effect: "A representation of some scrupling our way of adopting the Confession of Faith; upon which the Presbytery produced both the minutes of the Synod and Presbytery relating thereto, which seemed to give full satisfaction to the representers." There is no record on the minutes of the Synod relating to this subject except the adopting act itself, the account of the manner in which the members then present received the Confession, and the explanatory declaration of September 1730, interpreting the clauses relating to new members. If, therefore, "the representers" were fully satisfied with the Synod, they must have been satisfied with the above declarations, which leave the exceptions taken to the twentieth and twenty-third chapters in full force. This proves two things, first, that those exceptions were not the ground of dissatisfaction; and secondly, that these persons must have understood the Synod's declarations in the manner in which they are represented above.

The minutes of the Presbytery of Philadelphia, from 1717 to 1733 are lost. No information, therefore, relating to this subject can be gathered from the records still extant, except what may be inferred from the manner in which that Presbytery admitted new members. For example, it is said, Mr. Samuel Blair, "having given his assent to the Westminster Confession of Faith and Catechisms as the confession of his faith, was licensed to preach the gospel." p. 2. Charles Tennent "adopted the Westminster Confession of Faith and Catechisms, according to order of Synod." p. 19. David Cowell was ordained, "after he had adopted the Westminster Confession of Faith and Catechisms as the confession of his faith."* p. 28. Mr. McHenry was ordained, "adopting

* The ordination of Mr. Cowell, was by a committee consisting of Messrs. Andrews, D. Evans, Wales, and Treat, with Messrs. Dickinson, Pierson, and Morgan, correspondents. It is believed that not one of these gentlemen was either Scotch or Irish, unless it was Mr. Treat, and yet we find them employing the strict and comprehensive mode of adopting the Confession stated in the text.

the Confession of Faith, &c., according to the order of Synod." p. 35. Samuel Evans "adopted the Westminster Confession of Faith, Catechisms and Directory, according to the adopting act of Synod." p. 97. All these different forms are used as equivalent; the candidate adopted the Confession as the confession of his faith, according to the order of Synod, and according to the adopting act of Synod. The first is the most common, and the others merely state that the thing was done in obedience to the order, or the act of the superior judicatory.

The Presbytery of Donegal was formed in 1732. Their method of subscribing the Confession of Faith was as follows: "I, having seriously read and perused the Westminster Confession and Catechisms, do declare in the sight of God and all here present, that I do believe, and am fully persuaded, that so far as I can discern and understand said Confession and Catechisms, they are, in all things, agreeable to the word of God, taking them in the plain and obvious meaning of the words; and accordingly I do acknowledge them as the confession of my faith, and do promise, through divine assistance, for ever to adhere thereto. I also believe the Directory for the exercise of worship, discipline, and government, commonly annexed to said Confession, to be agreeable to the word of God, and I do promise to conform myself thereto in my practice, as far as in emergent circumstances I can attain unto." This is certainly strict enough.*

* Dr. Hill, after quoting the above formula, adds, "these are bold strides for new comers and a new Presbytery, and not very courteous and respectful to the Synod, the supreme judicatory of that day." The members of this Presbytery were Mr. Anderson, received as a member of Synod in 1710; Mr. John Thompson received in 1717; Mr. Robert Orr received in 1716; Mr Adam Boyd received in 1724; and Mr. William Bertram received in 1732. So that the last named was the only "new comer" in the Presbytery; the first three were among the oldest members of the Synod; and Mr. Boyd had been a member eight years. The Doctor proceeds: "the Synod had, in their qualified manner, adopted the Confession of Faith and Catechisms of the Westminster Assembly, but had said nothing about the Directory, and Form of Government, and Discipline." This is a mistake, as the Synod in 1729 said very nearly the same of the Directory that this Presbytery says of it. "But now these new comers, as Andrews calls them, (Mr. Andrews does not

The Presbytery of New Brunswick was formed in 1738. In 1741 they were excluded from the Synod. They immediately convened as a Presbytery, and were joined by several members of the Synod as correspondents, and determined to divide themselves into two Presbyteries. Before separating they adopted the following minute: "Forasmuch as the ministers who have protested against our being of their communion, do at least insinuate false reflections against us, endeavouring to make people suspect that we are receding from Presbyterian principles, for the satisfaction of such Christian people as may be stumbled by such false aspersions, we think it fit unanimously to declare, that we adhere as closely and fully to the Westminster Confession of Faith, and Catechisms, and Directory, as the Synod of Philadelphia in any of their public acts." The ministers present were Gilbert Tennent, William Tennent, Jun., Eleazar Wales, and John Rowland, members of the New Brunswick Presbytery, and William Tennent, Sen., Charles Tennent, Richard Treat, Samuel Blair, David Alexander, and Alexander Creaghead, correspondents. This declaration of an adherence to the Confession and Directory, as close as had ever been professed by the Synod of Philadelphia, it must be remembered, was made in 1741, after the adopting act of 1729; after the act of 1730 declaring, that new members must receive the whole Confession except the clauses specified in chapters twentieth and twenty-third; and after the thorough-going declaration of 1736, in which the Synod say they adhere "to the Westminster Confession of Faith, Catechisms, and Directory, without the least variation or

say a word about this Presbytery,) and this newly-formed Presbytery, go the whole length of adopting the form of government and discipline of the kirk of Scotland, in which they had been trained up in toto. They even surpass what the New Castle Presbytery had done. We see from this that bigoted reformers are bold fellows, they do not stick at trifles, &c." If the reader agrees with Dr. Hill, and we see not how he can help it, that the above declaration about the Directory is equivalent to adopting "the form of government and discipline of the kirk of Scotland in toto," he must admit that the Synod adopted that form in 1729 if never before; and that it was adopted by the new-side Synod as completely as by the old-side one. The proof of this will follow within a few pages.

alteration, and without any regard to the distinctions," in the adopting act, between essential and unessential articles. Such was the foundation-stone of the new Synod.

The records of the original Presbytery of Long Island have, it is understood, perished. Those now in existence commence with the reorganization of that Presbytery in 1747. It is believed also, that the early minutes of the Presbytery of East Jersey are lost; at least the writer has not been able to hear of them or to gain access to them. All, therefore, that can be known of the views and practice of those bodies in reference to this subject, must be gathered from the records of the Synod. It has already been stated, that Messrs. Dickinson, Pierson, and Bradner, adopted the whole of the Confession, except the often-specified clauses in 1729, and that Messrs. Pierson and Pemberton were present in 1730, when the Synod enacted that all new members should be required to adopt the Confession as strictly as they themselves had done. These Presbyteries, as well as the others, were in the habit of reporting their new members to the Synod and stating that they had adopted the Confession. Thus, in 1735, it is reported that Isaac Chalker, Simon Horton, and Samuel Blair, ordained by the Presbytery of East Jersey, had adopted the Westminster Confession of Faith, Catechisms, &c., according to the adopting act of Synod. And in 1738, the Presbytery of New York, as the united Presbyteries of Long Island and East Jersey were then called, reported that Aaron Burr and Walter Wilmot were ordained, and adopted the Westminster Confession, &c., according to the order of this Synod. The form in which these reports are made is the same in all the Presbyteries; the new members of Donegal and New Castle and East Jersey, are often included in the same minute, and the statement of their assent to the Confession is made in the same terms. Thus it appears that as the Synod was unanimous in their declarations in relation to this subject, so the Presbyteries were in the practical interpretation which they gave to those declarations. As far as the writer is aware, there is not the slightest evidence that any of the Presbyteries ever admitted, during the period under review, any minister who dissented from any of the doctrinal articles of the Confession of Faith.

Besides this documentary evidence of an official character, as to the original design and import of the adopting act, there is the testimony of cotemporary writers which remains to be considered. This, though of far inferior authority, is still not without interest and importance. A passage has already been quoted from Mr. Thompson's Reflections, in which he expresses his gratitude to God for the passage of that act in such a manner as shows his entire satisfaction with it. Yet such were the known opinions of the man, in relation to the subject, and such his avowed design in proposing the measure, that it is perfectly incredible that he should have been satisfied with the act in question, unless it was intended in the way in which the Synod subsequently explained it. The testimony of the Rev. Samuel Blair, however, is much more full and explicit. Soon after the schism in 1741, the Rev. Alexander Creaghead, one of the ejected members, renounced the Presbyterian Church, and published his reasons for so doing. These reasons were reviewed and answered by Mr. Blair. Mr. Creaghead's first reason for his secession was, that the Westminster Confession of Faith had never been adopted "in this province, either presbyterially or synodically as the confession of our faith in every article thereof, even to speak of no more at present but of the thirty-three articles therein contained." "By every article of the Confession of Faith," says Mr. Blair, "he means every chapter of it, and therefore calls the thirty-three chapters the thirty-three articles; whereas every chapter almost, contains several articles, all relating to some one general head. Now, whether Mr. Creaghead could suppose so or not, that neither Synod or Presbytery in this province did ever receive the Westminster Confession of Faith in every chapter of it, the thing itself is manifestly false in fact both ways. There never was any scruple, that ever I heard of, made by any member of the Synod about any part of the Confession of Faith, but only about some particular clauses in the twentieth and twenty-third chapters, and those clauses were excepted against in the Synod's act receiving the Confession of Faith, only in such a sense, which, for my part, I believe the reverend composers never intended in them, but which might notwithstanding be readily put upon them. Mr. Creaghead, to prove what he supposes, dwells much on what is called the Synod's preliminary act about the Confession of Faith made in 1729. But let that act be thought as insufficient as it can possibly admit, and granting that it was not sufficient for the securing of a sound orthodox ministry; yet that is no argument but the Confession of Faith has been sufficiently received by other acts. And so in fact it has been, by the Synod's act for the purpose, I think in the year 1730, [1729,] wherein the Synod declares, "all the ministers of the Synod now present, &c. &c."* "Here you see," continues Mr. Blair, "the Synod have received the whole of the Westminster Confession of Faith and Catechisms as the confession of their faith, save only some clauses in the twentieth and twenty-third chapters, which clauses it seems the Synod supposed might be understood as maintaining that magistrates have a controlling power over Synods in the exercise of their ministerial authority; a power to persecute persons for their religion; and that the popish Pretender had a right to the throne of Great Britain. And, now, if the declaration against receiving those clauses in such senses as these, be a good objection against the Synod, let any sober Protestant, especially Presbyterian, judge." This power of the civil magistrate, he adds, "is a great part of that unlawful supremacy and headship over the Church, which the Presbyterian Church has always protested against, and yet Mr. Creaghead finds fault with the Synod for this."† Nothing can be more explicit than this testimony, and nothing can be more unexceptionable. Mr. Blair is not a witness whose mouth can be stopped with the charge of heartless orthodoxy. He was one of the most zealous promoters of the great revival, and one of Mr. Tennent's most prominent supporters. In further refutation of Mr. Creaghead's

* Mr. Blair quotes at length the minute adopted on the afternoon of September 19, 1729, which has been already twice given above.

† Animadversions on the Reasons of Mr. Alexander Creaghead's receding from the judicatures of this church, together with its constitution. By Samuel Blair, Philadelphia, p. 8–11. This pamphlet is contained in No. 788 of the bound pamphlets of the Philadelphia Library. The copy is unfortunately defective, ending abruptly at the forty-eighth page. It is without date.

unreasonable charge, Mr. Blair says: "Moreover, in the year 1736, the Synod declare that they adopted and do still adhere to the Westminster Confession, Catechisms and Directory, without the least variation or alteration, and without any regard to the distinctions in the aforementioned preliminary act. It seems some people were jealous from the first preliminary act (without knowing or considering that the Synod had afterwards agreed in the solutions of all scruples which any of them had concerning any articles or expressions in the Confession of Faith, and so unanimously adopted and received it, in a fixed determinate manner as before related) that the Synod were about to vary and alter the Confession and Directory, and to set up new principles of religion and government contrary thereto. In answer to which jealousies, the Synod declares that they adhere to the Westminster Confession, Catechisms and Directory, without the least variation or alteration, which view of the case takes away all Mr. Creaghead's pretence for calling this declaration notoriously false. Mr. Creaghead may readily remember, that when our two Presbyteries were met together, June 3, 1741, after the separation of the Synod, we declared and recorded that we adhered to the Westminster Confession of Faith, Catechisms, and Directory, as closely and as fully as ever the Synod of Philadelphia in any of their public acts or agreements about them.* He may likewise remember, that the first time our Presbytery met by itself, after the separation, at White Clay Creek, we did unanimously agree and declare the Westminster Confession of Faith and Catechisms to be the confession of our faith, without any consideration of, or relation to any former act of the Synod whatever."†

Another of Mr. Creaghead's reasons, says Mr. Blair, is, "'That neither the government nor discipline of the Church is rightly

* For language far less strong respecting the Directory, the Presbytery of Donegal were charged with adopting the form of government and discipline of the kirk of Scotland in toto. Does language lose its meaning when uttered by a member of the "new-side" Synod? Or did they too adopt the Scottish system in toto?

† Animadversions, &c., p. 13.

administered by us.' And he proceeds to give his instances of such mismanagement; and the first is, 'that when we were first thrust out by a part of the Synod we did not begin to consider something of our principles and of some plan that we would adhere to in the government of the church.' This is really an odd story too! As if we had our principles to seek at that time of day; as if we had to begin to consider of them what they should be. When we were unjustly and arbitrarily thrust out by a part of the Synod, we had no new set of principles, nor any new plan of government then to devise. We were settled in these things long before that; we then declared adherence still to the Westminster Confession of Faith, Catechisms and Directory, as before related; we declared it to be our duty in those circumstances, as ministers and rulers in God's house, to carry on the government of the church, according to the rules of Presbyterian government."* "As to the scheme and pattern laid down in the Westminster Directory for the worship of God and the government and discipline of the church, we deny no part of it, as may be seen at large in our late declaration."†

Another cotemporary expounder of the adopting act is, as is supposed, the Rev. John Blair. The Rev. Samuel Harker, having been for several years under process by the New Brunswick Presbytery for certain Arminian opinions, was finally suspended by the Synod of New York and Philadelphia; whereupon he published an appeal to the Christian world. One of his grounds of complaint as to the sentence against him, was that it was "in violation of an act of Synod, A. D. 1729," which he calls, says the writer, "one of the great articles of their union, and which he thought sufficiently secured the rights of private judgment, wherein it is provided that a minister or candidate shall be admitted, notwithstanding his scruples respecting any article or articles the Synod shall judge not essential in doctrine, worship and government. But in order to improve this to his purpose, he takes the words 'essential' and 'necessary' in a sense in which it is plain the Synod never intended they should be taken. He would have them signify what is essential to communion

* Animadversions, &c., p. 29. † Ibid. p. 30.

with Jesus Christ, or to the being of grace in the heart; and accordingly supposes that no error can be essential which is not of such malignity as to exclude the advocate or maintainer of it from communion with Jesus Christ. But the Synod say essential in doctrine, worship, or government, *i. e.* essential to the system of doctrine contained in the Westminster Confession of Faith, considered as a system, and to the mode of worship and plan of government contained in our Directory. Now what unprejudiced man of sense is there who will not readily acknowledge that a point may be essential to a system of doctrine as such, to our mode of worship, and to Presbyterian government, which is not essential to a state of grace?"* "That, therefore, is an essential error in the Synod's sense, which is of such malignity as to subvert or greatly injure the system of doctrine and mode of worship and government, contained in the Westminster Confession of Faith and Directory."†

All that has hitherto been said refers to the former of the two questions proposed for consideration:—What was the meaning of the adopting act, as originally intended? It has been shown that it never was designed to fix the necessary doctrines of the gospel as the term of ministerial communion. It has been shown that this is not necessarily, nor even, when the whole document is taken together, naturally the meaning of the words; that this interpretation is contradicted by the mode in which the Synod themselves, in obedience to their own resolution, adopted the Westminster Confession and Catechisms; by the official and authoritative declaration of 1730, in which the Synod state that it was their intention, in the aforesaid act, to require every new member to receive the

* The Synod of New York and Philadelphia vindicated. In reply to Mr. Samuel Harker's appeal to the Christian world. By a member of the Synod, Philadelphia, 1764. See p. 10. In a copy of this pamphlet, which belonged to the father of the late Dr. Wilson of Philadelphia, the writer is said to have been the Rev. John Blair.

† Ibid. p. 11. This interpretation of the act is of course not official, and is below that given by the Synod itself in 1730, which allowed of no dissent except from the clauses so often referred to. Mr. Blair's interpretation is the most liberal for which there is any sanction in the declarations or practice of the church.

whole of the Confession, except the clauses relating to the power of the civil magistrates in matters of religion. This interpretation is still more explicitly contradicted by the official declaration of 1736, in which the Synod affirm that they received the Confession, &c. without the least regard to the distinction between essential and unessential articles, and that this was their meaning in their own adopting act of 1729. It is contradicted also by the action of the Presbyteries, who, in obedience to the order of the Synod, adopted the Confession of Faith. This, in no instance upon record was done by any Presbytery, or by any new member, in a way to limit the assent to the necessary doctrines of the gospel. And finally, the interpretation in question is contradicted by the explicit testimony of cotemporary writers.

The second question proposed was, What is, and ever has been, the condition of ministerial communion in our Church, as it relates to points of doctrine? This, as before remarked, is a very distinct question from the one already considered. It may be admitted, though it is distinctly denied, that the act of 1729 was intended to require of new members nothing more than assent to the essential doctrines of the gospel, and yet the doctrinal standard of the Church might be something very different and far higher. Those who are enamoured with what they take to be the meaning of that act, forgetful of their low opinion of the power of Synods, seem to regard it as unalterable. They speak as though the Synod of 1729 had authority not only over inferior judicatories, but over all succeeding Synods. This is certainly a strange assumption. Had the Synod of 1729 made the reception of the apostles' creed the condition of ministerial communion, that of 1730 had as good a right to require assent to every proposition in Calvin's Institutes and Commentaries. Let the act of 1729 mean what it may, what does it prove as to the doctrinal standard of our Church, unless it can be shown that the said act has never been modified or repealed? What prerogative had the Synod of 1729, which was not possessed by those of 1730 and 1736? If, therefore, the original act was ever so latitudinarian, it was repealed by the act of 1730, which required all new members to receive, as the Synod itself had done, the whole Confession of

Faith and Catechisms, a few specified clauses excepted. Where is there any repeal of this latter act? Where is there any official explanation lowering its demands? None such is to be found on the records of the Church, at least until the formation of the General Assembly. The act of 1736 re-affirmed the same standard with even still greater emphasis; greater plainness was unattainable. It remains now to be shown from subsequent official declarations, and from the administration of the discipline of the Church, that the standard thus fixed was unaltered, from 1730 to 1788, and that at no period of our history and in no section of the Church has assent to the essential doctrines of the gospel been made the condition of ministerial communion.

The period from 1741 to 1758, during which the Church was divided, might perhaps be omitted in a review, the design of which is to ascertain the doctrinal standard adopted by the whole Church. The opinions, however, of the separate portions of the Church, during this period, in relation to this subject, are a matter of too much interest to be passed over in silence. It is not necessary to raise the question, which of the two Synods was the proper representative of the Presbyterian Church; though there can be no doubt how it should be answered. However irregular or unjust the exclusion of the New Brunswick Presbytery in 1741 may have been, their rejection did not destroy the character of the Synod. That Presbytery and their early associates were a small portion of the whole body. Those who subsequently joined them, as for example the large Presbytery of New York, continued for several years after the separation, to meet with the old Synod, and to recognize its character. They finally peaceably withdrew, and with the excluded members formed a new Synod.

It will hardly be doubted that the old Synod, after the schism, continued to adhere to the Westminster Confession, or that they regarded the adopting act in the light in which it had previously been viewed. The separation took place at the meeting of Synod in 1741. After the New Brunswick brethren had withdrawn, an overture was introduced to the following effect: "That every member of this Synod, whether minister or elder, do, sincerely and heartily receive, acknowledge, or subscribe the Westminster Confession of Faith, and the Larger and Shorter Catechisms as the confession of his faith; and the Directory, as far as circumstances will allow in this infant church, for the rule of church order. Ordered, that every session do oblige their elders at their admission to do the same. This was readily approved *nem. con.*"* It is a little remarkable that this Synod, when all the members of the Presbytery of New York were absent, (none of whom attended this year,) and when the New Brunswick Presbytery and their associates were out of the house, avowed their adherence to the Confession and Directory in terms much less explicit and binding than those which had previously been unanimously adopted, when the members of both those bodies were present.

That the old Synod should adhere strictly to the Confession, is what might be expected. But how was it with the new Synod? It has already been shown, not only from the testimony of the Rev. Samuel Blair, who was one of their number, but from their own official statement, that all the excluded members and their associates adhered "as closely and fully to the Westminster Confession, Catechisms, and Directory, as the Synod of Philadelphia, in any of their public acts."† The Synod of New York was formed in 1745, and consisted of the Presbyteries of New York, New Brunswick, and New Castle. At their first meeting they adopted certain articles "as the plan and foundation of their Synodical union." The first of these articles is as follows: "They agree that the Westminster Confession of Faith, with the Larger and Shorter Catechisms, be the public confession of their faith, in such manner as was agreed upon by the Synod of Philadelphia in the year 1729, (and to be inserted in the latter end of this book,) and they declare their approbation of the Directory of the Assembly of Divines at Westminster, as the general plan of worship and discipline."‡ This of course, by itself, proves nothing as to the

* Minutes, vol. ii.

† Minutes of New Brunswick Presbytery, vol. i. p. 24.

‡ Minutes of the Synod of New York, p. 2.

manner in which the Synod adopted the Confession, unless it can be known how they understood the act of 1729. The opinions of Messrs. G. Tennent, William Tennent, Pierson, Pemberton, Samuel Blair, and John Blair, who were all present when these articles were formed, on this subject, have already been given, either in those explanatory acts of the Synod to which they assented, or in the citation of their own words on this point. Still, were this all we knew of the ground taken by this Synod in relation to this subject, it would at least remain doubtful how far they, as a body, required adherence to the Westminster Confession. It happened to them, however, as it did to the Synod of Philadelphia. The public were not satisfied with this ambiguous statement, and they were called upon to explain themselves. Within a few years, the Synod, in order to allay the jealousies of their neighbours, among the Dutch, say, "We do hereby declare and testify our constitution, order, and discipline, to be in harmony with the established Church of Scotland. The Westminster Confession, Catechisms, and Directory adopted by them, are in like manner adopted by us."* Again, in 1754, when writing to the Scottish General Assembly, they say, "That they conform to the constitution of the Church of Scotland, and have adopted her standards of doctrine, worship, and discipline."† What can be more explicit than this? It would be a poor service to the authors of these declarations to prove their liberality or latitudinarianism, as the reader may consider it, at the expense of their moral character. No honest man could adopt the language just quoted, unless he used it in the sense in which we know that those to whom it was addressed would understand it. For the Synod of New York to tell the Church of Scotland, that they had adopted her standards of doctrine, if they required nothing more than assent to the essential doctrines of the gospel, would have been a palpable untruth. Could any man, to repeat an illustration already employed, say that he adopted the standards of the Church of Rome, who assented to nothing but the

* Minutes of the Synod of New York, Appendix, p. 11.

† Ibid. Appendix, p. 13.

doctrines of the trinity, incarnation, and atonement? It is not possible to reconcile the above cited declarations of this Synod with candour and fair dealing, on any other assumption than that they required a strict adherence to the system of doctrines which they professed to adopt.

Another proof that the Synod of New York did not sanction the loose interpretation which has been put upon the adopting act is, that in the long negotiations between them and the Synod of Philadelphia, in reference to a union, there is no evidence of any difference of opinion as to the manner in which the Confession of Faith was to be received. These negotiations were continued through many years, and the papers which passed between the two bodies are very voluminous. The great difficulty in the way of a reconciliation, was the protestation which led to the exclusion of the New Brunswick Presbytery, and the testimony which the New York Synod wished should be rendered to the genuineness of the revival. The former was the main obstacle.* The Confession of Faith, or the mode of its adoption, was not a matter of dispute. In the communication made by the Synod of New York in 1749 to that of Philadelphia, they say, "We esteem mutual forbearance a duty, since we all profess the same Confession of Faith and Directory."† The Synod of Philadelphia in their communication of 1751, use precisely the same language. "Upon these terms (viz. the terms specified in their letter) we heartily agree with the Synod of New York, that since we profess the same Confession of Faith and Directory for worship, all our former differences be buried in perpetual oblivion."‡ One of the articles proposed in 1749, by the Synod of New York, was, "That every member assent unto and adopt the Confession of Faith and Directory according to the plan formerly agreed to by the Synod of Philadelphia in the years

* "The protestation made in 1741," says the Synod of New York, "appears to be a principal obstruction to the union of both Synods." — Minutes, p. 94. And in fact, as soon as they agreed about that point, the union took place.

† Minutes, p. 15. ‡ Minutes, Appendix, p. 6.

———." * This article is repeated in nearly the same form in all the subsequent proposals. Thus in 1751 the Philadelphia Synod proposed, as their second article, "That every member give his consent to the Westminster Confession of Faith and Directory, according to the plan agreed on in our Synod, and that no acts be made but concerning matters that appear to be plain duty, or concerning opinions that we believe relate to the great truths of religion, and that all public and fundamental agreements of this Synod stand safe." † In their reply, the Synod of New York do not make the slightest objection to the mode proposed of assenting to the Confession and Directory. But as the schism had arisen from the refusal of the New Brunswick Presbytery to submit to an act of Synod, which they said they could not in conscience obey, it was proposed that "no member or members should be obliged to withdraw from our communion upon his or their not being able actively to concur or passively submit, unless the matter be judged essential in doctrine or discipline." ‡ To this the other party assented; a similar provision being incorporated in the terms of union finally adopted.§ With regard to the proposal by the Synod of

* Minutes, p. 16. The years are not mentioned, but the only years in which the Synod of Philadelphia acted on the subject, were 1729, 1730, and 1736.

† Appendix, p. 3.

‡ Minutes, p. 36.

§ This article does not relate to the adoption of the Confession, or to the admission of new members, but to submission to the decisions of ecclesiastical judicatories. All their acts and determinations were to be concurred in or submitted to, unless conscience forbad it. In that case the dissentients should not be disowned, unless the Synod should think the matter essential to their doctrines or discipline.

It is in strict accordance with the spirit of the above article, that our present book of discipline, chapter v., section 13, &c., says, "Heresy and schism may be of such a nature as to infer deposition; but errors ought to be carefully considered; whether they strike at the vitals of religion, and are industriously spread, or whether they arise from the weakness of the human understanding, and are not likely to do much injury." This direction as to the administration of discipline, has been strangely appealed to in proof that a church which requires every candidate for the ministry to declare that he receives the "system of doctrine" taught in the Confession of Faith, does notwithstanding require nothing more than assent to the essential doctrines

Philadelphia, that "all fundamental agreements by this Synod stand safe;" the Synod of New York very properly said they could not agree to it, if it was "understood to refer to agreements made by said Synod [of Philadelphia] since the rupture happened." In making such agreements they had not concurred; it was therefore unfair that they should be bound by them. This very limitation, however, shows that they were willing that such as had been made before the schism, should remain. This would leave the important acts of 1730 and 1736, relating to the mode of adopting the Confession of Faith, in full force.

The decisive evidence that there was no material diversity of opinion between the two Synods in reference to the point under consideration, is the fact that both bodies unanimously adopted and ratified the following article as one of the terms of their union: "Both Synods having always approved and received the Westminster Confession of Faith, Larger and Shorter Catechisms, as an orthodox and excellent system of Christian doctrine, founded upon the word of God; we do still receive the same as the confession of our faith, and also adhere to the plan of worship, government, and discipline, contained in the Westminster Directory: strictly enjoining it on all our ministers and probationers for the ministry, that they preach and teach according to the form of sound words in the said Confession and Catechisms, and avoid and oppose all errors contrary thereto."* How decisive would this be considered if an enemy

of the gospel. This passage, however, has no relation to the admission of new members. It simply says, what it is presumed no one ever has denied, that deposition, the highest ecclesiastical censure, ought not to be inflicted for slight aberrations from our standards. All offences against the truth, morals, or order, should be punished according to their nature. It would be hard to visit a man with the same penalty for a hasty word, as for habitual drunkenness; and it would be equally preposterous to depose a minister who should deny that the Pope was antichrist, when you could inflict no higher penalty upon him for the avowal of complete infidelity. How a rule which inculcates this plain principle of justice can prove that every candidate should be admitted to the ministry who does not deny some essential doctrine of Christianity, it is difficult to perceive.

* Article I. of the plan of union agreed upon by the Synods of New York and Philadelphia, in 1758.

were endeavouring to fix on the two Synods the imputation of rigid Calvinism! Both bodies declare that they always have received, and do still receive the Westminster Confession as the confession of their faith; the very form of adoption in use in the strict Presbytery of New Castle, in the palmy days of Mr. Thompson and Mr. Gillespie. Every minister and probationer is strictly enjoined to avoid all errors contrary to the standards thus assumed. There must be an end of all confidence among men if such language can be used by those who make assent to the essential and necessary doctrines of the gospel, the term of ministerial communion; if an Arminian, Pelagian, Roman Catholic, or Quaker, can say that he receives a strictly Calvinistic creed as the confession of his faith!

That the doctrinal standard of our Church has not been changed since the time of the union of the Synods of New York and Philadelphia, appears from the following official acts and declarations. In 1763, application was made by a Presbytery in New York, to the east of the North river, to be incorporated with the Synod. "It was agreed to grant their request, provided that they agree to adopt our Westminster Confession of Faith, and engage to observe the Directory as a plan of worship, discipline, and government, according to the agreement of this Synod."* The last clause can refer to nothing but the first article of the plan of union just quoted, in which the united body adopt the Confession of Faith as the confession of their faith!

In 1770, a letter was written to the Presbytery of South Carolina, in answer to an application for an union between the two bodies, in which the Synod say: "The conditions which we require are only what we suppose you are already agreed on, viz.: That all your ministers acknowledge and adopt as the standard of doctrine, the Westminster Confession of Faith and Catechisms, and the Directory as the plan of your worship and discipline. The Church of Scotland is considered by this Synod as their pattern in general, but we have not as yet expressly adopted by resolution of Synod, or bound ourselves to any other of the standing laws or forms of

* Minutes of the Synod of New York and Philadelphia, p. 60.

the Church of Scotland, than those above mentioned, intending to lay down such rules for ourselves, upon Presbyterian principles in general, as circumstances shall, from time to time, show to be expedient." Such were the conditions which our Church used to insist upon in all cases of union with foreign bodies; adherence to her standards, both as to doctrine and order. In the above record, it is not only stated that the Westminster Confession and Catechisms were the standard of doctrine in our Church, and the Directory the plan of worship and discipline, but still farther, that as the General Assembly of the Church of Scotland had made many standing laws suited to the circumstances of the Church in that country, so the Synod proposed to lay down rules suited to our circumstances. The right to make such rules is assumed as perfectly familiar and undoubted.

In 1786, a committee was appointed to meet similar committees from the Synods of the Dutch, and Associate Reformed Churches, with the view of negotiating some plan of union between the several bodies. When this convention met, it directed the several committees of which it was composed, to state explicitly "what the formulas of doctrine and worship are, to which each of the Synods respectively adheres, and the mode in which they testify their adherence, and prevent and punish any departure from them." "On the part of the Synod of New York and Philadelphia, the reply is contained in the representation given in by their committee, articles first and fifth; viz.

"The Synod of New York and Philadelphia adopt, according to the known and established meaning of the terms, the Westminster Confession of Faith as the confession of their faith; save that every candidate for the gospel ministry is permitted to except against so much of the twenty-third chapter as gives authority to the civil magistrate in matters of religion. The Presbyterian Church in America considers the Church of Christ as a spiritual society entirely distinct from the civil government; and as having the right to regulate their own ecclesiastical polity independently of the interposition of the civil magistrate.

"The Synod also receives the Directory for public worship, and form of Church government recommended by the Westminster Assembly, as in substance agreeable to the institutions of the New Testament. This mode of adoption we use because we believe the general platform of our government to be agreeable to the sacred Scriptures; but we do not believe that God has been pleased so to reveal and enjoin every minute circumstance of ecclesiastical government and discipline as not to leave room for orthodox churches of Christ in these *minutiæ*, to differ with charity from each other.

"The rules of our discipline and the form of process in our church judicatures are contained in Pardevan's, alias Stewart's Collections, in conjunction with the acts of our own Synod; the power of which, in matters merely ecclesiastical, we consider as equal to the power of any Synod or General Assembly in the world. Our church judicatories, like those in the Church of Scotland, from which we derive our origin, are church sessions, Presbyteries, and Synods, to which it is now in contemplation to add a national or General Assembly."*

This document, considered merely as containing the testimony of competent witnesses as to the constitution of our Church, is of the highest authority. It was delivered under circumstances which rendered both accuracy and fidelity indispensable. Its authors were negotiating a treaty with other churches, who had a right to know the opinions and principles of those with whom they contemplated a union. Any ambiguity of statement or want of candour would, under such circumstances, be an unpardonable offence. The above document, however, is something more than the testimony of a committee. It is that testimony approved and sanctioned by the Synod. This report was presented and accepted, it was spread out upon the minutes, the conduct of the committee approved, no one of their acts or statements disallowed, and the efforts for a union still farther prosecuted.

As to the document itself, it is impossible for language to be more explicit as to all the points to which it relates. The Confession of Faith is said to be the confession of the faith of the Synod,

* Minutes of the Synod of New York and Philadelphia, for 1786.

save that new members were allowed to object to certain clauses in the twenty-third chapter. The very exception greatly strengthens the case. That the new members were required to adopt the Confession, except those clauses, shows that nothing else was allowed to be rejected. This is precisely what the old Synod twice, unanimously and authoritatively, in 1730 and in 1736, declared was the mode in which the Confession was to be adopted. This was the condition of ministerial communion then established, and which the Synod in 1786 declared they still adhered to. The evidence as to this point is the stronger from what is said of the manner in which the Directory was adopted. The Confession of Faith was received entirely, with the single exception specified, according to the known and established meaning of the words; but the Directory was received only for substance, and the reason is given for this mode of adoption. It has already been stated, that the Directory was of such a nature, abounding so much with prescriptions relating to local and temporary circumstances, that the strict Presbytery of Donegal could not adopt it more fully than the whole Synod did.

It is to be remarked farther on this document, that the "acts of Synod" are declared to be standing rules, regulating the administration of discipline, and the power of that body in matters merely ecclesiastical is declared to be equal to the power of any Synod or General Assembly in the world. If this is not full-grown Presbyterianism, it would be difficult to know where to find it. The committee which drew up these declarations, were Drs. Rodgers, Witherspoon, McWhorter, and Samuel Smith, and Messrs. Nathan Kerr, and John Woodhull. There is no obnoxious Mr. Thompson, Anderson, or Gillespie here, to be upbraided for "swallowing the Confession whole." Yet which of the last-named gentlemen ever uttered such sweeping declarations as are here made by Drs. Rodgers and McWhorter?

Again, in 1787, the committee previously appointed for the purpose, presented the draught of a Form of Government and Discipline for the Church. The same year the Synod made some slight alterations in the twentieth and twenty-third chapters of the Westminster Confession; and in the following year, "the Synod having fully considered the draught of the Form of Government and Discipline, did on the review of the whole, and hereby do ratify and adopt the same, as now altered and amended, as the Constitution of the Presbyterian Church in America, and order the same to be considered and strictly observed as a rule of their proceedings by all the inferior judicatories belonging to this body. And they order that a corrected copy be printed, and the Westminster Confession of Faith, as now altered, to be printed in full along with it, as making part of the Constitution. Resolved, That the true intent and meaning of the above ratification of Synod is, that the Form of Government and Discipline, and the Confession of Faith, as now ratified, is to continue to be our constitution, and the confession of our faith, unless two-thirds of the Presbyteries under the care of the General Assembly propose alterations or amendments, and such alterations and amendments shall be agreed to and enacted by the General Assembly."*

In this dying act of the Synod of New York and Philadelphia, that body put forth all its power. There is not on the records of the Church, unless in the analogous cases of the several adopting acts, such an illustration of the power assumed by the supreme judicatory of the Church. The constitution was the work of their own hands; it was revised, corrected, adopted and imposed by them, and made unalterable without the concurrence of two-thirds of the Presbyteries, and the sanction of the General Assembly. Though the draught had been circulated among the Presbyteries and churches for their suggestions and advice, it was of no force but as ratified by the Synod, who ordered all the inferior judicatories to make it the rule of their proceedings. It is not to be supposed that the General Assembly has fallen heir to all the power of the old Synod. Far from it. The acts of the latter body were part of the constitution of the Church. They adopted the Westminster Confession, and it was ever afterwards, unless the rule was repealed, to be adopted by all new members. When they saw fit they altered that Confession, and it became, as altered, part of the constitution of the Church. The Assembly has no such power. It

* Minutes of the Synod of New York and Philadelphia, pp. 450, 451.

acts under a constitution which greatly limits its authority. It cannot alter or add to that fundamental code. Its great office is to see that the constitution is faithfully adhered to, both as to doctrine and order, in all parts of the Church. Its acts and decisions, when they do not transcend the limits set to its authority, are of general obligation, until properly repealed or reversed. But it stands in a very different relation to the Church, from that sustained by the old Synod.

The present object of inquiry, however, is the doctrinal standard of our Church. What light is thrown upon this point by the document just quoted? What is meant by the Westminster Confession of Faith being a part of our constitution? Who ever heard of adopting a constitution for substance? Is the constitution of the United States thus adopted or thus interpreted? It is on the contrary the supreme law of the land; and all who take office under it are bound to observe it in all its parts. If then the Westminster Confession is a part of our constitution, we are bound to abide by it, or rightfully to get it altered. Ever since the solemn enactment under consideration, every new member or candidate for the ministry has been required to give his assent to this confession, as containing the system of doctrines taught in the word of God. He assents not merely to absolutely essential and necessary articles of the gospel, but to the whole concatenated statement of doctrines contained in the Confession. This, whether right or wrong, liberal or illiberal, is the constitutional and fundamental principle of our ecclesiastical compact.

Besides the above official and authoritative declarations, the actual administration of discipline in our Church proves what standard of doctrine has been assumed and enforced. Ministerial communion has been repeatedly refused to those who, though they denied no one of the essential and necessary doctrines of the gospel, yet rejected some of the doctrinal articles of the Confession of Faith. Thus, as already stated, the Rev. Mr. Harker was long under process and finally disowned for teaching "that, according to the tenor of the covenant of grace, God has bound himself by promise to bestow saving blessings upon the faith and endeavours of unregenerate men; and that God has predestinated persons to salvation on the foresight of faith and good works, or compliance with the terms of the covenant."* Mr. Blair, in his above-cited defence of the Synod against Mr. Harker's appeal to the public, says: "Mr. Harker makes no distinction between ministerial and Christian communion. 'To admit me,' says he, 'to stand well in the communion with the Christian church, and at the same time to expel, and exclude me communion with the Synod (as a minister, as I suppose he means), would in my opinion involve the consequence, that the Synod were no Christians.' That is, the Synod must admit every one (male and female I suppose), into the pulpit, whom they would admit to the Lord's table."†

In 1798, a reference was made to the General Assembly, by the Synod of the Carolinas, in relation to a creed published by the Rev. Hezekiah Balch. The most important errors contained in that creed, as specified by the committee to whom it was referred, were the following: First, his "making disinterested benevolence the only definition of holiness or true religion." Second, his "representing personal corruption as not derived from Adam; making Adam's sin to be imputed to his posterity in consequence of a corrupt nature already possessed; and derived," say the committee, "from we know not what; thus in effect setting aside the idea of Adam's being the federal head and representative of his descendants; and the whole doctrine of the covenant of works." Thirdly, "asserting that the formal cause of a believer's justification is the imputation of the fruits and effects of Christ's righteousness, and not the righteousness itself." The Assembly condemned these and other minor errors, and decided that Mr. Balch could retain his ministerial standing in the church, only on the condition that he publicly renounced them.‡

In 1810, another reference was made by the Synod of the Carolinas, to the General Assembly, requesting their attention to a late

* See Minutes of Synod for 1760, for the doctrine of Mr. Harker, and those of 1763, for the sentence passed upon him.

† Vindication of the Synod of New York, &c. p. 12.

‡ Minutes of the Assembly, vol. i. pp. 175, 176. Digest, 129–134.

publication, entitled 'The Gospel Plan,' by the Rev. William C. Davis. The book was referred to a committee, who reported the following, among other propositions, as contained in it. First, that the active obedience of Christ constitutes no part of the righteousness by which a sinner is justified. Second, that obedience to the moral law was not required as the condition of the covenant of works. Third, that God could not make Adam, or any other creature, either holy or unholy. Fourth, that regeneration must be a consequence of faith. Faith precedes regeneration. Fifth, that faith, in the first act of it, is not an holy act. Sixth, that if God has to plant all the principal parts of salvation in a sinner's heart, to enable him to believe, the gospel plan is quite out of his reach, and consequently does not suit his case; and it must be impossible for God to condemn a man for unbelief; for no just law condemns or criminates any person for not doing what he cannot do. The Assembly declared all these doctrines to be contrary to the Confession of Faith of our Church. Other parts of the work are censured as incautiously expressed and as of dangerous tendency. They further judged that the preaching or publishing the doctrines above stated "ought to subject the person or persons so doing to be dealt with by their respective Presbyteries, according to the discipline of the Church relative to the propagation of error." *

If then, explicit official declarations and the actual administration of discipline can decide the question, it is clear that our Church has always required adherence to the system of doctrine contained in the Westminster Confession of Faith as a condition of ministerial communion. From the adopting act of 1729 to the present hour, there is not a line upon our records which, either directly or indirectly, teaches that nothing beyond the essential and necessary doctrines of the gospel was to be required of its ministers.† On

* Minutes of the General Assembly, pp. 334, 335.

† It will be remembered that the Assembly of 1836 did not decide that the errors charged upon Mr. Barnes were undeserving of censure. On the contrary, they declared that they were not to be tolerated in the Presbyterian Church. That gentleman was acquitted on the ground that he did not hold the errors charged.

the contrary the very ambiguity of the adopting act was the occasion of that doctrine being repudiated, and a strict adherence to the Confession enjoined with a frequency and clearness which otherwise would not have been called for. Thus, in 1730 it was declared that every new member must adopt the whole of the Confession except certain clauses relating to the power of the civil magistrate. The same declaration was made with like unanimity and still greater emphasis in 1736. In 1741, the Synod repeated their unqualified adoption of the Confession, and the ejected members declared that they also adhered to it with equal strictness. The Synod of New York, during the schism, declared that they had the same standards of doctrine, worship, and discipline, as the Church of Scotland; and the two Synods, at the time of the union, unanimously declared, without limitation or qualification, the Westminster Confession to be the confession of their faith. In 1786, a committee of Synod, in negotiating with two other Christian bodies, inform them that the Synod of New York and Philadelphia receive the Westminster Confession, save that every candidate is allowed to object to certain parts of the twenty-third chapter. When the General Assembly was formed, the Confession as then altered, and as it now exists, was declared to be a part of the constitution of the Church. Had these facts and documents been known and regarded, the assertion that it is a constitutional principle of our Church to demand of its ministers nothing more than assent to the essential doctrines of the gospel, never could have been made. If they do not ascertain and prove the condition of ministerial communion in the Presbyterian Church in the United States, to be adherence to the system of doctrine contained in the Westminster Confession, no set of men can, in future, hope to make their intentions understood.

This question about the conditions of ministerial communion has been so much connected with the exposition of the adopting act of 1729, that it was deemed expedient to disregard, in this case, a mere chronological arrangement, and to bring together in one view, all the documents which serve either to fix the meaning of that act, or to decide what is the doctrinal standard of our Church. It is hoped that the importance of the subject will be considered a sufficient apology for the length of the discussion. It is now time, however, to return to the consideration of the period which is more particularly under review.

Agreeably to the settled principle and common understanding of Presbyterian government, such an act as that of 1729, when once passed, remains obligatory upon all the inferior judicatories until properly repealed. We accordingly find that, after 1729, the adoption of the Confession of Faith by all new members was regularly required by every Presbytery, and regularly reported to the Synod. Thus, in 1730, it is recorded that "Mr. Elmer desiring time last Synod to consider of the Synod's declaring to the Westminster Confession, Catechisms, &c.; and Mr. Morgan and Mr. Pemberton being absent, do all now report that they have declared before the Presbytery, and desire their names be inserted in our Synodical records."* In the following year, Mr. Cross, who had been absent from the two preceding meetings of Synod, was called upon to signify his opinion of the Synod's acts, &c.; "the said Mr. Cross did declare his hearty concurrence with all that the Synod had done in that affair, and that he did adopt the said Confession of Faith and Catechisms as the confession of his faith."† In 1732, it is said of Mr. Bertram, of the Presbytery of Bangor in Ireland, "after declaring his full and free assent unto the Westminster Confession of Faith and Catechisms, the Synod did unanimously and cheerfully comply with his desire of admission as a member of this Synod."‡ On the same page it is recorded, that "the Moderator (Mr. Steward) and Mr. Orme, not having opportunity before, either in Presbytery or Synod, did now declare their hearty assent unto the Confession of Faith and Catechisms, and adopted them as the confession of their faith." In 1734, it was ordered, that the Synod make a particular inquiry during the time of their meeting every year, whether such ministers as have been received as members since the foregoing meeting of the Synod have adopted, or been required by the Synod, or by their respective Presbyteries, to adopt the Westminster Confession of Faith and Catechisms, with the

* Minutes, vol. ii. p. 14. † Ibid. vol. ii. p. 19. ‡ Ibid. vol. ii. p. 21.

Directory, according to the acts of the Synod made some years since for that purpose; and also, that the report made to Synod in answer to said inquiry, be recorded on our minutes.

"Mr. Samuel Pumry, Mr. James Martin, Mr. Robert Jamison, and Mr. Samuel Hemphill, declared for and adopted the Westminster Confession of Faith, Catechisms, and Directory commonly annexed; the former as the confession of their faith, the latter as the guide of their practice in matters of discipline as far as may be agreeable to the rules of prudence, &c., as in the adopting acts of Synod is directed.

"Pursuant to the act of Synod found upon inquiry, Mr. William Tennent, Jun., Mr. Andrew Archbold, ordained, and Mr. Samuel Blair, licensed, did each and every of them declare their assent and consent to the Westminster Confession of Faith, Catechisms, and Directory annexed, according to the intent of the act of Synod, in that case made and provided."*

In the minutes for 1735, it is recorded that, "inquiry being made according to the order of last Synod, whether those admitted into any of our Presbyteries since last Synod, have adopted the Westminster Confession, Catechisms, &c., according to the adopting act of the Synod, it was found that Messrs. Isaac Chalker, Simon Horton, and Samuel Blair, ordained by the Presbytery of East Jersey, and Mr. Hugh Carlisle, admitted into the Presbytery of New Castle, have done it, according to the order aforesaid."† Similar entries appear after this almost every year.‡

* Minutes, vol. ii. p. 31.

† Minutes, vol. ii. p. 35.

‡ Annexed is a list of Ministers who entered the Presbyterian Church from 1729 to 1741. The writer has not the means of making this list complete or satisfactory. The records of the Synod rarely state, either the place of settlement or origin of the new members; and the minutes of the several Presbyteries from which this information might be obtained, are, for the most part, defective, lost, or inaccessible.

Rev. Daniel Elmer, Fairfield, New Jersey; first mentioned as a member of Synod 1729. He was from New England, as stated on a previous page.

Rev. John Wilson, —— 1729, from Ireland, as stated above.

Rev. John Tennent, licensed by the New Castle Presbytery, and was settled for a short time at Freehold, New Jersey, where he died early in life. He came from Ireland with his father, the Rev. William Tennent, Sen.

With regard to the administration of the discipline and government of the church, the same characteristics which marked the preceding period, are to be found also in that from 1729 to 1741. As might be expected, the Synod continued to exercise all the ordinary Synodical powers. The records of the several Presbyteries were regularly called for and revised, and approved or censured, as the occasion demanded. Appeals, references, and complaints were

Rev. Ebenezer Gould, Greenwich, New Jersey, 1730, probably from Long Island or New England.

Rev. Eleazar Wales, Allentown, Pennsylvania, afterwards at Kingston, New Jersey, 1731.

Rev. Richard Treat, Abington, Pennsylvania, 1732.

Rev. Robert Cathcart, —— 1732, a member of the Presbytery of New Castle, and probably from Ireland.

Rev. William Bertram, Derry and Paxton, 1732, received as a minister from the Presbytery of Bangor, Ireland. Minutes, vol. ii. p. 21.

Rev. John Cross, Baskingridge, 1733, became a member of the New Brunswick Presbytery. He was probably from Ireland.

Rev. Benjamin Campbell, —— 1730. In the minutes of the Presbytery of New Castle, p. 157, it is recorded, "Mr. Campbell and Mr. Legat, students in divinity from Ireland, presented to the Presbytery their respective testimonials."

Rev. John Nutman, East Hanover, New Jersey, 1733. Probably from Newark, New Jersey, as that was the residence of an extended family of that name.

Rev. Samuel Hemphill, —— 1734, received as a minister from the Presbytery of Straban, Ireland. He was disowned for heresy in 1735.

Rev. Andrew Archbold, —— 1734, reported to the Synod as ordained; probably by the Presbytery of New Castle. See minutes, p. 31.

Rev. James Martin, Lewes, Delaware, 1734, from Ireland.

Rev. Robert Jamison, —— 1734. He was a member of the Presbytery of Lewes, and was probably from Ireland.

Rev. Samuel Blair, Shrewsbury, New Jersey, Londonderry, Pennsylvania, and principal of the academy at Fagg's Manor, 1735. He was a native of Ireland. See Dr. Miller's Retrospect, vol. iii. p. 204.

Rev. Simon Horton, —— 1735. It is believed that he was settled in East Jersey, and that he was from New England.

Rev. Isaac Chalker, Wallkill, New York, 1735, from Long Island.

Rev. Hugh Carlisle, —— 1735, probably from Ireland.

Rev. William Tennent, Jun., Freehold, New Jersey, 1735. Born in Ireland.

Rev. Patrick Glasgow, Monokin, Maryland, 1736; ordained by the Presbytery of Lewes.

received and decided. For example, in 1736, "an appeal from a part of the Rev. William Tennent's people from the judgment of the Presbytery of Philadelphia was brought in and read, together with a supplication of said persons to the Presbytery of Philadelphia, and their judgment upon it. After that, Mr. Tennent, the appellants, and the members of the Presbytery were heard at length; at last all parties were ordered to remove, and the Synod entered upon a debate upon the affair, and at last agreed in the following unanimous judgment, viz.: 'That it appears evident to the Synod,

Rev. Alexander Creaghead, Pequa, 1736; ordained by the Presbytery of Donegal.

Rev. John Paul, Nottingham, 1736; from Ireland. Minutes, vol. ii. p. 43.

Rev. John McDowell was received as a probationer from the Presbytery of Temple Patrick, Ireland. Minutes, vol. ii. p. 43.

Rev. Francis Allison, Chester county, Pennsylvania, afterwards vice-provost of the University of Pennsylvania, 1737. He was born and educated in Ireland. Dr. Miller's Retrospect, vol. iii. pp. 201, 204.

Rev. Samuel Black, Forks of Brandywine, 1737; received as a probationer from Ireland. See minutes of Donegal Presbytery, p. 117.

Rev. Aaron Burr, Newark; president of the College of New Jersey, 1738. He was a native of Connecticut, and was ordained by the Presbytery of New York.

Rev. John Elder, Paxton, Pennsylvania, 1738, ordained by the Presbytery of Donegal.

Rev. Walter Wilmot, —— 1738, ordained by the Presbytery of New York.

Rev. Charles Tennent, —— 1738, ordained by the Presbytery of New Castle. Born in Ireland.

Rev. Richard Sanckey, —— 1739, ordained by the Presbytery of Donegal, removed with his congregation to Prince Edward, Virginia, where he died at a very advanced age.

Rev. David Alexander, Pequa, 1739, ordained by the Presbytery of Donegal.

Rev. John Thompson, Jun. —— 1739, ordained by the Presbytery of Donegal.

Rev. Joseph Leonard, Goshen, 1739, ordained by the Presbytery of New York. He was from New England. MS. history.

Rev. James McCrea, Lamberton, New Jersey, 1739. MS. history.

Rev. Samuel Thompson, Carlisle and Silver Spring, 1740. He was from Ireland. Minutes of Donegal Presbytery, p. 153.

Rev. Samuel Cavin, —— 1740, ordained by the Presbytery of Donegal. He was from Ireland. Minutes of Donegal Presbytery, p. 153.

that Mr. Tennent having in all respects acted and been esteemed and looked upon, not only by this Synod, but also by the congregation of Neshaminy, and particularly by the appellants themselves, as the minister and pastor of the people of Neshaminy, that he is still to be esteemed the pastor of that people, notwithstanding the want of a formal installation among them, (which omission, though the Synod doth not justify, yet it is far from nullifying the pastoral relation between Mr. Tennent and the said people,) and consequently that the Synod doth justify the judgment of the Presbytery of Philadelphia in reference to the matter; and that the appellants had no just cause of complaining against, or appealing from the said judgment of the Presbytery."*

It was also in the exercise of the usual powers of such bodies, that the Synod erected new Presbyteries or divided old ones, as occasion required. In 1732, "it being overtured by the committee of overtures, that an erection of a new Presbytery in Lancaster county should be appointed by the Synod, it was voted by a great majority that Masters Anderson, Thompson, Orr, Boyd, and Bertram, be members of a Presbytery by the name of Donegal Presbytery."† In 1733, an overture was presented by the committee for a division of the Presbytery of Philadelphia, which was approved, and it was "agreed that Messrs. Andrews, Morgan, Evans, Tennent, Treat, Elmer, Gould, and Wales, be the Presbytery of Philadelphia, and that the rest of the members now in said Presbytery be the Presbytery of East Jersey."‡ In 1735, a request was made by Messrs. Hook, Jamison, Stevenson, and Martin, that they might be set off from the Presbytery of New Castle, "and erected into a Presbytery by themselves; the Synod do agree that they become a Presbytery under the name of the Presbytery of Lewestown, and do order them to meet and constitute the 19th day of November next, at Lewestown."§ In 1738, it is recorded that "the Presbytery of Long Island being reduced so that a quorum cannot statedly meet about business, 'tis ordered that they be united with the Presbytery of East Jersey, and be henceforth known by the name of the

* Minutes, vol. ii. p. 46. † Ibid. vol. ii. p. 22.
‡ Ibid. vol. ii. p. 26. § Ibid. vol. ii. p. 38.

Presbytery of New York."* The same year, "upon a supplication of some members of the Presbytery of New York, to be erected into a new Presbytery, with some members of the Presbytery of Philadelphia, overtured that their petition be granted, and all to the northward of Maidenhead and Hopewell unto the Raritan river, including also Staten Island, Piscatawa, Amboy, Boundbrook, Baskingridge, Turkey, Rocksitius, Minisinks, Pequally, and Crosswicks, be the bounds of that Presbytery, and that the said Presbytery be known by the name of the Presbytery of New Brunswick, and that the time of their meeting be the second Tuesday of August next, at New Brunswick. This overture was approved."†

It was stated in the preceding chapter, as one of the peculiarities of our first Synod, that, in accordance with the Scottish system, it exercised all Presbyterial powers. The examples of the exercise of such powers, during the period under review, are very numerous. The Synod was in the habit, for example, of receiving and disposing of ministers and candidates who had not connected themselves with any of our Presbyteries. In 1730, Mr. John Peter Miller, a Dutch probationer, recently arrived in the country, was received, and left to the care of the Philadelphia Presbytery. In 1732, the Rev. Mr. Bertram was received from the Presbytery of Bangor in Ireland. In 1736, Mr. John McDowell presented his credentials from the Presbytery of Temple Patrick in Ireland, and "was received by the Synod as a probationer," and recommended to any Presbytery to which he might choose to apply. The Synod likewise ordained, censured, removed, and suspended ministers without the intervention of a Presbytery. Thus, in 1735, "a supplication being brought into Synod from the people of Goshen, and also a letter from Mr. Tudor, a candidate for the ministry there, both signifying that he is ready to adopt the Westminster Confession of Faith, &c. and to submit to Presbyterial rules; and also desiring Synod would, as soon as possibly may be, send a committee to the said place to attend the ordination of Mr. Tudor there, "the Synod" it is said "do accordingly appoint Mr. Robert Cross, Mr. Pumry, Mr. Webb, Mr. Nutman, Mr. John Cross, and Mr. Chalker, to meet at Goshen,

* Minutes, vol. ii. p. 56. † Ibid. vol. ii. p. 58.

the last Wednesday of the next month, October, to attend to the said ordination, and that Mr. Robert Cross preside in the said affair. And the Synod do further appoint for the trials of Mr. Tudor, that he make an exegesis in Latin upon that question, *An lex naturæ sit sufficiens ad salutem?* and that he preach a popular sermon upon Rom. ii. 6." The following year, the above committee reported that they did not ordain Mr. Tudor "because of his insufficiency."

In 1735, the Rev. Mr. Hemphill was tried by the commission of Synod for false doctrines, and the case upon their report came before the Synod, who passed the following sentence: "The Synod from the consideration of his contumacy in his errors; his disregard of the censures of the commission; and rejecting our communion; do declare him unqualified for any further exercise of his ministry within our bounds, and that this be intimated to all our congregations, by each respective minister. Approved *nem. con.*"*

The Synod also frequently acted in reference to the congregations in the capacity of a Presbytery. Thus, in 1733, "Mr. Andrews made a motion to the committee of overtures that an assistant be allowed unto him in the work of the ministry in this city, and the committee after discoursing upon it, having recommended the consideration thereof to the Synod, upon the proviso, that if the said motion be allowed or approved, there be first a sufficient provision made for an honourable maintenance of Mr. Andrews, during his continuance among this people, and the Synod entered upon the consideration of the said motion . . . and it was carried in the affirmative, *nem. con.*" It was then overtured "that the congregation be allowed to call an assistant to Mr. Andrews," which was also agreed to. In 1734, it appears an application was made to the commission for the removal of Mr. Robert Cross from Jamaica to Philadelphia. The matter was thus brought before Synod, when the commissioners from the two congregations interested in the business, were heard, and after public notice had been given to the people of the First Church, that if any of them had "any thing to object against Mr. Cross' being settled here in Philadelphia, they may appear and offer what they had to say in the

* Minutes, vol. ii. p. 38.

affair," Synod decided against his removal. The following year it is recorded that "a supplication being brought into the Synod from one part of the Presbyterian congregation of Philadelphia, desiring Mr. Robert Cross to be granted for their minister; also another paper to strengthen the supplication; and also another supplication from another part of the said congregation desiring Mr. Jonathan Dickinson to be their minister, the Synod not having time to issue that affair at present, do defer the consideration of it till to-morrow morning." The following day, however, a petition was presented by the friends of Mr. Cross to be erected into a new congregation, which was deferred for future consideration. The next morning the motion for a new erection "was carried in the affirmative by a great majority. Mr. John Smith of Bethlehem, in the Highlands of New York, desired that his dissent might be entered on our minutes." This decision having produced dissatisfaction, it was re-considered in the afternoon, and re-affirmed. Messrs. Dickinson, Pemberton, Webb, Elmer, Chalker, and Wales, dissenting. The Synod then declared that they did not intend by their decision "to oblige the said people to erect themselves into a new congregation, but only that the Synod allowed them to do so."* The following summer, a new congregation was formed by the Synod's commission; and in 1737, a call from the new erection in this city," it is said, "to the Rev. Mr. Robert Cross, together with a supplication to the Synod containing arguments to move the Synod to concur with the designs of the said call, were read." The call was handed to Mr. Cross and his sentiments desired in relation to it. In answer to which he said 'that he was clearly convinced and persuaded in his judgment, as things now appear, that it is his duty to remain with the people of Jamaica, and he thought the Synod could not determine this matter until his people be apprized thereof, and have opportunity to declare themselves concerning it.' The Synod then agreed that "the clerk and Mr. Elmer, each of them by himself, should endeavour to prepare an overture upon the affair to be brought in the afternoon, to be considered by the Synod." This overture, which was unanimously adopted, proposed to defer the question of Mr.

* Minutes, vol. ii. p. 42.

Cross' removal until the next meeting of the Synod; that in the meantime he should preach two months for the new congregation; that the Synod should appoint supplies for the people of Jamaica during Mr. Cross' absence, &c. &c. In 1737, a supplication was again presented to the Synod for Mr. Cross, "the purport whereof was to invalidate what was offered in the supplication from Jamaica." Mr. Cross having submitted himself wholly to the judgment of the Synod; after considerable debate, and "after solemn calling upon God for light and direction, it was decided *nem. con.*, to transfer Mr. Cross to Philadelphia." * In the following year it was reported to the Synod "that the Rev. Robert Cross was installed since our last meeting, according to the Synod's appointment, and that the two congregations in Philadelphia were since united." In all this protracted business, neither the Presbytery of New York to which Mr. Cross belonged, nor that of Philadelphia with which the congregation was connected, is so much as named. So completely did the Synod act on the Scottish principle, that the higher court has all the powers of the lower ones.

The Synod continued to transact much of its business by committees, which were sometimes designed merely to collect information, but most commonly were clothed with full powers. Thus, in 1731, some difficulty having occurred between Mr. Bradner of Goshen and one of his church members, the Synod "appointed a committee to go to Goshen, with the full power of the Synod, to hear and determine that business." † In 1734, "an appeal being brought in by Mr. John Kirkpatrick and Mr. John Moor from the Presbytery of Donegal, the Synod appointed that Messrs. Andrews, William Tennent, Treat, Alexander Hucheson, George Gillespie, Thomas Evans, and Henry Hook, be a committee to meet on the first Wednesday in November next to hear the said appeal, and determine it by the authority of Synod, and that they bring an account of their transactions therein to the next Synod. And the Synod do also empower the said committee to hear any matter *de novo*, that shall be brought before them by the said John Kirk-

* Minutes, vol. ii. p. 53.

† Ibid. vol. ii. p. 20.

patrick and John Moor, with relation to the affair aforesaid, and authoritatively to determine thereupon; appointing also that if either party shall appeal from the determination of the said committee, they shall enter their appeal immediately, that it may be finally determined by the next Synod."* In 1737, we find the following record: "Overtured on Mr. Morgan's affair, that inasmuch as it would be both difficult and tedious for the Synod to make a particular inquiry into the whole affair, the Synod appoint the Presbyteries of Philadelphia and East Jersey to meet as a committee at Maidenhead and judge of the said affair, and absolve Mr. Morgan from the censure he lies under, if he appear suitably penitent, and no new accusations be advanced against him; and Mr. Morgan to continue under suspension until the said committee meet, and that at least three members of each Presbytery be a quorum. The first Wednesday of August next to be the time of meeting; and it is ordered that every minister do endeavour to bring an elder with him. Approved *nem. con.*"†

The following minute affords an illustration of one other peculiarity in the mode of action adopted by the Synod. A reference was made in 1738 by the Presbytery of Philadelphia of some difficulty between them and the congregation of Hopewell and Maidenhead. The Synod censured the conduct of the people, and "wholly disallowed the said complainants being erected into a new congregation, until they do first submit the determination of the place for erecting a new meeting-house to their Presbytery, as was agreed upon between them and their neighbours, as a condition of their being a separate congregation. This overture was approved by a large majority. And it is further ordered by the Synod, that when the Presbytery of Philadelphia meet at Hopewell and Maidenhead, to fix the place of a new meeting-house, they shall call the following correspondents: Messrs. John Pierson, John Nutman, Samuel Blair, Aaron Burr, Nathaniel Hubbell, and Eleazar Wales."‡

There is not much in the powers granted to the committee, in the following illustration, beyond what is now customary; but the case is interesting and instructive. In 1738, "Mr. Gilbert Ten-

* Minutes, vol. ii. p. 30. † Ibid. vol. ii. p. 52. ‡ Ibid. vol. ii. p. 68.

nent represented to the committee that there had been differing sentiments in some points of doctrine, between himself and Mr. David Cowell, upon which there had been sundry large letters passed between them, concerning which it is overtured: That this affair be considered by a committee appointed by the Synod, who shall be directed to converse with Mr. Tennent and Mr. Cowell together, that they may see whether they so widely differ in their sentiments as is supposed, and if there be necessity, distinctly to consider the papers, that Mr. Tennent and Mr. Cowell be both directed to refrain all public discourse upon the controversy, and all methods of spreading it among the populace, until the committee have made their report to the Synod; and that no other member take notice of, or divulge the affair. The above mentioned committee were Messrs. J. Dickinson, Pierson, Pemberton, Thompson, Anderson, Boyd, and the moderator (Richard Treat)." It would be thought rather singular for any Synod in our day thus to lay an interdict upon theological controversy. In the afternoon of the day on which they were appointed, the committee reported that they had heard Mr. Tennent and Mr. Cowell explain themselves on the points in debate, and requested to be allowed to report to the next Synod. This request was granted, and Mr. Robert Cross was added to the committee.* The next year they "brought in the following overture, which being read, the Synod had the great satisfaction to find that the contending parties fully agreed in their sentiments on the point in controversy, according to the doctrine contained in the said overture, viz. Though they apprehend that there are some incautious and unguarded expressions used by both the contending parties, yet they have ground to hope that the principal controversy between them flows from their not having clear ideas of the subject they so earnestly debate about, and not from any dangerous errors they entertain, since they both own that the glory of God is the great ultimate end of all things. And as the point under debate concerns an important doctrine of religion, we would take the liberty to express our thoughts with respect to it, in a few words, which we

* Minutes, p. 60.

hope will be agreeable to the sentiments of the Synod, and readily agreed to by the parties concerned in this dispute. We apprehend that the glory of God was the only motive that influenced him to all his external operations. For since nothing else had an existence, nothing certainly could influence him from without himself. By his declarative glory we mean the manifestation of his essential and adorable perfections for the great and excellent ends he designed in this manifestation. It is the indispensable duty of every creature, according to its utmost capacity, to aim at the same end, which the blessed God has in view; and to endeavour to direct all his actions unto it. The method in which the great God has required us to prosecute this end is by conformity to his image and example, and a sincere and universal obedience to his laws. In his infinite and astonishing grace he has been pleased inseparably to connect our happiness with the prosecution of this end. This obedience which we are to pay to the divine law, and by which alone we can glorify him, must be performed by us, not only because it is the way to happiness, but because it is infinitely just and reasonable in itself, agreeable to the blessed God, whom we are under indissoluble obligations to obey and carry on the same design which he has been pleased to propose in all his actions. And these designs of the glory of God and our own happiness are so inseparably connected that they must never be placed in opposition to each other. For in all cases, he that actively glorifies God promotes his own happiness, and by a conformity to the divine statutes and laws, which is the only way to happiness, we, in the best manner we are capable of, glorify God." * This is surely sound doctrine. The glory of God is the ultimate end of all things. To promote that glory is the highest duty, and should be the governing purpose of all intelligent beings; and their own happiness is inseparably connected with their aiming at this end, and being governed by this motive. This, no doubt, was the doctrine which Mr. Tennent had so much at heart. He was satisfied with the Synod's assertion of it, though he was, or at least became, greatly dissatisfied that the opposite doctrine, that happiness was the grand

* Minutes, p. 66.

end of existence, and its attainment the proper governing motive of all rational creatures, which he supposed Mr. Cowell to hold, was not more pointedly condemned.

That Mr. Tennent was not pleased with the issue of this dispute is evident from the fact, that when the minutes were read at the next meeting of the Synod, he moved that all the papers relating to the controversy should be read, and the whole subject be considered by the Synod. This motion after considerable debate was rejected by a large majority. This no doubt increased his dissatisfaction. The following year, 1740, when from various causes he felt constrained to read before the Synod a paper containing his reasons for thinking that a large portion of his brethren were unconverted men, he assigned as the first reason "Their unsoundness in some of the principal doctrines of Christianity that relate to experience and practice; as particularly in the following points; First, that there is no distinction between the glory of God and our happiness; that self-love is the foundation of all obedience. These doctrines," he says, "do in my opinion entirely overset, if true, all supernatural religion; render regeneration a vain and needless thing; involve a crimson blasphemy against the blessed God, by putting ourselves upon a level with him. Secondly, that there is a certainty of salvation annexed to the labours of natural men. This doctrine in my opinion supposes the greatest falsehood, viz. that there is a free will in man naturally to acceptable good. . . . As these opinions are contrary to the express testimony of holy Scripture, our Confession of Faith and Christian experience, they give me reason to suspect, at least, that those who hold them are rotten-hearted hypocrites, and utter strangers to the saving knowledge of God, and of their own hearts." The first of these doctrines was the one involved in his controversy with Mr. Cowell. Why he should charge it upon the Synod, seeing they so explicitly teach the opposite doctrine in the minute above cited, does not appear. As to the second point, Mr. Thompson, in his reply to Mr. Tennent, says he did not know a single man in the whole Synod whom he even suspected of holding it. How strongly Mr. Tennent felt on this subject is still more evident from a subsequent charge against the Synod, viz. that they had so much "more zeal for outward order than for the main points of practical religion. Witness the committee slighting and shuffling the late debate about the glory of God, and their present contention about the committee-act;" (that is, the act for the examination of candidates by a committee of Synod.) Considering the composition of the committee against whom this complaint is directed, and the character of their award, it must be regarded as a little singular. Had this good man lived in our day, his ardent temper could hardly have kept within bounds, when he saw the doctrines that "self-love is the foundation of all obedience," and that "there is a free will in man to acceptable good," made the key-stone of a whole system of theology.*

There is scarcely any period in the history of our Church more prolific in acts and overtures than the one now under consideration. These acts proceeded in nearly equal proportions from each of the two parties into which the Synod now began to be divided. Neither party questioned the right of the Synod to make such acts, as both freely availed themselves of the power. Several of the most important of these measures are so intimately connected with the great schism of 1741, that they will be more properly considered in detail, in connection with that event, though chronologically belonging to the present period.

In the minutes for 1733, there is the following record: "Upon an overture to the Synod in pursuance of an order of the committee to that purpose, viz.: to use some proper means to revive the declining power of godliness, the Synod do earnestly recommend it to all ministers and members to take particular care about

* The former of these doctrines the reader may see presented with most revolting plainness in the closing number of the Christian Spectator. He who reads the paper in that number on the foundation of moral obligation will cease to wonder at the strong language of Mr. Tennent in relation to this point. For the doctrine that the ultimate ground of moral obligation is the tendency of virtue to promote *our own* happiness; and that the highest reason why we are bound to obey God, is, that he is wiser than we, and therefore knows best what will make us happy, must excite abhorrence in every pious heart, whose feelings have not been drugged into insensibility.

ministerial visiting of families, and press family and social worship, according to the Westminster Directory; and they also recommend it to every Presbytery at proper seasons, to inquire concerning the diligence of each of their members in such particulars. This overture was approved *nem. con.* Ordered, that each Presbytery take a copy of said overture, together with this order, and insert the same in their Presbytery books."*

In 1735, "Mr. Gilbert Tennent brought some overtures into the Synod with respect to trials of candidates both for the ministry and for the Lord's supper, that there be due care taken to examine into the evidences of the grace of God in them, as well as of their other necessary qualifications. The Synod doth unanimously agree, 'That as it has been our principle and practice, and as it is recommended in the Directory for worship and government, to be careful in this matter, so it awfully concerns us to be most serious and solemn in trying both sorts of candidates above mentioned. And this Synod does, therefore, in the name and fear of God, exhort and obtest all our Presbyteries to take special care not to admit into the sacred office, loose, careless, and irreligious persons, but that they particularly inquire into the conversation, conduct, and behaviour of such as offer themselves to the ministry; and that they diligently examine all the candidates for the ministry in their experience of a work of sanctifying grace in their hearts; and that they admit none to the sacred trust that are not, in the eye of charity, serious Christians. And the Synod does also seriously and solemnly admonish all the ministers within our bounds to make it their awful, constant, and diligent care to approve themselves to God, to their own consciences, and to their hearers, serious, faithful stewards of the mysteries of God, and of holy and exemplary conversation. And the Synod does also exhort all the ministers within our bounds to use due care in examining those whom they admit to the Lord's supper. This admonition was approved by the whole Synod. And the Synod further recommends unanimously to all our Presbyteries, to take effectual care that each of their ministers is faithful in the discharge of his awful trust. And in particular,

* See Minutes, vol. ii. p. 26.

that they frequently examine with respect to their members, into their life and conversation, their diligence in their work, and their method of discharging their ministerial calling; particularly that each Presbytery do, at least once a year, examine into the manner of each minister's preaching; whether he insists in his ministry upon the great articles of Christianity, and in the course of his preaching recommends a crucified Saviour to his hearers as the only foundation of hope, and the absolute necessity of the omnipotent influences of Divine grace to enable them to accept of this Saviour; whether he does, in the most solemn and affecting manner he can, endeavour to convince his hearers of their lost and perishing state whilst unconverted, and put them upon the diligent use of those means necessary, in order to obtain the sanctifying influences of the Spirit of God; whether he does, and how far he does discharge his duty towards the young people and children of his congregation, in a way of catechizing and familiar instruction; whether he does, and in what manner he does visit his flock and instruct them from house to house. And the Synod hereby orders, that a copy of this minute be inserted in the books of each of our Presbyteries, and be read at each of their Presbyterial meetings; and a record of its being read be minuted at the beginning of every session, and that there be also an annual record in each Presbytery book of a correspondence with this minute. And in case any minister within our bounds shall be found defective in any of the aforementioned cases, he shall be subject to the censure of the Presbytery; and if he refuse subjection to such censure, the Presbytery are hereby directed to report his case to the next Synod. And the Synod recommends to each of the ministers within our bounds, to be as much in catechetical doctrines as they in prudence may think proper."*

It is obvious that neither the knowledge nor power of evangelical religion could be dead in a church which was willing and able to issue such admonitions as the above. There may have been, and probably was a great declension in practical religion, but there was no denial of evangelical principles. The public sentiment of the

* Minutes, p. 31.

Church must have been in favour of genuine experimental godliness. The above overture so far illustrates the relation in which the Synod stood to its own members and the several Presbyteries, as it contains not only the solemn admonitions of the governing body, insisting upon the performance of specific duties, but directions as to the mode of their performance, and requisitions with which the Presbyteries were called upon to comply. That these bodies felt these orders to be obligatory upon them, is obvious from their obedience. This overture is recorded at length in the Presbytery book of Philadelphia; and in the minutes of their nextsubsequent meeting it is stated, "the minute of Synod ordered to be recorded in the Presbyteries, was read according to order of Synod, and by proper inquiries of the several members, it was found that the design of the said minute was in a good degree complied with." A nearly similar entry is made frequently in the minutes for subsequent years. That the Presbytery of East Jersey complied with the above directions appears from the following record in the synodical book: "There having been a complaint made by some members of the Presbytery of East Jersey, that the Presbytery are incapable to comply with the excellent design of the act of the last Synod with respect to the trials of candidates for the ministry, and of the fidelity of their own members in the discharge of their ministerial trust, by reason that several of their members, and Mr. John Cross in particular, neglected to attend the stated meetings of the Presbytery; and that Mr. John Cross has, without the concurrence of the Presbytery, removed from one congregation to another: the Synod do declare the conduct of such ministers as do neglect attendance on the meetings of the Presbytery without necessity, or that take charge of any congregation without the Presbytery's concurrence, to be disorderly, and justly worthy of Presbyterial censure, and do admonish said Mr. Cross to be no further chargeable with such irregularities for the future."*

How Mr. Tennent regarded this matter, and what authority he attributed to the act of Synod, may be inferred from what he says in the paper read to that body in 1740, and before referred to. He

* Minutes, vol. ii. p. 36.

therein complains of some of his brethren for "setting out men to the ministry without so much as examining them about their Christian experiences, notwithstanding of a late canon of this Synod enjoining the same. How contrary is this practice to the Scriptures, and to our Directory, and of how dangerous tendency to the Church of God! Is it probable that truly gracious persons would thus slight the precious souls of men?"*

In the year 1734, the following order was inserted on the minutes: "The Synod determines that no minister of our persuasion, in the government of Pennsylvania, or the lower counties, from this time forward, marry by any license from the government, till the form of them be altered and brought into a nearer conformity to those of the neighbouring governments of New York and New Jersey, and particularly till they are altered in such a manner as hath no peculiar respect to the ministers of the Church of England, nor oblige us to any of the forms and ceremonies peculiar to that Church. And we do further agree to refer it to the Presbyteries of New Castle and Donegal, to make what regulations they see cause for upon the affair of licenses with respect to their own members." In 1735, it is recorded that "upon reading last year's minutes relating to marriages by licenses, it is supposed there may be some exempt instances, wherein the restraints of that act may be found too severe. The Synod, therefore, order that each particular Presbytery shall have full liberty to determine upon, and direct in such exempt cases as they shall think convenient, provided always that no minister within our bounds shall be allowed to marry by license any members of our established congregations, or others known to be of our communion, without certificates from the ministers of such congregations; or in case of the absence of the minister, or of the congregation's being without a minister, from some other substantial persons, that such marriage is regular, and that there is no just bar in the way of it."† The Synod it seems felt no hesitation in assuming the right to control all its members in the exercise of one of their official functions; or, when the rule pre-

* Quoted by Mr. Thompson in his Government of the Church, p. 20.

† Minutes, pp. 32, 36.

scribed was found too strict, to order that the several Presbyteries "should have full liberty" to determine what cases should be exempted from its operation.

In the following year we find a still more extraordinary record. "Upon motion made by a member, the Synod do agree that if any of our members shall see cause to prepare any thing for the press upon any controversy in religious matters, before such member publish what he hath thus prepared, he shall submit the same to be perused by persons appointed for that purpose, and that Messrs. Andrews, Dickinson, Robert Cross, Pemberton, and Pierson, be appointed for this purpose in the bounds of the Synod to the northward of Philadelphia; and Messrs. Anderson, Thomas Evans, Cathcart, Stevenson, and Thompson, in the bounds of the Synod to the southward of Philadelphia. Approved."* Here then is an actual censorship of the press. This is almost equal to the Presbyterianism of France; where the national Synods made and enforced similar regulations.† All the gentlemen above named, except Mr. Pierson, were present at this meeting of the Synod; and yet no protest against what we should regard as a most extraordinary stretch of Synodical power is even hinted; and no refusal of Mr. Andrews, Mr. Dickinson, Mr. Evans, or Mr. Pemberton, to act on such a committee, and thus sanction the legality of its appointment. Surely they must be under a delusion, who, in their aspirations after advisory councils, long for the return of the early days of our Church.

The same year, (1736,) a long overture was introduced, no doubt, judging from the style and sentiments, by Mr. Thompson, against heresy. It alludes particularly to the case of Mr. Hemphill, who had been unanimously disowned by the Synod, as before stated. It urges, "seeing we are likely to have most of our supply of ministers to fill our vacancies, from the north of Ireland, and seeing it is too plain to be denied or called in question that we are in danger of being imposed upon by ministers and preachers from thence, though sufficiently furnished with all the formalities of Presbyterial credentials," the adoption of various expedients for guarding against

* Minutes, p. 38.

† Quick's Synodicon, vol. ii. pp. 111 & 349.

the danger. It also testifies against the custom of some of the Irish Presbyteries of ordaining men *siné titulo* before they come to this country, thus depriving the Presbyteries here of their right of judging of their fitness for the sacred office. In consequence of this overture it is recorded: "The Synod do agree that no minister ordained in Ireland *sine titulo* be received to the exercise of the ministry among us, until he submit to such trials as the Presbytery among whom he resides shall think proper to order and appoint, and the Synod do also advertise the general Synod in Ireland, that their ordaining any such *sine titulo* before their sending them hither for the future, will be very disagreeable and disobliging to us. And the Synod do appoint Messrs. Robert Cross, John Thompson, and Joseph Houston, to send the above overture and appointment to the general Synod in Ireland, inclosed in a proper letter unto them."* On a subsequent page it is stated that "inquiry being made of the several Presbyteries whether they had complied with an order of Synod, touching the admission of foreign ministers and candidates that come from Europe, it was found that the order has been complied with." It is evident from the above overture, and from various other sources, that the Irish members in their zeal against error were not actuated by any sectional jealousies. Their efforts were directed against their own countrymen. There was no desire to gain or confirm an ascendency in the Synod for men of their own origin. The very persons most prominent in these measures are found writing urgent letters to New England for suitable ministers to supply their vacant churches. Under these circumstances it is impossible to question either the sincerity of their professions, or the purity of their motives.

In 1737, an overture was introduced and approved in reference to itinerant preachers. This act forbad a licentiate to preach in any vacant congregation without the order of the Presbytery to which he belonged, or of the Presbytery under whose care the congregation was placed. It forbad also the congregations to invite any minister or probationer without the concurrence of their Presbytery;† &c. In the following year this order was so modified as

* Minutes, p. 40.

† Ibid. p. 54.

to forbid any minister belonging to the Synod "to preach in any congregation belonging to another Presbytery," after being warned by any member of the Presbytery that his so preaching would be likely to cause division. To this was added the explanation, that this prohibition by one member was to be merely temporary. If the Presbytery to which the congregation belonged gave the stranger liberty to preach, he might do so. Thus explained, it was agreed to *nemine contradicente.** In 1739, it is stated that "The act made last year with respect to ministers preaching out of their own bounds being taken under a review, the Synod determine that if any minister in the bounds of any of our Presbyteries judge that the preaching of any minister or candidate of a neighboring Presbytery has had a tendency to promote division among them, he shall complain to the Presbytery in whose bounds the said congregation is; and that the minister who is supposed to be the cause of the aforesaid division shall be obliged to appear before them, and it shall be left to them to determine whether he shall preach any more in the bounds of that congregation; and he shall be bound to stand to their determination, until they shall see cause to remove their prohibition; or the Synod shall have an opportunity to take the affair under cognizance. Approved *nem. con.*" † In 1740, the Synod say that although this agreement had at the time it was passed met with universal acceptance, yet as some of the brethren had become dissatisfied with it, and some of their people misinterpreted it, supposing it to be intended against all itinerant preaching, they agreed to repeal it, and thus avoid all contention on the subject.‡

This act is not so much an illustration of the power of the Synod, as it is a declaration, and enforcing the rights of Presbyteries. It merely provided that no man should preach in any congregation against the will of the Presbytery under whose care such congregation was placed. This is a principle fully recognized in our present constitution. If a congregation is vacant, it applies to the Presbytery for supplies, or obtains permission to fill its own pulpit. That the Presbytery has the right to watch over and pro-

* Minutes, p. 58. † Ibid. p. 66. ‡ Ibid. p. 72.

vide for the religious instruction of its churches is one of the most familiar principles of our form of government. It very clearly shows at once the agitation existing in those days, and the moderation of Synod, that they were willing to waive this principle, though twice unanimously sanctioned, for the sake of peace. The opposition to this rule seems to have proceeded principally from Mr. Tennent. No man was, under ordinary circumstances, more disposed than that gentleman to enforce the obligation of such rules, and even to push them to extremes. But when he thought they stood in the way of the interests of religion, he trampled them under his feet. To create a division in the congregation of a converted pastor, or to preach against his consent within his bounds, was, in his eyes, a high ecclesiastical offence. But to preach the gospel to the people of a graceless minister, in despite of his remonstrances, was a matter of duty; and he would have done it, in despite of all the Synods in the world. In this he was clearly right, as far as the principle is concerned. There are obligations superior to those of mere ecclesiastical order; and there are times when it is a duty to disregard rules, which we admit to be legitimate both in their own nature, and in respect to the authority whence they proceed. It was on this principle that the apostles and the reformers acted. It is analogous to the right of revolution in civil communities; and consequently the cases are very rare in which it can be resorted to, with a good conscience. Because the reformers rightfully trampled on the ecclesiastical authorities to which they were subject, it does not follow that every wandering evangelist, who thinks that he is a better man or better preacher than his brethren, may properly enter into parishes, divide congregations, and unsettle pastors at pleasure. Whether Mr. Tennent was right in applying his principle in the way he did, is a very difficult question, which belongs properly to a subsequent period of our history.

It is worthy of remark that the same circumstances which called forth this act of the Synod, under the different system of the Connecticut churches, led to the interference of the civil authorities. In May 1742, the General Assembly of Connecticut passed a law, in which, after a long preamble, they enacted that any settled minister who should preach within the parish of another minister, unless invited by the latter and by the major part of the people, should be deprived of all the benefit of the law for the support of the clergy; that if any one, not a minister or licentiate, should teach or exhort in any parish, without being properly invited, he should be bound over in the penal sum of one hundred pounds; and if any stranger not an inhabitant of the colony should transgress in like manner he was to be sent as a vagrant from constable to constable out of the bounds of the colony.*

In the year 1738, the Presbytery of Lewes brought in an overture respecting the examination of candidates for the ministry. After reciting the various disadvantages under which such candidates then laboured in the prosecution of their studies, and the dangers arising from the admission of uneducated men into the ministry, it proposed that the Synod should agree that all the Presbyteries should require every candidate, before being taken upon trial, to be furnished with a diploma from some European or New England college; or in case he had not enjoyed the advantage of a college education, he should be examined by a committee of Synod, who should give him a certificate of competent scholarship, when they found him to merit it. This overture was approved by a great majority; and Messrs. John Thompson, George Gillespie, James Anderson, Thomas Evans, Henry Hook, James Martin, and Francis Allison, were appointed the committee of examination for the Presbyteries to the south of Philadelphia; and Messrs. Andrews, Robert Cross, G. Tennent, E. Pemberton, J. Dickinson, D. Cowell, and J. Pierson for the Presbyteries to the north of Philadelphia.†

In 1739, "the New Brunswick Presbytery having brought a paper of objections against the act of last year, touching the previous examination of candidates, the Synod consented to review

* Trumbull's History, vol. ii. p. 162–4. For this law the Association of New Haven county tendered their hearty thanks to the Assembly, and prayed that it might be continued in force.

† Minutes, p. 61.

that act, and upon deliberation agreed to the following overture, which they substitute in the place of it, viz.: It being the first article in our excellent Directory for the examination of candidates for the sacred ministry, that they be inquired of what degrees they have taken in the university, &c.; and it being oftentimes impracticable for us in these remote parts of the earth, to obtain an answer to these questions of those who propose themselves for examination, many of our candidates not having enjoyed the advantage of an university education; and it being our desire to come to the nearest conformity to the incomparable prescriptions of the Directory that our circumstances will admit of; and after long deliberation of the most proper expedients to comply with the intentions of the Directory where we cannot exactly fulfil the letter of it, the Synod agree and determine that every person who proposes himself for trial as a candidate for the ministry, and who has not a diploma or the usual certificate from an European or New England university, shall be examined by the whole Synod, or its commission, as to those preparatory studies which are generally passed through at the college, and if they find him qualified, shall give him a certificate which shall be received by our respective Presbyteries as equivalent to a diploma or certificate from the college. This, we trust, will have a happy tendency to prevent unqualified men from creeping in among us, and answer, in the best manner our present circumstances are capable of, the design which our Directory has in view, and to which by inclination and duty we are all bound to comply to our utmost ability. This was agreed to by a great majority." *

Against the above act, Messrs. Gilbert Tennent, William Tennent, Sen., William Tennent, Jun., Charles Tennent, Samuel Blair, and Eleazar Wales, together with four elders, protested. It is stated in the minutes of the next year, that various proposals were made with the view of reconciling these protesting brethren. As these efforts were not successful, "the Synod," it is said, "still desiring that that unhappy difference may be accommodated, recommend it to any brethren of the Synod to consider any further expedient to

* Minutes, p. 66.

that end, to be brought in at the next *sederunt*." What these expedients were, the records do not inform us. Two of them may be learned from other sources. Mr. Dickinson proposed that "there should, by consent of both parties, be drawn up a fair representation of the state of the case debated, and sent to the General Assembly of the Church of Scotland or their commission; to the general Synod of Ireland or their commission; or to the ministers of our profession in London or Boston, to obtain their judgment or advice."* This proposal was rejected by Mr. Tennent, because, besides other reasons, the persons specified were mostly "dead formalists."† Another expedient was suggested by Mr. Gillespie, which at first seemed likely to succeed. He proposed, "that if a Presbytery admit a man, they shall report his trials to the Synod for their satisfaction on his taking his seat. When Mr. Tennent was asked by Mr. Dickinson, whether, in case of the Synod's dissatisfaction, he would allow a re-examination or censure, he said, No. He would consent to the Presbytery being censured, but not to the candidate being examined or censured. The matter was then dropped, as Mr. Tennent claimed the right of imposing what members he pleased upon the Synod."‡ After these and other efforts for an accommodation had failed, "it was put to vote whether the said agreement (about candidates) should be repealed, or continued until some other expedient could be found to the Synod's satisfaction; and it was voted that it continue at present. The protesting brethren renewed their former protest," and were joined by Mr. John Cross and Mr. Alexander Creaghead, ministers, and eleven elders. The Rev. George Gillespie, and the Rev. Alexander Hucheson dissented.§ The Synod then passed the following explanatory

* See Protest presented to the Synod of Philadelphia, June 1, 1741. Printed and sold by Benjamin Franklin, 1741. In the preface to this Protest the above fact is stated.

† Remarks on the Protest examined and answered, p. 12. ‡ Ibid. 16.

§ Minutes, p. 72. The names of the ministers and elders are not distinguished in the above minute. By a reference to the list of members at the opening of the Synod, it is ascertained that the only additional clerical protesters were Mr. Cross of the Presbytery of New Brunswick, and Mr. Alexander Creaghead of the Presbytery of Donegal.

declaration: "That they do not hereby call in question the right of inferior Presbyteries to ordain ministers, but only assert their own right to judge of the qualification of their own members; and though they do not deny but that such as are brought into the ministry contrary to this agreement, may be truly gospel ministers, yet, inasmuch as they cannot but think the said agreement needful to be insisted on in order to the well-being of this part of the Church of Christ, they cannot admit them, when so brought into the ministry, to be members of this Synod, until they submit to the said agreement, though they do consent that they be in all other respects treated and considered as ministers of the Gospel; any thing that they be otherwise construed in any of our former proceedings notwithstanding."

As this act was the immediate occasion of the schism which occurred in 1741, the consideration of it, as a constitutional question, must be reserved until the causes and merits of that great controversy come to be examined. It may, however, be remarked here, what indeed cannot fail to attract the reader's attention, that the opposition to this measure was not so much of an ecclesiastical as of a religious character; that is, it did not arise so much from difference of opinion as to the power of the Synod, as from the supposed bearing of the act upon the interests of religion. This is evident from the character of its opponents. They were all, unless Mr. Wales be an exception, Irishmen or Scotchmen.* That the New England members took side with the majority in all this matter, appears from the absence of their names from the list of either protestants or dissenters; from the open effort of Mr. Dick-

* This remark refers of course only to the clergymen. The four Tennents and Mr. Blair were Irish; so it is believed was Mr. John Cross. Mr. Alexander Creaghead, (who is not to be confounded with Mr. Thomas Creaghead,) soon after this time became a Cameronian. These, together with Mr. Wales, whose origin is not known, were all the protesters. The two dissentients, Messrs. Gillespie and Hucheson, were both Scotchmen. Mr. Gillespie is the gentleman to whom Dr. Hill refers when he says "*even* Gillespie, &c.," with the design of showing that in the lowest depths of Presbyterianism, a lower still might be found. It may fairly be inferred, therefore, that the opposition in which Mr. Gillespie joined, did not arise from any lack of Presbyterianism.

inson to conciliate Mr. Tennent's consent to some compromise; and especially from the fact that when the Synod of New York was formed, to which the New England members in the general attached themselves, it was made one of its fundamental principles, that the Synod should be obeyed. This provision, which has already been referred to, and which subsequently was incorporated into the terms of union between the two Synods, was evidently intended to meet just such cases as the present. It stated that if any member could not with a good conscience, either actively concur in, or passively submit to, any determination of the Synod, he should peaceably withdraw, without attempting to make any schism, provided the Synod insisted upon their determination as essential to their doctrine or government. In reference to the act about itinerant preachers, the Synod, though the matter had twice been unanimously concurred in, and though clearly in the right, declined to insist, when they saw the opposition springing up among some of their members and people. In relation to the act about the examination of candidates, they first adopted a modification, then proposed one expedient after another for a compromise, but refused to give it up. As the other party thought they could not, with a good conscience, yield, a division became inevitable, and it therefore took place, though not in the Christian manner in which the article just referred to afterwards provided for. This schism, however, never would have taken place, neither party would have been so unyielding, had they not, in a great measure, lost their confidence in each other, and become embittered in their feelings.

The motive therefore of Mr. Tennent's opposition to this act was not dislike of the ecclesiastical principle on which it was founded, but dislike of the object at which he thought it aimed. He believed it was adapted, and probably designed, to keep evangelical men out of the ministry, and therefore he would not submit to it.* The arguments by which he and his friends justified their opposition; the

* In a letter from the Synod to President Clapp of Yale College, it is stated when this act was passed, "Mr. Gilbert Tennent cried out, that this was to prevent his father's school from training gracious men for the ministry." Minutes, vol. iii. p. 17.

ecclesiastical principles which they advocated, how far these differ, or whether they differed at all from those of their opponents, are questions which belong to a subsequent period of our history. It would be strange if Gillespie, Hucheson, and Creaghead, who sided more or less with Mr. Tennent, held a more lax system of Presbyterianism than Dickinson, Pemberton, and Pierson, who as far as appears, were on the other side. The reader will not, of course, confound the question as to the validity of the act respecting the examination of candidates, with the propriety of the exclusion of the New Brunswick Presbytery, by a simple protest. Many who sanctioned the former measure, remonstrated against the latter.

The review of the whole period which has now been passed over, must, it is believed, lead the reader to at least the three following conclusions.

First, that the Presbyterian Church in the United States does not owe its existence to Congregationalists. From the middle of the seventeenth to the middle of the eighteenth century, Presbyterians were the most numerous class of emigrants to this country, and probably more numerous than all other classes combined. Our church is but one branch of this extended Presbyterian family, and owes its origin to the English, Scotch, and Irish Presbyterians, who sought on these shores a refuge from the persecutions or penury which awaited them at home. The Congregationalists who associated with them, who were few in number, ceased to be Congregationalists. They entered the church under the name and with the profession of Presbyterians, promising "to submit to Presbyterian rules."

Second, that our Church was, during this whole period, strictly and properly Presbyterian. There was less irregularity in the organization of the congregations than among the churches of Scotland during the corresponding period of their history. The great majority of our ministers were presbyterially educated and ordained. The Presbytery and Synod not only exercised uniformly and without opposition all the powers which are now recognized as belonging to such bodies, but in many respects greatly exceeded them. In all the particulars in which they differed from the Presbyteries and

Synods of the present day, they conformed to the principles and usages of the Church of Scotland.

Third, that assent to the system of doctrine contained in the Westminster Confession of Faith, has always been a condition of ministerial communion in the Presbyterian Church. Before 1729, this was, in effect, the case; after that time, it was the publicly asserted and uniformly enforced condition of admission into the ministry in our communion.

www.ingramcontent.com/pod-product-compliance
Lightning Source LLC
LaVergne TN
LVHW011210110826
845150LV00006B/1385

* 9 7 8 1 4 2 5 5 1 8 0 2 8 *